TWAYNE'S WORLD LEADERS SERIES

EDITORS OF THIS VOLUME

Arthur W. Brown
*Baruch College, The City University
of New York*
and
Thomas S. Knight
Adelphi University

Walter Lippmann

TWLS 58

Walter Lippmann

WALTER LIPPMANN

By LARRY L. ADAMS

Baruch College of the City University of New York

TWAYNE PUBLISHERS

A DIVISION OF G. K. HALL & CO., BOSTON

Copyright © 1977 by G. K. Hall & Co.
All Rights Reserved
First Printing

Library of Congress Cataloging in Publication Data

Adams, Larry L
  Walter Lippmann.

  (Twayne's world leaders series ; TWLS 58)
  Bibliography: p. 221–24.
  Includes index.
  1.   Lippmann, Walter, 1889–1974.
JC251.L55A64   320.5'092'4   76-54721
ISBN 0-8057-7709-1

MANUFACTURED IN THE UNITED STATES OF AMERICA

For my parents

Contents

About the Author

Larry Adams received the Ph.D. in political science from the University of California, Santa Barbara. He is currently on the faculty of Baruch College, City University of New York.

Dr. Adams teaching and research interests are modern political philosophy and American political thought. The topic of his doctoral dissertation was a comparison of the ideas of Edmund Burke and Sigmund Freud.

Preface

This book is designed to introduce the reader to the social and political theory of Walter Lippmann, beyond question the most widely read American social thinker of the twentieth century and one of the most respected. One student of his work placed the minimum readership of his thrice weekly syndicated newspaper column in the United States at one and one-half million people. Several of his twenty-two books went through multiple editions.

Lippmann never scorned the term "popularizer," and he did not rise to the level of an original philosopher. He accepted forums from *Senior Scholastic* to *Foreign Affairs*, from *Life* magazine to the Brookings Institution, from college commencements to the General Assembly of the United Nations.

His vocation was that of journalist and author, and he never lost his desire to have an impact upon public opinion and political leaders. He lived through and theorized upon the events of six decades in the twentieth century. The first American President to praise Lippmann, and then bitterly break with him, was Theodore Roosevelt; the last was Lyndon Johnson. Arthur Schlesinger, Jr., relates that during the Depression, the *New Yorker* magazine noted the founding of the American Monarchist Party with the observation that Walter Lippmann could probably easily win election as king. A famous *New Yorker* cartoon of the same era showed two matrons at breakfast, one of whom, immersed in her newspaper, was saying, "Of course I only take a cup of coffee in the morning. A cup of coffee and Walter Lippmann is all I need."

Most students of Lippmann's work have been troubled by what they find to be a lack of consistency in his work, contradictions which reach his fundamental assumptions. The titles of some of the books on Lippmann reveal the unease of some of his intellectual biographers: *The Intellectual Odyssey of Walter Lippmann; Twentieth Century Pilgrimage; Five Public Philosophies of Walter Lippmann.* One commentator concludes that "Certainly he has varied more widely in his views than any other significant political theorist of his time."

This book takes a different view, according Lippmann a presumption of intellectual and moral coherence whenever it seems reasonably possible to do so. To read him in this way is not to place him beyond criticism, but I believe it does allow the reader to obtain the greatest possible illumination from the interplay of Lippmann's mind and times.

Chapter 1 deals with his early development and the first major statements of his thought in the closing years of the Progressive era, when he was optimistic about the prospects for domestic social reform.

Chapter 2 is the only chapter which covers the entire time span of Lippmann's thought. It does so within the area of international relations. The basic categories he develops are considered: sovereignty and nationalism; imperialism; war; balance of power; international organization. I draw primarily upon his books rather than from his newspaper and periodical essays for reasons of economy of space, and because it seems fair to assume that his books present considered judgments, upon which he had some period of time to reflect.

The balance of Lippmann's theoretical production is taken up chronologically. The development of his concerns over time crystallized those concerns in three major books, which provide the principal focus for chapters 3, 4, and 5. The major works examined in these chapters are, in order: *Public Opinion* (1922), *A Preface to Morals* (1929), and *Essays in the Public Philosophy* (1955). The first of these books deals with the subject which most continuously engaged Lippmann's theoretical attention over the years. The second exposes relationships between his political theory and his social theory more broadly construed. The third he hoped would stand as a summation of the final form of his theorizing. There are numerous strands of theory which cut across these works and bind them together; the most important is a fine but strong thread of Neoplatonism.

The inconsistencies in Lippmann's lifework are interesting and important; but of more enduring interest is their underlying unity, which mirrors his own search for meaning and coherence in a chaotic century.

Acknowledgments

Adequate thanks to all whose efforts, learning, and example contributed to this book would quickly become a tedious autobiography. So I shall express my appreciation only to those most immediately implicated. (Errors in execution of course are mine.) Particular thanks belong to my original mentor D. Mackenzie Brown; my former teacher and co-worker, the late Harry Girvetz; my esteemed professor and adviser, the late William Ebenstein; the teacher who introduced me to Walter Lippmann and much else, Gordon Baker; my skilled and understanding editor, Arthur Brown; and one whose care brought the manuscript through many difficulties, Mrs. Elaine Berry.

Chronology

1889 Born in New York City.

1896 Enrolled in Dr. Julius Sachs' School for Boys.

1906 Enters Harvard.

1908 Becomes contributor to *Harvard Illustrated, Harvard Advocate*. Plays active role in Harvard Socialist Club.

1909 Meets William James.

1910 Serves as teaching assistant for George Santayana. Takes seminar with Graham Wallas. Works as reporter on Boston *Common*. Becomes assistant to Lincoln Steffens on *Everybody's Magazine*.

1912 Serves as Executive Secretary to George R. Lunn, Socialist mayor of Schenectady, New York.

1913 Publishes *A Preface to Politics*.

1914 *Drift and Mastery*. Joins editorial board of *New Republic* magazine.

1915 *The Stakes of Diplomacy*.

1917 Marries Faye Albertson. Appointed Assistant Secretary of War. Appointed Secretary to the Inquiry.

1918 Commissioned captain in Army Military Intelligence. Helps draw up explanation of Fourteen Points. Appointed member of American Commission to Negotiate Peace.

1919 Returns to *New Republic*.

1920 Takes leave of absence from *New Republic* to write next book.

1921 Employed as editorial writer for New York *World*.

1922 *Public Opinion*.

1923 Promoted to editor of New York *World*.

1929 *A Preface to Morals*.

1931 Begins column "Today and Tomorrow" for the New York *Herald Tribune*.

1937 *The Good Society*.

1938 Divorced; marries Helen Byrne Armstrong.

1943 *U.S. Foreign Policy: Shield of the Republic*.

1955 *Essays in the Public Philosophy*.

1958 Awarded Pulitzer Prize.

1962   Awarded second Pulitzer Prize. Recipient of George Foster
        Peabody Award.
1963   Begins column for *Newsweek* magazine.
1964   Receives Presidential Medal of Freedom.
1974   Dies in New York City.

CHAPTER 1

The Young Progressive

I

WALTER Lippmann was eleven years old at the turn of the century. During the next seventy-four years he led a remarkable public career, as assistant to the great investigative journalist Lincoln Steffens, executive secretary to a socialist mayor, member of the original editorial board of one of the leading journals of political opinion, advisor to the Wilson Administration in four different offices, editor of one of the foremost newspapers of the 1920s, syndicated columnist for thirty-five years, author of some twenty-two books, and friend and colleague to a host of the distinguished and powerful figures in American society in this century. But biographical data are remarkably scanty on so public a man as this one because of his personal reticence.

No one who knew Lippmann personally has said that he was a self-revealing person. The impressions of his friends and associates mark a uniform refrain: he was composed, reserved, dignified, self-assured. To some, his self-assurance, particularly in his younger, more radical years, seemed to border on arrogance. To others, his sense of propriety seemed prudish at times. Lippmann generally enjoyed the company of the bohemians and intellectuals who attended the salon gatherings at Mabel Dodge's home, nicely situated on Fifth Avenue in Greenwich Village. Lippmann himself presented some of the theories of Sigmund Freud at more than one of these parties. Mabel Dodge found Lippmann "strong," and "succinctly male," but possessing "no incontinence and no flowing sensuality." Once, she recalled, the young Lippmann was so offended by the conduct of the dancer Isadora Duncan that he left the party early and wrote to his hostess from the more proper surroundings of his quarters at the Harvard Club: "If this is Greece and Joy and the Aegean Isles and the Influence of Music, I don't want anything to do with it."[1]

15

John Reed, who knew Lippmann at Harvard as well as in Mabel Dodge's salon gatherings, sums up, wistfully and satirically, Lippmann's Olympian qualities:

> And with him *Lippmann*,—calm, inscrutable,
> Thinking and writing clearly, soundly, well;
> All snarls of falseness swiftly piercing through,
> His keen mind leaps like lightning to the True;
> His face is almost placid—but his eye,—
> There is a vision born to prophecy!
> He sits in silence, as one who has said:
> "I waste not living words among the dead!"
> Our all-unchallenged Chief. But were there one
> Who builds a world, and leaves out all the fun,—
> Who dreams a pageant, gorgeous, infinite,
> And then leaves all the color out of it,—
> Who wants to make the human race, and me,
> March to a geometric Q.E.D.—
> Who but must laugh, if such a man there be?
> Who would not weep, if *Walter L.* were he?[2]

At the same time, few American social theorists have been more self-revealing in their writing than Walter Lippmann. Autobiography always creeps into philosophy, he observed, and precisely because he was such an interior person, his theories were necessarily self-disclosing. He wrote of Woodrow Wilson words which might aptly be applied to his own work: "Like all essentially contemplative men, the world has to be reflected in the medium of his intellect before he can grapple with it."[3]

Lippmann recognized his emotional distance from others and sought to compensate for it in a variety of ways. But he also accepted his inwardness and intellectuality and sought to develop them as strengths and resources. "We forge gradually our greatest instrument for understanding the world—introspection,"[4] he observed. While the remark was intended to apply to society at large, it was clearly autobiographical. Lippmann's program for society transformed was a representation of his own inner life. To make conscious our purposes, to refine our instincts, to socialize our motives, to exert mastery over the future through reasoned choice and plan—these aims were the heart of his conception of social reform. The theorist's values always guide his perceptions and description of reality, he wrote at another point. An admirer of Plato, Freud, and James, Lippmann would necessarily be sensitive to this understanding.

The decisive experiences and encounters in Lippmann's early years reflect a keen ethical awareness: the biographical markers of his first thirty years may be seen as a series of ethical choices which brought his life into contact, and into parallel, with the movements and leaders of the first two decades of the twentieth century.

Although he later casually characterized his home as middle class, Walter Lippmann was born into advantaged circumstances. His parents were both of German Jewish descent. From his grandfather, who emigrated from Europe after the abortive Liberal uprisings of 1848, Walter as a child learned to believe that "Wherever the American flag was planted, there tyranny must disappear."[5] Walter's father, Jacob, was a clothing manufacturer and real estate broker, whose investments were sufficiently successful to permit him to retire early. He hoped that Walter might pursue the study of law; but Walter's mother, a graduate of Hunter College, encouraged the youth's interest in the arts, and he went off to Harvard with the intention of becoming an art critic.[6] That he chose to become a social critic instead may be partially ascribed to the personalities and theories of his teachers and to his own college achievements. Still, his interest in the arts, and in the larger cultural setting of politics, never left him.

In what might be a wistful autobiographical observation, he once wrote: "Art enlarges life, by admitting us to the experience of others." And he remained adamantly opposed to political writers who found art irrelevant, or even opposed, to radical change. He urged his readers to "remember the close alliance of art, science, and politics in Athens, in Florence, and Venice at their zenith. We in America have divorced them completely: both art and politics exist in a condition of unnatural celibacy."[7] To an American socialist who contended that the quest for beauty should be suspended in an unliberated world—that the beauty of justice now alone mattered—Lippmann replied: "Without a literature the people is dumb, without novels and poems, plays and criticism, without books of philosophy, there is neither . . . the imagination to conceive, nor the understanding of a common purpose. Without culture you can knock down governments, overturn property relations . . . but you cannot create a genuine revolution in the lives of men."[8] It is evident that Lippmann was not making a utilitarian argument that art is a useful tool for the revolutionary; but he was arguing that any social transformation worth gaining will be an extension of a much longer and larger civilizing process.

As an only child, Walter was the focal point of his parents' attention and affection. He distinguished himself as a student at Dr. Sachs' School for Boys, attended largely by the sons of well-to-do German Jewish families. With his parents, he attended Temple Emmanu-El, where he received religious instruction in Reform Judaism and was confirmed in 1905. He regularly took summer holiday trips to Europe with his parents, once journeying as far as Russia; and he developed an easy familiarity with European architecture, sculpture, painting, languages, and history. Like any well-educated, well-traveled resident of Fifth Avenue, the youthful Lippmann took on traits of reserved urbanity which were to distinguish his later life and thought.[9]

In 1906, at the age of seventeen, Lippmann entered Harvard, from whence he graduated Phi Beta Kappa in three years. It was his good fortune to attend the University during one of its "golden ages." President Charles W. Eliot had drawn together a distinguished faculty. Among the students with whom Lippmann shared those years were John Reed, who was to chronicle the Russian Revolution and be buried in honor beneath the Kremlin's walls; the poet T. S. Eliot; humorist Robert Benchley; journalist Heywood Broun; authors Conrad Aiken and Stuart Chase; future New Deal Secretary of Labor Francis Biddle; and historian Samuel Eliot Morison.[10] Most of these men were to play some role in the crises of institutions and values which were to preoccupy Lippmann's professional life.

Lippmann's intellectual gifts and attainments might seem to have made an academic career a logical choice, but changes were stirring him. He was seeking new experiences and understanding of life in more than intellectual ways. Having grown up in a "cottoned and cushioned" home life, Lippmann now began to work as a volunteer poverty worker at civic welfare institutions—Hale House and Civic Service House—in downtown Boston. In 1908, he was given a prolonged exposure to the destitution, helplessness, and suffering of the poor as he worked for several days in the Chelsea slums, where a major fire had raged on Palm Sunday, destroying many homes.[11] The lasting concern for the poor which Lippmann carried away from these experiences is reflected in several ways in his later writings. He was rare, almost alone, among later progressives in defending the New York City "machine" of Tammany Hall. ". . . Tammany has a better perception of human need, and comes nearer to being what a government should be," he wrote, than any model of reform developed by middle- and upper-class reformers.[12] Of the Tammany leader, Tim Sullivan, Lippmann said that he expressed the meaning of statesmanship much more fully than most middle-class reformers. Sullivan did not patronize the poor, Lippmann declared: he understood their needs, defended them against the inequities of a legal system they could not comprehend, and generally humanized the painful process of their building homes and careers in an American society alien to them. It is true that he expected their votes and their political loyalty in return—what officeholder would expect less?[13]

To his early sensitivity to poverty may be traced an important part of Lippmann's vigorous support of the struggle of organized labor. In *Drift and Mastery,* he writes:

There are certain preliminaries of civilization which the great mass of workingmen have not yet won. They have not yet won a living wage, they have not won anything like security of employment, they have not yet won respect from the government, they have not yet won the right to be consulted as to the conditions under which they work. Until they do, it is idle to talk about industrial peace. . . .[14]

Labor violence was defensive violence, he concluded, and unavoidable until basic reforms were forthcoming: ". . . the scab is a traitor to the economic foundations of democracy. . . . Democracies of workingmen have to fight him out of sheer self-protection . . . the clubbing of scabs is not a pretty thing; the importation of scabs is an uglier one."[15]

Another idea which can reasonably be attributed to Lippmann's wrenching college experience of working among the poor was his enthusiasm for syndicalism, which some of his friends and teachers, notably Graham Wallas, mistook for an admiration for the irrationalism of Georges Sorel, the leader of the movement. Lippmann made the basis of his enthusiasm for syndicalism clear in 1910, and through the prewar years he continued to interchange "syndicalism" and "socialism" casually as synonymous terms. "The most cruel of all denials," he wrote, "is to deprive a human being of joyous activity. Syndicalism is shot through with the assertion that imposed drudgery is intolerable. . . ." Such an assertion represented a new kind of revolt, he argued, and one perhaps more dangerous to capitalism than demands for higher wages.[16]

Lippmann lucidly analyzed the fashion in which poverty was bound up in myriad ways with the American socioeconomic system. One reason he was so deeply opposed to William Jennings Bryan and Populism was that he believed the Populists wished to impose forcibly upon the urban poor an outmoded regional and class morality by outlawing dance halls, gambling, alcohol, and prostitution. In Chicago, for example, a commission to study the problem of prostitution in the metropolis summarized its recommendations in a slogan: "Constant and persistent repression of prostitution the immediate method; absolute annihilation the ultimate ideal."[17]

The conclusions and recommendations of the Chicago Vice Report, as it was known, called forth from Lippmann an anguished protest, a fine blend of eloquence and analysis. What person, he inquired, who has

. . . put himself into any imaginative understanding of conditions can escape seeing that prostitution today is organic to our industrial life, our marriage sanctions, and our social customs? Low wages, fatigue, and the wretched monotony of the factory—these must go before prostitution can go. And behind these stand the facts of woman's entrance into industry—facts that have one source at least in the general poverty of the family. And that poverty is deeply bound up with the economic system under which we live. In the man's problem, the growing impossibility of early marriages is directly related to the business situation. Nor can we speak of the degradation of religion and the arts, of amusement, of the general morale of the people without referring that degradation to industrial conditions. You cannot look at civilization as a row of institutions each external to the other.[18]

By 1910, Lippmann had also become familiar with the slums of New York City as well as of Boston. "The only practical ideals in a democracy are a fine expression of natural wants," he observed. "This happens to be a thoroughly Greek attitude. But I learned it first from the Bowery."[19]

In summary, it is reasonable to surmise that Lippmann's experience with poverty, against the backdrop of his advantaged urban upbringing, was a primary source of one of his basic conclusions as a young Progressive: the state as enforcer of the taboos of agrarian and middle-class morality upon the urban poor was giving way to the positive state as provider of social services. Lippmann's work in the settlement houses and slums of Chelsea had a more immediate effect as well: the young student redoubled his contributions to Harvard's student literary publications, in particular defending socialism; and became President of the Harvard Socialist Club. Under his leadership, the Socialist Club became considerably more than a discussion circle. It drew up a socialist platform for local elections, criticized the university for not paying its menial employees a living wage, and lobbied for social reform bills in the Massachusetts legislature.[20]

II

Three members of the Harvard faculty had an exceptional impact upon Lippmann: William James, George Santayana, and Graham Wallas. They were remarkably dissimilar men, and their contributions to Lippmann's thought will be discussed below; but it is appropriate here to mention the nature of Lippmann's encounter and relationship with each.

For the Harvard *Illustrated Review*, Lippmann wrote a book review sharply critical of Barrett Wendell's *The Priviliged Classes* because of its defense of the prerogatives of wealth. One afternoon soon thereafter, Lippmann responded to a knock on his door in Weld Hall to find standing before him William James, elderly but alert with his well-barbered beard, and full of praise for Lippmann's essay. Lippmann was captivated by James's warmth and, he later confessed, "almost worshipped him." Though James had retired from teaching, and was to die the year Lippmann left Harvard, Lippmann visited him regularly and often at James's home on Irving Street. Lippmann was excited by the intellectual openness of James, one of the great humanistic psychologists in America.[21]

George Santayana differed from James both in temperament and in his theories: where James was warm, Santayana was cool; where James had what Lippmann termed a "come hither" personality, Santayana preserved his distance; where James's emphasis was on the flow of experience, Santayana's was on the form. Santayana was as thoroughly an aristocrat as James was a democrat. Lippmann was ready to acknowledge that he could understand Santayana, ". . . when he says of the Platonists, 'their theories are so extravagant, yet their wisdom seems so great. Platonism is a very refined and beautiful expression of our natural instincts, it embodies conscience and utters our inmost hopes.'"[22] In this statement the reader can sense Lippmann drawing together James and Santayana—Pragmatism and Platonism.

The Platonist is committed—as Lippmann was to be in the final stage of his social thought—to an invisible, immutable, higher order of reality, which structures and governs the flux of human experience. The Platonist would insist that he is giving expression to a discovery, not a hope, and he would indignantly repudiate the Pragmatic or Freudian suggestion that platonic theories are simply refined expressions of our biological natures. Nonetheless, the Pragmatist and the Platonist agree upon the need for structure in human experience, and its universality. Where they part company is on the central questions of whether the structure is socially constructed and provisional, as the Pragmatist would have it, or beyond convention and change, as the Platonist believes.

Lippmann never grew emotionally close to Santayana, as he had to James, but he stayed on at Harvard to begin postgraduate work as a teaching assistant for Santayana. The philosopher's profound effect on him, Lippmann said later, would have been just as great had he never known him personally. It was Santayana, Lippmann later believed, who prevented him from becoming a Pragmatist.[23]

Lippmann joined a seminar in 1910 which was given by Graham Wallas; and this "drooping, scholarly, fastidiously lucid" man, this "rather slovenly, slightly pedantic, noble spirited," person (as H. G. Wells described him),[24] had a special impact. Like James, Wallas insisted that an understanding of human motivation was indispensable to an understanding of human life; but beyond the usual concerns of James, Wallas was intent upon politics and social reconstruction. His approach was empirical, and his practical experience was impressive. He had stood for office in several London municipal elections and had worked in numerous Parliamentary contests. He had collaborated as an equal with the Fabians, Beatrice and Sidney Webb; Sidney Olivier (Sir Laurence's uncle); and the twin *enfants terribles* of British Socialism, H. G. Wells and George Bernard Shaw. Here was a voice which spoke to Lippmann from within the political whirlwind. Here was ethical theory developed in conjunction with political action to alleviate social suffering. The two men, separated by thirty years, discovered and respected one another immediately.[25]

In the spring of 1910, Lippmann resolved to leave Harvard after a term of postgraduate study, during which he served as assistant to Santayana in the philosophy department. The decision may not have been an easy one for him to make. He had led a comfortable home life, among adults, in a family which was largely centered upon him. He had always been an avid reader, intellectually precocious, and academically successful. Poised and persuasive, in discussion, on debating teams, and in written work, he had enjoyed the admiration and deference of his teachers and fellow students—"our all-unchallenged chief." He clearly bore the marks of the intellectual, and it is not difficult to imagine him enjoying extraordinary distinction in an academic career. Moreover, other avenues of activity, camaraderie, and success were not so open to him. Except for tennis, he displayed no love or aptitude for athletics. He was not adept at banter or at "being one of the boys," a deficiency which was likely to have been intensified for him by his exclusion from Harvard's prestigious social clubs on the grounds that he was a Jew.

Despite all these considerations, Lippmann chose to leave Harvard in June, 1910, and venture upon a much less assured course into the future. He went to work as a reporter for a reformist monthly, *The Boston Common*. Why? I would suggest that the decision was an ethical one, whose meaning is the red thread running through the entire body of Lippmann's published work. The decision arose from Lippmann's conviction that ideas can make a difference in social life—in the course of nations, the conduct of institutions, and in the lives of individual men and women—and that furthermore, he, Walter Lippmann, could make such a difference as a thinker. In a limited sense, Lippmann recaptured and revised the precepts of the Enlightenment—that a humane politics is possible in a large and diversified nation-state and that the success of a humane politics depends upon the rule of law, which is a compound of reasoning, representation, persuasion, and acceptance of majority decisions which do not invade the selfhood of individuals.

Lippmann was with *The Boston Common* only six weeks, enduring torments of boredom with routine reporting, before Lincoln

Steffens, the muckraking journalist—whom we should today more respectfully term an investigative reporter—called Lippmann to be his assistant as an editor of a major national magazine, *Everybody's*. Lippmann accepted gratefully. For the next two years he learned much—not only about the economics and editorial management of a large periodical but about how to write clearly and succinctly, to harness imagination and skepticism, and to investigate social institutions.[26]

Steffens, Lippmann later explained, inducted him into a project in which the two men "were looking not for the evils of Big Business, but for its anatomy." This experience reinforced Lippmann's predilection to seek understanding first, and only later, if at all, to form working moral judgments in accord with the human realities of a given social situation. As he once remarked caustically of the Chicago Vice Commission, "A scientist who began an investigation by saying that his results must be moral or constitutional would be a joke."[27]

On the subject of the analysis of "Big Business"—which included industrial corporations, railroads, insurance companies, banks, and labor unions—Steffens "made a bold and brilliant guess, an hypothesis." Private organizations required government just as certainly as did the public polity—and in private organizations, as with public institutions, the formal charter and structuring of offices was not a wholly true representation of power relationships. Sometimes actual power would thrust its way out of the formal organization through historical chance, and sometimes the disparity was a matter of deliberate deception, of propping up an administrative dummy to conceal actual relationships. "We found," Lippmann related, "that the anatomy of Big Business was strikingly like that of Tammany Hall: the same pyramiding of influence, the same tendency of power to center on individuals who did not necessarily sit in the official seats, the same effect of human organization to grow independently of legal relationships."[28] The analogy with Tammany Hall, the "machine" of New York City politics, is a highly imperfect one. It serves to soften the deeper meaning of the researches of Steffens and Lippmann in this period: that the organization and control of private property in America was becoming more concentrated, divorced from ownership through the public stock company, and steadily loosened from accountability to the public's elected governors. Property "is controlled," Lippmann wrote, "by groups of men whose influence extends like a web to smaller tributary groups, cutting across all official boundaries and designations, making short work of all legal formulae, and exercising sovereignty regardless of the little fences we erect to keep it in bounds."[29]

Through Steffens, Lippmann was introduced to the writers most committed and distinguished in the field of muckraking; but "As Lippmann viewed them, in belief even more than in age, they belonged to another era of history."[30] And Steffens himself was deeply uneasy and anxious. "We have been the blind leading the blind," Steffens guessed wistfully, "but we have led, and not so very far astray, and we are beginning to see the light. I suppose some young fellow like Lippmann will expose us some day, and I say, let 'em expose us. No one can throw more dirt on some of us than we have eaten in our private humility."[31] It has been argued that muckraking was bound to exhaust itself because it had no positive theory of government. The muckrakers themselves were not reformers, but Lippmann, a socialist, was a reformer.

In January, 1912, after Steffens retired from *Everybody's,* Lippmann "jumped" at the opportunity to join the municipal administration of the Reverend George Lunn, newly elected Socialist mayor of Schenectady, New York. This too proved a disenchanting experience, on two levels. In the first place, Lippmann could not abide the pettiness and vainglory of local politicians. He was dismayed "at the grim way in which committee meetings, verbose reports, flamboyant speeches, requests, and delegations hold the statesman in a mind-destroying grasp."[32] Moreover, the Schenectady socialists, while victorious at the polls, lacked what H. G. Wells called a supporting hinterland, a surrounding body of attentive active adherents. "On no important measure," Lippmann concluded, "could the administration expect popular understanding."[33]

Lippmann's apprenticeship in practical American socialist politics lasted only three months. After resigning as secretary to Mayor Lunn, he was free to ponder the future. Within a matter of months, reading and reflecting, he had decided: he would maintain his independent stance; he would try his hand as an author. He drew upon his wide reading as well as his firsthand involvement to compose *A Preface to Politics* and *Drift and Mastery,* which forcefully summarized, analyzed, and projected from his experience. In 1914, at

the ripe young age of twenty-five, in the twilight of the Progressive
Era, these two books swiftly elevated him to national prominence as
one of the nation's foremost political thinkers and commentators.

III

Having looked at the leading events in the first quarter century of
his life, we are now in a position to examine more systematically
Lippmann's social and political thinking in the Progressive era,
down to the outbreak of World War I.

The most important characteristic of American society in the first
two decades of the twentieth century, Lippmann believed, was social growth. Growth meant not only change, but enlargement, adap-
tation, and improvement—progress. The changes through which
American life was passing, and the individual's life span—and attention span—were so circumscribed that most people understandably
did not appreciate the pace and scale of the transformation. The
same had always held true in history, declared Lippmann: "What
looks to us like an incredible rush of events sloping towards a great
historical crisis was to our ancestors little else than the occasional
punctuation of daily life with an exciting incident."[34]

For Lippmann the vital question concerning this time of unprecedented social change was the extent to which it would, or would
not, be met and led by reason—reason in the persons of political
leaders and political analysts, reason in the form of social planning.
He commented: "The measure of our self-consciousness will more
or less determine whether we are to be the victims or the masters of
change. Without philosophy we stumble along. The old routines
and the old taboos are breaking up anyway, social forces are emerging which seek autonomy and struggle against slavery to nonhuman
purposes."[35]

Lippmann's conception of social change, then, was multicausal at
best, fuzzy and diffuse at worst. The "social forces" to which he
refers were what he elsewhere called the great "movements" of the
time—changes within corporate capitalism, the labor movement
and socialism, the movement for women's rights, and consumerism.

Were there forces or principles of social causation deeper than
these social movements? Lippmann strongly implied that there
were—the movements were social institutions and associations animated by common interests, and quite likely the creatures as well as
the bearers of social change. He pointed to a number of possible

deeper causes—the spread of information and education; the ease of travel, which invited cross-cultural criticism; the large surplus of wealth generated by industrial capitalism.[36] But the cause to which Lippmann most often returned was technology—"invention" and "machines." He casually remarked, "We have still to explore the new scale of human life which machinery has thrust upon us."[37] Again, "We are homeless in a jungle of machines. . . ."[38] And "concentration is a world-wide tendency, made possible at first by mechanical inventions. . . ."[39]

These statements imply that Lippmann accepted, in some form, the view shared by most Liberals, most socialists, and Marxists, that the origins of social change, if not exclusively imbedded in the economic process, are predominantly located there, as opposed to the state, in the "private sector" of economy and society rather than in the "public sector." "I venture to suggest," Lippmann wrote, "that much of what is called 'corruption' is the odor of a decaying political system done to death by an economic growth."[40]

Though this statement may ring like the argument of the *Communist Manifesto*—that the old Liberal political order will be done to death by the strength of economic developments it has sought to exploit—Lippmann was never a Marxist.

His argument that economic transformations would force political change stands on three legs. The first is that basic social change can never be wholly anticipated and hence can never be wholly peaceful:

We are not civilized enough to meet an issue before it becomes acute. We were not intelligent enough to free the slaves peacefully—we are not intelligent enough today to meet the industrial problem before it develops a crisis. . . . no honest student of politics can plead that social movements should confine themselves to argument and debate, abandoning the militancy of the strike, the insurrection, the strategy of social conflict.[41]

The second leg of Lippmann's argument for the economic origins of social change is that the legal system, in America and elsewhere, tends to be a fossilized framework of the values of the past, rigid and irrelevant to the needs and problems of the present and future. This view in turn had two or three sources in Lippmann's development, but Marx was certainly not one of these. In the first place, Lippmann could see the biased use of the law in his own day, by judges who wished to break strikes, defeat the organization of labor, and protect corporate wealth. "It is the bad sociology of judges and their class prejudices that are destroying the prestige of the bench," Lippmann objected,[42] applauding Roscoe Pound's remark that the courts were "doing nothing and obstructing everything."[43] Lippmann further expressed deep distrust of the clockwork devices of the American Constitution, inspired, he agreed with Woodrow Wilson, by the Founding Fathers' admiration of the "mechanical" Newtonian explanation of mass and motion.[44] What the Founding Fathers wanted was to construct a timeless "machine" of government, when human nature was in fact organic and continually evolving. The United States Constitution was a series of "fantastic attempts to circumvent human folly by balancing it with vetoes and checks."[45] This bad situation was made worse by allowing judges to claim to base their judgments on a sort of mystical divining of the meaning today, in utterly unforeseeable circumstances, of the fallible authors of that imperfect legal charter of an earlier century.

The third support for Lippmann's negative view of the originating power of the political-legal process was derived from his understanding of William Jennings Bryan, in the light of the theory of Sigmund Freud. Bryan represented the family farm and the family business firm: he represented America's agrarian past, not her industrial future. Lippmann could remember as a child awaiting "with beating pulse" the results of the election of 1896.[46] Bryan was to be feared, we may suppose, because he was the enemy of all that Jacob Lippmann was: a city dweller, son of immigrants, a merchant, a non-Christian. Bryan and the Populists, then, were reactionary. They sought to reverse the course of America's economic and demographic development. And the method of the Populists, to a lesser extent the method of all legislatures, was "the method of the taboo, as naive as barbarism, as ancient as human failure."[47] It was an effort on the part of lawgivers, of the ruling segment of America—very often white, rural, and Protestant—"to ostracize the desires it cannot manage."[48] To Lippmann, there was a compelling analogy between the Sherman Anti-Trust Act and blue laws which forbade selling liquor, or gambling, or dancing. Both discriminated against actual practice, against life as it was lived, whether in the slums or in the offices of corporate management. Part of the problem may have lain with the rural and Protestant predilections of the legislators, but part of it was also to be found in their training. Who were the legislators?—psychologists? economists? educators? authorities in public health? No—they were attorneys, trained to vindicate logic against experience, the past against the present, privilege against the powerless. Faced with a departure from established norms, Lippmann declared, "They issued a legislative curse, and called upon the district attorney to do the rest."[49]

So it was that Lippmann could open his first work, *A Preface to Politics*, with the assertion that sumptuary legislation, enforced morality, more ". . . than any other fetish, . . . has ruined our sense of values by glorifying the pharisee with his vain cruelty to individuals. . . ."[50] For Lippmann had accepted the premise that we live in a pluralistic society, in which men have agreed not to enforce ultimate moral choices upon one another, and in what his mentor William James called "a pluralistic universe," from which we can abstract only working ideas and tentative conclusions. "Those who have some simpler method than the one I have sketched," Lippmann wrote tartly, "are, it seems to me, either unaware of the nature of the problem [of social reconstruction], interested only in some one phase of it, or unconsciously impatient with the limitations of democracy."[51]

IV

A consideration of what Lippmann believed to be the dominant movements of the prewar decades will reveal that the first in importance—for the political leader, and in terms of its historical impact upon the other movements—was the development of the trust, or more generally, the development of corporate concentration. It may seem strange to label corporate concentration a "social movement," but it bore some of the marks normally associated with that term, at least so far as Lippmann was concerned. Moreover, Lippmann, like his mentor James, considered himself an evolutionary naturalist, for whom any phenomenon bore some utility and was therefore never to be condemned *a priori*. Lippmann's view of social development carried a resemblance to James's view of mental life, as Santayana depicted it: "He saw that experience, as we endure it, is not a mosaic of distinct . . . [phenomena]. It fades gradually in the rear, like the wake of a ship, and bites into the future, like the bow cutting the water."[52] For Lippmann, any major institutional development met some need, bore some clue as to the future, provided some opportunity for the political leader.

We had known for two generations, he pointed out, "that the trust was a natural economic growth." It was central to the theory of Marx, and others had developed the idea as well.[53] From the neutral vantage point of sheer curiosity, the coming of the trust signified a greatly enlarged scale of economic activity and far more complexity in economic life as a consequence.

"The scope of human endeavor," Lippmann wrote, "is enormously larger, and with it has come, as Graham Wallas says, a general change of social scale. Human thought has had to enlarge its scale in order to meet the situation." That is why the rigid received "perennial" wisdom is no longer workable, Lippmann argued. Take the Golden Rule, for instance: "I might possibly treat my neighbor as myself, but in this vast modern world the greatest problem that confronts me is to find my neighbor at all. The size and intricacy with which we have to deal have done more than anything else . . . to wreck the simple generalizations of our ancestors."[54] More succinctly he wrote, ". . . tradition will not work in the complexity of modern life."[55] In part, what the new scale and complexity require is a substitution of political planning for religious creeds. "Government can play a leading part in this work," Lippmann asserted, "for with the decadence of the church it [government] has become the only truly catholic organization in the land."[56]

But whatever problems corporate concentration brought with it, Lippmann agreed that it had gone a long way "to bring order out of chaos, and forge an instrument for a nation's business."[57] Here it is Lippmann the dispassionate observer speaking. Denunciations of specific business abuses he believed appropriate. A blanket condemnation of the course of corporate history was not: "It has been said that no trust could have been created without breaking the law. Neither could astronomy in the time of Galileo."[58] The trusts had to be recognized and studied for the dominant social force they were. "When you see how business controls politics, it certainly is not very illuminating to call the successful business men of a nation criminals,"[59] stated Lippmann. Yet this was what the trustbusters were insisting upon, and should they succeed, they would have mounted ". . . one of the most destructive agitations that America has known."[60] Of the Sherman Act, he wrote caustically, "The spectacle of an enlightened people trying in vain for 25 years to find out the intention of a statute that it has enacted—that is one of those episodes that only madmen can appreciate."[61]

It was, in large part, Woodrow Wilson's support of antitrust legislation that caused Lippmann to denounce him as a reactionary. Wilson was not under the spell of Bryan, not even a part of the old Progressive movement; Wilson was "an outsider capable of skilled interpretation."[62] Wilson stood for Bourbonism, for restoration of the old "village patriotism" of the agrarian radicals. Wilson recognized that America had been swept by profound economic change, from top to bottom. Yet rather than domesticating and riding the beast, he sought to cage it, to arrest the widening division of labor, the new efficiencies and new promises of the larger economic units. "The ideal is the old ideal, the ideal of Bryan, the method is the new one of government interference. That, I believe, is the inner contradiction of Woodrow Wilson,"[63] Lippmann concluded.

Wilson, in an address, had rhetorically asked Americans whether they were not eager for the day when their sons should be able to look forward to becoming, instead of workers, "heads of some small, it may be, but hopeful business . . . ?" Lippmann responded with acid skepticism: "But to what percentage of the population can be held out that hope? How many small but hopeful steel mills, coal mines, telegraph systems, oil refineries, copper mines, can this country support?"[64] Lippmann recognized the bitter irony represented by the rise of the trusts: "We are just about to establish a democratic state, and we find that capitalism has become international. It seems as if we were always a little too late for the facts."[65] But he was not ready to concede that the moment for political reform had passed, that ". . . American voters are not intelligent enough or powerful enough to dominate great industrial organizations."[66] What specific political measures would be most efficacious would depend upon circumstance and experimentation. Some industries might require public ownership, and others consumers' cooperatives, and still others direction by regulating commission. No single method would work in all cases.[67]

It was the Pragmatist in Lippmann which left him impatient with programmatic solutions:

. . . as a matter of fact there can be no such thing as a "solution" in the sense which most people understand the word. When you solve a puzzle, you've done with it, but the industrial puzzle has no single key. Nor is there such a thing for it as a remedy or a cure. You have in a very literal sense to educate the industrial situation, to draw out its promise, discipline and strengthen it.[68]

The promise of "Big Business" was threefold for Lippmann. Its first resource was what he called the social surplus, wealth generated by industrial capitalism which was being applied neither to human need nor to economic growth through productive reinvestment. An immediate parallel suggests itself between Lippmann's social surplus and Karl Marx's surplus value, the value given to a commodity by wage labor which was expropriated by the capitalist. Once again, the analogy between Lippmann's thought and Marx's is inapposite. The social surplus, "the legitimate fund of progress," was drawn from inefficient workers, unnecessary jobbers and "middlemen," and rent for land. Just as Lippmann was persuaded that the time was "sure to come, when the government will be operating the basic industries, railroads, mines, and so forth," so he believed that the "landlord is an old-fashioned instrument to be superseded as fast as a less costly one can be devised."[69] Profits might or might not be part of the social surplus. Lippmann never attacked the concentration of wealth as such, nor did he make redistribution of income a central tenet of his Progressivism. There were ways, however, in which he called into question the claims of owners to their wealth. For one thing, he gave moral priority to the claims of the workers to the wealth they produced, in particular the social surplus:

Now the working class has very excellent uses for money that it can secure. It invests directly in human life, in the food, clothing, shelter, and recreation which are its basis. So the pressure of the labor movement is a force that can make for a wiser use of wealth. If employers find that they "cannot" pay higher wages, their real business is not to resist labor, but to increase the efficiency of production so that they can. They will have to learn to finance industry better, they will have to eliminate the sinecures of their cousins and their uncles, they will have to scale down capitalization, and do without the hundred and one middlemen who extract a profit.[70]

Another point Lippmann made was that where private property is concerned, "There is no question of inalienable rights. It is a question of good use and bad use. . . ." If the benefactors of great wealth had less good effect than they might, confiscatory taxation was entirely appropriate. Could the government make better social use of Mr. Carnegie's vast fortune than Mr. Carnegie himself did? If so, ". . . then the government is entirely justified in substituting itself for Mr. Carnegie as a dispenser of libraries and peace palaces."[71]

The claim of the wealthy to the fruits of corporate sales, according to Lippmann, was further weakened by the fact that while the ". . . trusts have concentrated control and management, . . . ownership they have diluted till it means very little." "The stockholders," he contended, "deprived of their property rights are being transformed into money-lenders."[72] Lippmann here was anticipating by a generation the thesis amplified by Adolph Berle and Gardiner Means during the New Deal: a dominant and novel development in the twentieth-century corporation is the separation of the ownership of private property from management of it. "The trust movement is doing," Lippmann presciently observed, "what no conspirator or revolutionist could ever do: it is sucking the life out of private property."[73] The shareholder, he believed, was losing attributes of ownership which had been used to defend the institution of private property from Aristotle to John Stuart Mill:

He may never see *his* property. He may not know where his property is situated. He is not consulted as to its management. He would be utterly incapable of advice if he were consulted. Contact with his property is limited to reading in the newspapers what it is worth each day, and hoping that dividends will be paid. The processes which make him rich in the morning and poor in the evening . . . are inscrutable mysteries.[74]

It was an abstract, ascetic, dysfunctional mode of ownership. *Sic transit gloria entrepreneur.*

But if this drastic alteration in the mode of ownership strengthened the moral, political, and economic claims of labor as opposed to management, if it brought a much enlarged justification for government intervention in the economy,[75] it carried one further basic benefit which Lippmann believed might be more fundamental still. The professional business administrator was coming to supplant the old profit-taking owner-manager. Modern industry had been created by "the profiteer"—but the businessman had never been a universally accepted hero, and now he was not only under challenge, he was being displaced. The "profit system has never commanded the whole-hearted assent of the people who lived under it," he wrote. "There has been a continuing effort to overthrow it." It is noteworthy that Lippmann's roll call of rebels does not include Marx and Kautsky, but Owen, Mill, Ruskin, and Morris.[76] Lippmann remained the Progressive, not a Marxist.

The complexity of the corporate division of labor was bringing about a revolution of incentives. In a way that Adam Smith had never forseen, Lippmann clearly saw that the development of one of Smith's cardinal features of the market economy—division of labor—was strangling another of its central traits, the profit motive, or economic self-interest, as a guide to conduct. The complexity of industrial society meant that the business administrators must possess—or enjoy access to—knowledge of physics, chemistry, and engineering; knowledge of organized labor; knowledge of the credit market; knowledge of the care and feeding of stockholders; knowledge of the political and legislative environment; and, Lippmann concluded, "perhaps at times they may have to dabble in Latin-American revolutions."[77]

Business administration—Lippmann did not hesitate to call it "administrative science"—was emerging to eclipse "the old commercial morality of the exploiter and profiteer."[78] The large-scale complexities of concentrated corporate capitalism had "created a demand for a new type of businessman—for a man whose motives resemble those of the applied scientist and whose responsibility is that of a public servant."[79] What Lippmann wished to stress was precisely the shift in motivation accompanying the new expertise:

. . . men enter the profession by undergoing a special discipline to develop a personal talent. So their lives seem more interesting, their incentives more genuine. The business man may feel the scientist content with a modest salary is an improvident ass. But he also feels some sense of inferiority in the scientist's presence. For at the bottom there is a difference of quality in their lives,—in the scientist's a dignity which the scramble for profits can never assume. . . . a community of interest, a sense of craftsmanship, and a more permanent place in the larger reaches of the imagination.[80]

The concept of scientists—professionals—as a ruling elite which Lippmann advances here is as old as the work of Auguste Comte or of Plato; and as current as the writings of Don Price, Daniel Bell, John Kenneth Galbraith, and Robert Heilbroner. Perhaps the environmental crisis will at last elevate the scientist to the partnership in policymaking which has so long been proclaimed as rightly his. In any event, Lippmann did stop short of announcing the likely death of the profit motive, and the coronation of the disinterested professional. The new professionals were still "surrounded" by the ethos—and the persons—of the old "economic absolutism,"[81] he observed. "The only dispute is whether these [professional] motives can be extended and made effective. It is, I think, a crucial question. It lies at the root of most theoretical objections to socialism in the famous 'human nature' argument."[82] Lippmann himself was convinced that scientific detachment, craftsmanship, and humane cooperation could, and must, replace the supremacy of acquisitiveness and competitiveness. The ". . . old economists were bad psychologists and superficial observers when they described man as a slot machine set in motion by inserting a coin,"[83] asserted Lippmann. But to say that the new structure of motivation *could* win out—even to say that it *must* win out—was not to say that it would, or that it had. Lippmann's deliberate sense of skepticism was never absent from even his most intimate and intense wishes for society. That "business men are undergoing a change of heart," he observed, "is just what an endless number of American reformers are shouting. . . ." But, he warned, "The notion seems to be that workers, politicians, consumers and the rest are to have no real part in the glorious revolution which is to be consummated for their benefit."[84] The transformation of an elite was insufficient to satisfy the democratic Lippmann. All would hinge upon how this "movement" reacted with the other movements stirring America—labor, consumerism, and feminism in particular. Ultimately, an equitable and productive relationship among them all would depend upon political leadership, and a new method in social theory.

In his writings on the labor movement Lippmann allowed the fullest and warmest display of his hopes for social reconstruction. For example, he wrote with feeling of the strength of spirit of Big Bill Haywood, leader of the International Workers of the World, or "Wobblies." Lippmann was arguing that social reform depended on passion as well as imagination, that one should "saturate feeling with ideas. That is the only way in which men can tap their own power,—by passionate ideas."[85] Haywood, he declared, was a fine example:

. . . he sees the unskilled laborer, the genuine proletarian without property in things or in craft; he sees the outcast, the convict, the casual, the bum, the peon, with such wonderful warmth and great understanding that they have come to embody for him the whole social problem. What are the troubles of a business man harassed by a bad credit system to these ultimate miseries in which are concentrated the failures of our civilization? Do you think there will be any "reason" for Haywood in a social philosophy which

seems to forget the very things which fill his sky? He has only to take a walk
through Union Square to feel what fools his critics are.[86]

Rarely does such a display of emotion break through in the writings
of Lippmann even in his youth. By the same token, a few of the rare
displays of bitterness in his writings are reserved for the tactics to
which ownership has resorted to against labor: "They have been
known to refuse advertising to papers which were friendly to organized labor—on the highest grounds, of course, such high
grounds being a refusal 'to pander to the unthrifty class.'" He continued vehemently:

They have been known to use the black-list, though of course they do not
approve of it. They have been known to place spies in labor unions, to
protect workers against themselves. They have been known to use what
revolutionists call the "provocateur." . . . There have been some actual
"planting" of dynamite as at Lawrence, a little beating up as at Calumet,
kidnapping, private armies, Gatling guns and armored trains as at West
Virginia and Colorado.[87]

Employers fight labor, Lippmann argued, as monarchs fight con-
stitutions, as the nobility fought the bourgeoisie to prevent the
middle class from sharing political power through the vote.[88] He
recognized the existence of a class struggle; indeed, he wrote
". . . class interests are the driving forces which keep public life
centered upon essentials."[89] But Lippmann developed no rigorous
definition of class, no unified economic theory of historical development. "I have not been able to convince myself," he wrote in
words William James would have applauded, "that . . . one party,
one class, or one set of tactics is as fertile as human need."[90]
Moreover, Lippmann would broach no determinism of a Marxist
variety or of any other. "For while it is illuminating to see how
environment moulds men," he wrote, "it is absolutely essential that
men regard themselves as moulders of their environment. A new
philosophical basis is becoming increasingly necessary to
socialism—one that may not be 'truer' than the old [Marxist]
materialism but shall simply be more useful."[91]
    Lippmann could quite fairly be called a socialist in his prewar
writings, and "socialist" was no idle term in those days. In 1912 the
American Socialist Party had 118,000 members, 323 publications,
and held twelve hundred offices in thirty-four states, including

seventy-nine mayors in twenty-four states. But it is equally significant that the Socialist Party candidate for President in that year of reform ferment polled only six percent of the vote; and the term "socialist" was so widely and diffusely used that it was applied to a very wide range of humanitarian reformers, who should not in strict usage then have been so called, and would not be in popular usage today.[92]

However, Lippmann's detachment, his rationalism, his individuality, and his Pragmatism barred him from accepting any political creed, even if it was dedicated to the eradication of the misery of poverty, where his feelings were deeply engaged. He found Marx inadequate because of the strength of agrarianism, and most especially of the middle class, in America. Lippmann saw at work in Progressivism "an unexpected burst of sheerly democratic impulse which blurs class lines."[93] He disavowed any "intention of casting any doubts upon the historic service of Karl Marx." The recent developments which have rendered Marx obsolete, he declared, demonstrate "that the probabilities have changed, and . . . only by expressing that fact can *our* social science be built up."[94]

Lippmann regarded Marx as both time-bound and utopian, and he reserved some of his harshest words for utopians of every stripe. Utopians have "an infinite faith in moulds" for human nature, he said: they simply wish to substitute another routinized conservatism for our present routinized conservatism.[95] Warming to his subject, Lippmann was later to say that utopians—naming Plato, More, Bacon, Campanella, Fourier, Bellamy, Wells—have uniformly proposed tyrannies. "But why are the utopias tyrannical?" he asked. His answer was drawn from Freud: "I imagine it is because the dreamer's notion of perfection is a place where everything and everybody is the puppet of his will. In a happy dream the dreamer is omnipotent: that is why it is a happy dream."[96] Utopias, then, are dreams, and not just harmless dreams—infantile dreams where omnipotence and impotence are fantasized, or, in more rational terms, where there is perfectly harmonious regimentation. At best, Lippmann observed, the dream deflects attention from reality, and may leave the dreamer "uncompromising in his dreams, and acquiescent in his deeds."[97]

What Lippmann abhorred most in socialist (and other) utopias was their tendency to "forcible scrubbing and arranging"—the enforced asceticism he had despised in the Populists. Some socialists definitely wished to have the state "become a censor of morals . . . like the benevolent employers. . . . Without any doubt socialism has within it the germs of . . . bureaucratic tyranny. . . ."[98]

If Lippmann's conceptions about the labor movement are pulled together, what was the central thrust of his theorizing about its present estate and its future role? That labor was woefully disadvantaged in the Progressive era, he had no doubt: "They have no share in the country, they have 'nothing to lose but their chains.' But with the tactics open to them they haven't 'a world to win.'"[99] The victory of organized labor was by no means assured. Employers were well organized against them, pitting poor against poor, race against race, religion against religion, native-born against immigrant, denying constitutional rights of speech and assembly, using simultaneously violence and the judicial process to bar the advance of labor. "I don't know, no one knows, whether labor can realize its promises," Lippmann reported.[100] For these reasons, he believed that the time when peaceful tactics could be ethically demanded of the labor movement had not yet arrived. Peace prior to the attainment of power for labor would mean not justice, but continued exploitation. "Perhaps when society has learned to respect labor, then society and labor will disarm. But that day is not our day," Lippmann wrote.[101] Here he anticipated by twenty years the argument of Reinhold Niebuhr in *Moral Man and Immoral Society*.[102] While Niebuhr believed that the community at large had the most to fear from organized group aggression, he argued that the Christian, like the Marxist, could not condemn violence *per se,* since the law, backed by the coercive power of the state, had latent violence within it. The violence of insurrection might have to be raised against the violence of the state in order to obtain justice. Dictatorships, after all, are among the most peaceable of polities.

To be heard, Lippmann argued, reason must speak from power. That is one of the sad truisms of politics. Group cooperation is possible only where the strength of the groups involved has some comparability. Another, perhaps more hopeful, way of stating the dilemma, was to point out that "Guerilla warfare is the only tactic open to weakness."[103] And here Lippmann felt constrained to condemn Bill Haywood and the International Workers of the World: "I have heard Haywood say that when a union had something to lose, the spontaneity of rebellion was gone. . . . The I.W.W. prefers revolt to solidarity—of course, it imagines that it can have workers united and militant too. But in practice it is quite ready to destroy union for the sake of militancy.[104]

The gradual winning of workers' benefits might actually be opposed by militant labor leaders, then, for fear of undermining the prospects of rebellion and radical change. In point of fact, Lippmann countered, those unions that the militants scorned as "conservative," such as the railway brotherhoods, were precisely those unions that had won the most tangible real-world benefits.[105] The crucial benefit for labor was a partnership in management, and quite possibly a partnership in profits.[106]

Without successful unions American classes would become fixed and polarized, Lippmann argued: ". . . it is labor alone that can stand between America and the creation of a permanent servile class. Without unions industrial democracy is unthinkable. Without democracy in industry, that is, where it counts most, there is no such thing as democracy in America."[107] The stakes could scarcely be higher.

Yet Lippmann was hopeful concerning the ultimate outcome. This social problem, like all others, he viewed as a task in applied social education. He once remarked of his experience in the Schenectady office of Mayor Nunn that his socialist colleagues used to contend they were struggling against special privilege. But Lippmann's understanding of the situation was quite different. "I understood then," he related, ". . . what [H. G.] Wells meant when he said that he wanted 'no longer to "fix up," as people say, human affairs,' but to devote his forces to the development of that needed intellectual life without which all his shallow attempts at fixing up are futile."[108]

Lippmann's interest in "the feminist agitation" for equal rights for women reached back, it will be recalled, to his college days. The industrial revolution, by destroying cottage industry, had forced millions of women out of the home, into mine, factory, and office, and left millions more idle and bereft within the home.[109] Lippmann particularly sympathized with women seeking liberation, because, like freed slaves, they had not only to contend with the prejudices of the dominant (male) group, but with their own inner bewilderment.[110]

It was not lost on Lippmann that those women who were championing the right of women to work were almost invariably of the upper class, because of inherited wealth, exceptional talents, or both. He supported the view that "a woman's place is in the home," not for the usual reasons advanced by males, but because of the critical nature of the home as an educational institution. It was in the home, if anywhere, that socialist motives and a humane set of political concerns had to be nurtured. Recognizing that money is power, Lippmann proposed that the division of labor be extended to the home, and that women be paid for the valuable social tasks they perform: "The idea of having forty kitchens, forty furnaces, forty laundries, and forty useless backyards in one square block, managed by forty separate overworked women, each going helplessly to market, each bringing up children by rule of thumb,—all that is a kind of individualism which the world will get away from."[111]

Lippmann borrowed from Freud in suggesting that the present bleak and constricted house life imposed upon women led to their working out their aggressive and antisocial desires vicariously, through their husband's careers and powers in society.[112]

What Lippmann sensed to be the gathering power of feminism was one of his chief reasons for believing firmly in the rise of the consumer movement. "The mass of women do not look at the world as workers," he pointed out; "in America, at least their prime interest is as consumers. It is they . . . who do the shopping; it is they who have to make the family budget go around; it is they who feel shabbiness and fraud and high prices most directly. They have more politics than men. . . ."[113]

Women's free time, their availability for political activism, was a key to the situation; for only by the political process, only by binding legislation, could the consumer movement succeed against the entrenched advantages of the manufacturer and the retailer. The opportunities for legislation were enhanced by the ongoing process of corporate concentration, which increased the visibility of the retail outlets through the rise of the "chain" store and the mail-order house, standardized products and pricing. These developments unified the interests of the consumers, and brought regulation and accountability within easier reach.[114]

But the obstacles to the growth of consumerism were formidable. There was the mythology of open markets and free competition and consumer sovereignty, supported by the academic economists. Lippmann variously termed their theories "brutal fictions," "romantic," "Platonic," and "laughable."[115] There was the reality of monopoly and oligopoly, which had the consequence of depriving the consumer of the knowledge or the power to make the seller-buyer bargain a fair one.[116] And there was the rapidly growing power of advertising, producing what John Kenneth Galbraith delicately terms the "revised sequence." Demand no longer welled up spontaneously from myriad small consuming units, calling forth supply: demand was cynically manipulated by advertising, Lippmann declared. Demand in fact was being manufactured and was becoming one of the vital commodities of the corporate economy.[117]

The realization of the potential of these movements—corporate concentration, labor organizing, feminism, and consumerism—was not assured; "destiny is one of the aliases of drift," Lippmann warned. Political leadership was needed to develop and reconcile the human potential latent in these movements. Just because Progressivism had no charter or manifesto, Lippmann could proclaim himself a Progressive:

> The sanctity of property, the patriarchal family, hereditary caste, the dogma of sin, obedience to authority—the rock of ages, in brief, has been blasted for us. . . . The adjective "progressive" is what we like, and the word "new." . . . The business man has stepped down from his shrine; he is no longer an oracle. . . . We have scotched the romance of success . . . the husband is not regarded as the proprietor of his wife nor the parents as autocrats over the children . . . the body is not a filthy thing, and . . . to implant in a child the sense of sin is a poor preparation for a temperate life. The battle for us . . . does not lie against crusted prejudice, but against the chaos of a new freedom.[118]

Lippmann argued that the basic insight of eighteenth-century American political theory was that that government is best that governs least. It is equally true—and a truth discerned in the twentieth century—he declared, that that government is best that provides most. These two maxims needed to be held, together, and acted upon together, by political leaders. Woodrow Wilson had really understood only the eighteenth-century insight, Lippmann believed; and Theodore Roosevelt understood them both.[119] Wilson was a democratic reactionary and could not act in concert with the dominant movements of the time but would only seek to impede them. Roosevelt, on the other hand, had performed the task of leadership, a task with two dimensions: "By becoming part of the dynamics of unrest he gathered a power of effectiveness: by formulating a program for insurgency he translated it into terms of public service."[120] Roosevelt's actions in behalf of conservation were a model of the statesman at work: "He recognized the need . . . , made it public, crystallized its force and delegated the technical accomplishment. . . ."[121] Roosevelt had exhibited the indispensable qualification of the statesman: "mastery."

Many writers have expressed misgivings concerning Lippmann's admiration of Roosevelt, of leadership and mastery, of technical experts. Has not Lippmann been a skeptic concerning public opinion and dubious of democracy all along? Do not his later writings simply reveal in blatant form an elitism which was latent from the outset? A consideration of Lippmann's later writings must await subsequent chapters, but the issue deserves to be addressed initially here, in the setting of Lippmann's Progressive thought.

Lippmann did admire Roosevelt deeply, with an ardor he surely would not have expressed as a man of greater age. He probably also experienced anxiety about the slender range of alternatives permitted by the American political system in its selection of leaders. The two-party system was not a necessity, he urged: European parliamentary experience had demonstrated that.[122] Yet Lippmann's concern on this score must have been deepening by 1913, as it began to appear that the Progressive "Bull Moose" Party of Theodore Roosevelt would not survive. "The two party system," he complained anxiously, "chokes off the cry of a minority—perhaps the best way there is of precipitating an explosion."[123] (A "return to normalcy" was a more dreadful possibility which the young Lippmann did not descend to examine.) Furthermore, Lippmann did have misgivings about the ability of the possessors of power and wealth to deceive and manipulate public opinion, "For the majority in these semi-democratic times is often as not a cloak for the ruling oligarchy."[124]

But on the record of his early writings Lippmann was indeed a democrat. Of course he reserved the right to exercise his critical faculties; he knew, he said, of no democracy in history that inspired unquestioning enthusiasm.[125] And he was not a "mystical democrat" who believed that elections were completely accurate and adequate expressions of the will of the people. But, he pointed out, "Mystical democrats are rare. Looked at closely an election shows the quantitative division of the people on several alternatives. That choice is not necessarily wise, but it is wise to heed that choice."[126] It was advisable to heed the choice for two reasons: the first was that dissent and discussion are permitted: the minority's dignity and its essential right to one day become a majority are observed. "So *we who are democrats* need not believe that the people are necessarily right in their choice: some of us are always in the minority, and not a little proud of the distinction,"[127] he wrote.

The second rationale Lippmann proposed for majority rule also bore the stamp of the Enlightenment: ". . . of all governments democracy is the most relevant" because "Only humane laws can be successfully enforced; and they are the only ones really worth enforcing."[128]

The central responsibility of the leader, then, was to encourage, as Lippmann said, literally to educate, to draw out, of the dominant movements their potential for civility and social service—their capacity for encouraging human growth. Thus leadership was a necessary but not a sufficient condition of a successful democratic polity: "The real problem of collectivism"—of the future of society—"is the difficulty of combining popular control with administrative power."[129] How power was to be shared, divided, and checked, between the competing and cooperating groups, carried Lippmann back closer to the "fantastic vetoes and checks" of the United States Constitution than he was aware or willing to concede.

That Lippmann was not advocating blind adherence to the whims or dictates of leadership can be grasped in another way. Not only did he discern an objective social situation, not only did he bear many of the distinguishing characteristics of the American democratic socialist; but he argued for a method—a method of proceeding for the leader, and for the social theorist. Lippmann's method was in large part absorbed from his teachers. It was a blend of psychology, education, science, and democracy, and of the correlations between them. The method is never stated altogether or in a single passage, but it represents Lippmann's deepest early understanding of social life and its possibilities.

Some prefatory thoughts are useful in introducing this Progressive "method." First, it should be recalled that Lippmann himself, in behavior and thought, was a highly methodical person, who prized thoroughness and order. Second, though it might not appear relevant at first blush, Lippmann was deeply disturbed by the political apathy and unawareness he encountered at Harvard, in the Mayor's office in Schenectady, and elsewhere. He opened *A Preface to Politics*, with the statement, "The most incisive comment on politics today is indifference."[130] Later, he drew the conclusion that "Only those who are really at home in their world find life more interesting as they mature."[131] But the ". . . modern world is brain-splitting in its complexity,"[132] and many persons prefer emotional "drift" to sustained thinking about society. One of the leading forms of this emotional drift is to be found in the idealization of the American past as a "golden age." The American past is idealized in the images evoked by Adam Smith and Thomas Jefferson: the unfettered individual, preindustrial America, life on the family scale, economic goods supplied by open competition, strictly limited government. "In the Sherman Act is symbolized this deliberate attempt to recreate an undeliberate society," he wrote.[133] For the American democrat, Lippmann continued, drift means the dream that the undisciplined man is the salt of the earth. For the American capitalist, large or small, drift means the dream of laissez-faire, of being let alone, of having the public good result from the individual's pursuit of personal interest and gratification.[134] All these golden ages are rooted in "each man's wistful sense of his own childhood." Each is in some sense infantile and leaves the individual politically uninterested and immobile.[135] For Lippmann, such a lack of interest and action, then, was a dreaming "drift"; its opposite and remedy was "mastery" or method. "The democratic experiment is the only one that requires . . . willful humanistic culture. . . . An aristocracy flourishes where the people find a vicarious enjoyment. . . ."[136] Lippmann's debt to Freud is again evident in this line of reasoning.

The first step in the method Lippmann introduces is the recognition that in industrial society, ". . . men have to substitute purpose for tradition: and that is, I believe the profoundest change that has ever taken place in human history. In endless ways we put intention where custom has reigned. We break up routines, make decisions, choose our ends, select means."[137] It should be pointed out that for William James, one of Lippmann's mentors, mental life was defined by purposiveness: the essence of mental life is the choice of means for the attainment of future ends.[138] This "profoundest change," then, is one which is simultaneously social and psychological. And it is a difficult and painful change, fraught with unforseeable consequences. Modern men, if they are reflective, are required, says Lippmann, "to break with habits rooted in the animal loyalties of

their childhood. . . . The scars are very deep, even the most successful rebel is somewhat crippled."[139]

As a consequence, he argues, anticipating Erich Fromm's famous
thesis of twenty-five years later, many citizens of republics fear
freedom and may seek some new authority to which they may submit, some absolutism in exchange for security. George Bernard
Shaw had expressed the same idea, Lippmann noted: "It was a
profound observation when Bernard Shaw said that men dread liberty because of the bewildering responsibility it imposes. . . ."[140]
Lippmann stated the matter more vividly and inclusively:
"Liberalism suffuses our lives, and the outstanding fact is the decay
of authority. But this doesn't mean for one minute that we are able
to command ourselves. In fact . . . [our time] has lost authority and
retained the need of it. We are freer than we are strong. We have
more responsibility than we have capacity."[141]

V

Yet Lippmann had no counsel of despair or acquiescence, neither
to scale and complexity, nor to the chaos of the new freedom. He
counseled mastery, which he defined as ". . . the substitution of
conscious intention for unconscious striving."[142] So defined, mastery referred to the Enlightenment trinity of the autonomous individual, scientific method, and democratic politics. "There is nothing
accidental . . . in the fact," Lippmann argued, "that democracy in
politics is the twin brother of scientific thinking. They had to
come together. As absolutism falls, science arises. It *is* self-
government."[143]

Lippmann was fully aware how difficult personal mastery, personal self-government, is for most persons. The "exorcising of
bogeys" was "an intricate part of the effort at self-government."[144]
By "bogeys," he referred to the regimen of superstition, of lies and
shame, which has constituted a large, if not a dominant, part of
human mental life in the Progressive present as well as in all ages
past. This regimen has to do most intimately with sexuality, he
declared, but it has also to do with the imagined wrath of God, and
with the "fear economy" which capitalism has established, wherein
the dignity of work, the ability to support oneself and one's family,
may be snatched away at any moment.[145] The more humane society
of the future would require the drastic reduction of "economic and
sexual terror."[146]

According to Lippmann, what was needed was an enlarged acceptance of humanity as we find it;[147] the only thing sacred should be
human experience, the only thing sanctified, human desire.[148] He
concluded, "We have to build up a disciplined love of the real
world. It is no easy task."[149]

There is, then, in Lippmann's Progressive period, a transparent
committment to social reconstruction. Reconstruction, however,
had subjective foundations, he believed. He was deeply concerned
with human rationality, with political psychology, with the inner
dimension of politics, so long neglected by Liberals. Of his teacher,
Graham Wallas, Lippmann wrote, "Mr. Wallas has called a halt. I
think we may say that his is the distinction of having turned the
study of politics back to the humane tradition of Plato and
Machiavelli—of having made man the center of political investigation."[150] The purpose of politics, Lippmann insisted, ". . . is to
provide opportunities, not to announce ultimate values; to remove
oppressive evil and to invent new resources for enjoyment. With
the enjoyment itself it can have no concern. That must be lived by
each individual. In a sense the politician can never know his own
success, for it is registered in men's inner lives and is largely in-
communicable."[151]

When Lippmann discussed this method, this "new way of going at
all problems,"[152] the names he most frequently mentioned as its
pioneers were Darwin, Freud, Wallas, and James. "The impetus of
Freud," he acknowledged, "is perhaps the greatest advance ever
made towards the understanding and control of human character.
But," he added, "for the complexities of politics it is not yet
ready."[153] Lippmann's own first book drew a highly favorable review by Ernest Jones, Freud's British disciple and biographer, in
Imago, a journal of the International Psychoanalytic Association.
Jones praised Lippmann for his application of Freudianism to social
and political problems.[154]

But as Lippmann was no Marxist, neither was he ever a full
Freudian. In truth, he was a youthful, eclectic thinker, borrowing
from several of the leading thinkers of his day in an effort to synthe-
size and popularize theories he hoped would exert a profound social
impact in the years ahead.

The clearest conceptual tie between psychology and programmatic politics he found not in Freud or Wallas but in William James.
James had written an essay in which he decried pacifism for not

granting the reality of human aggressiveness. James proposed instead the consideration of "moral equivalents" for war. The Civilian Conservation Corps of the New Deal and the Peace Corps in the early 1960s are sometimes suggested as examples of what James had in mind: discipline, sacrifice, community, and strenuous effort given over to some shared goal other than the killing of enemies. Lippmann eagerly took up what he understood to be James's underlying assumption (and one of Freud's, as well): ". . . that every lust is capable of some civilized expression." He wrote: "The older moralists, the taboo philosophers believed that the desires themselves were inherently evil. To us they are the energies of the soul, neither good nor bad in themselves. Like dynamite, they are capable of all sorts of uses. . . ."[155]

While all disciplines and institutions had a part to play in this process the Freudians called "sublimation," moral substitution was the essence of statecraft, and the devising of moral equivalents was the goal of philosophy rightly conceived.[156]

Such a political psychology links the leader with the philosopher and conceives of politics as an educative process. "Politics would be like education—an effort to develop, train, and nurture men's impulses," Lippmann said. "As Montessori is building the school around the child, so politics would build all of social life around the human being."[157] That Lippmann saw the politician as educator is further evidence of his being first and last a good democrat, because he had in mind genuine education, not indoctrination:

To govern a democracy you have to educate it: that contact with great masses of men reciprocates by educating the leader. The consent of the governed' is more than a safeguard against ignorant tyrants: it is an insurance against benevolent despots . . . with many exceptions, democracy compels law to approximate human need.[158]

Ever the skeptic, Lippmann was ready to concede that this grand educational opportunity might be lost or defeated—the "modern world is brain-splitting in its complexity"[159]—and the process of deception by special interests was well established. "It is a great question whether our intellects can grasp the subject," he said. "Are we perhaps like a child whose hand is too small to span an octave on the piano?"[160] But Lippmann surmounted these doubts with a characteristically American affirmation: "Experience will reveal our mistakes; research and criticism may convert them into wisdom."[161] It was through the fructifying interplay of theory and practice that the age would earn finally the full right to be called "Progressive." Learning would take place in the classroom and the library, but also in the laboratory, the factory, the legislature and the courtroom, in psychological researches and in the home. "Men made bridges before there was a science of bridge-building," he wrote; "they cured disease before they knew medicine."[162] Here was a new inference to be drawn from defining politics as the art of the possible: the future must be constructed out of the materials of the present.

Any social theorist who is both an optimist and a voluntarist has a rationalist lurking inside him. Any social theorist who places his central confidence in education to improve not only society but the human condition is under the influence of that lurking rationalist within. A rationalist is one who believes in the power of ideas. On the first page of *Drift and Mastery*, Lippmann argued that the social revolution impending in America would not require bullets and bayonets. It was not directed against any external tyrant, he said. According to Lippmann, Americans had ". . . to face the fact in America that what thwarts the growth of our civilization is not the uncanny, malicious contrivance of the plutocracy, but the faltering method, the distracted soul, and the murky vision of what we call grandiloquently the will of the people."[163] Lippmann's rationalism, and his attention to psychology, had the effect of allowing him to be radical without endorsing or envisioning massive violence. Not an armed struggle with the plutocracy, but method, concentration, and clear vision were required to bring into being a transformed society. Even as a young man in the field, in the Socialist municipal administration of Schenectady, Lippmann recalled that whereas his colleagues saw their difficulties as part of the ongoing struggle with the "Great Beast," "Special Privilege," he had believed their defeats and frustrations were due to the lack of educated Socialist support among the general public.[164] And at different points, Lippmann ascribed both the tyranny of rulers and the terrorism engaged in by some of the dispossessed to "ignorance"—a Socratic and rationalistic view of evil.[165]

Graham Wallas and others expressed concern that Lippmann's *A Preface to Politics* might have disclosed a latent admiration of irrationalism. Certainly William James was a nominalist; and Lippmann expressed admiration as well for Henri Bergson, Sigmund Freud, and Georges Sorel. Wallas had, in his *Human Nature and Politics*, sharply criticized the excessive "intellectualism" of nineteenth-century social psychology and political theory, and Lippmann had drunk deeply at Wallas's well. Might not Lippmann's acceptance of all these thinkers, coupled with his admiration for the leader figure in general, and the rather swashbuckling Theodore Roosevelt in particular, signal a serious acceptance of irrationalism? Wallas himself composed the preface to his next work, *The Great Society*, in the form of an open letter to Lippmann, in which he pointedly suggested that twentieth-century anti-intellectualism was a problem to be examined alongside nineteenth-century intellectualism.[166] Wallas and the others need not have worried. Lippmann had not only the influence of Santayana to rely upon but his own innate skepticism and thoroughly cerebral approach to life.

Lippmann did indeed write, "It seems like topsy-turvyland to make reason serve the irrational. Yet that is just what it has always done, and ought always to do."[167] He was making both a descriptive and a prescriptive statement here. He was saying that in the past and in the present, theories were the servants of latent purpose: the values of the theorist or the aims of a class or an institution. Men's "motives were deeper than their intellects."[168] But this was simply what Freud and James were saying: that our perceptions are selective, that to some extent at least we see what we prefer to see, and that we develop theories to serve some agenda of values. As Lippmann pointed out, we are apt to resist such a view, at least of our own cherished theories, because our "intellectual honor" seems at stake: ". . . we think we must aim at final truth, and not allow autobiography to creep into speculation." But ". . . autobiography creeps in anyway. The more we censor it, the more likely it is to appear disguised, to fool us subtly and perhaps dangerously." Men like James, who show us the willful origins of theory, are benefactors, "in reality the best watchers of the citadel of truth."[169]

This must be read, in part, as a confessional statement. Since this is a generalization about theorists, and Lippmann himself is an aspiring theorist, the statement not only includes him but must also have been confirmed by his self-experience. Yet it is not a simple statement of the supremacy of the emotional over the rational in human affairs. Lippmann qualifies it in vital ways. The first one is that he is contending that theory serves purpose. Purpose for Lippmann has an element of volition, or sheer will; it also has conceptual and ethical components. This point of view is evident in Lippmann's treatment of leadership, in which his admiration of Theodore Roosevelt comes to the fore:

Statesmanship cannot rest upon the good sense of its program. It must find popular feeling, organize it, and make that the motive power of government. If you study the success of Roosevelt the point is reenforced. He is a man of will in whom millions of people have felt the embodiment of their own will. . . . For visions alone organize popular passions.[170]

There is operating here what we might call a backdoor rationalism. Lippmann first asserts that in politics passion predominates over the reasoned content, the "good sense," of a "program." But the matter does not rest there. Popular passions, if they are to have effect, must be organized by the "vision" of a "leader." It is only vision that can perform this task. And "vision," Lippmann specifies in this discussion, is a synonym for "purpose." So while passion is the master of reason in politics, it will find a constructive outlet, a human expression, only if it is put in order through the medium of the vision and purpose articulated by a leader. Thus Lippmann confesses the ethical wish underlying his own theory, and argues that conceptualization and ethics, as well as will, play essential roles in the drama of politics.

Lippmann matured during the twilight of Progressivism— uniformly mistaken by the Progressives for the dawn—as a chastened rationalist. Wallas taught him that psychology is essential for the study of politics—that human experience is the alpha and omega of any sound political theory. James too taught that thought is enveloped in experience and that ideas are only provisional constructs of that experience, reflecting aspiration as well as curiosity. From Freud Lippmann heard again the message of naturalism, of scientific method, and of the acceptance of these as bridges to personal harmony and social cooperation. "Where there is id, there shall be ego," Freud wrote, meaning that reason could come to a larger acceptance and mastery of the instincts simultaneously. Lippmann, on a parallel path of reasoning, hoped for radical social change and a more equitable human future without large-scale violence. And he hoped for a better human future without being required to subscribe to any fixed idea of human goodness and benevolence.

VI

The events of the twentieth century did not gratify such humane hopes, and the place of the man of reason is insecure in times of conflict. National and global crises were to test severely Lippmann's faith that it would be best "if among us there are men who have stood apart, who refused to be anxious or too much concerned, who were cool and inquiring, and had their eyes fixed on a longer future."[171]

Lippmann was never quite so removed as that description of the dispassionate political philosopher implied. He cultivated detachment, it is true, but as a means to influencing men and events as well as a means to understanding them. He lived his professional life in close proximity to power. In his youth he even elected to grasp it for a time, in a series of secondary but significant offices. After America's entry into World War I, he accepted an appointment as Assistant to the Secretary of War, Newton Baker. After a few months in that position he was invited by Colonel House to serve as Secretary to the Inquiry, a confidential panel of scholars on whom President Wilson would rely for information and recommendations in framing the American peace proposals. This position was followed by European service as a commissioned officer in Army Intelligence. Finally, after helping to draft an explanation of Wilson's Fourteen Points for the Allies, Lippmann was given a place on the United States delegation to the Versailles peace conference. None of these positions seems fully to have satisfied Lippmann, though for a man not yet thirty years of age they represent rare distinction. In actuality, he probably possessed more power as a member of the editorial board of *New Republic* in regular communication with Colonel House. As the *New Republic* gradually swung away from Theodore Roosevelt in 1915–1916, to an endorsement of Woodrow Wilson for reelection, the White House had been acutely aware of the stature of this new journal of American Liberalism, and aware too of the prestige of the youngest of its editors.

In any event, his wartime experience provided Lippmann with the stimulus and materials for his most original work, *Public Opinion*. Indeed, in the decade following the war he had the opportunity to reflect and compose the two books which were most independent of the immediate stream of events—*Public Opinion* in 1922 and *A Preface to Morals* in 1929.

Yet his critics and friends alike fretted. Herbert Croly at the *New Republic* was openly distressed that Lippmann had returned to the "fleshpots" of New York City in 1921 to accept a post as editorial writer for the New York *World*. Two years later Lippmann assumed full editorship. In 1931, when the *World* failed financially and Lippmann contracted to write a column for Ogden Reid's *Herald Tribune* and its syndicate, many Liberals felt betrayed. The *World's* editorial page had been the foremost voice of the Democratic Party, exposing the oil and land scandals of the Harding years, strongly supporting the Presidential candidacies of John W. Davis in 1924 and Al Smith in 1928, campaigning against the Ku Klux Klan and in behalf of better living conditions for the miners of West Virginia. From advocacy of these causes Lippmann had moved to the leading organ of Wall Street Republicanism. Liberals were angered that Lippmann would lend the considerable prestige of his name to the *Herald Tribune,* and were not at all mollified by the newspaper's announcement that he would be allowed to "write freely upon such topics as he selects, expressing whatever opinions he holds."[172]

Lippmann's "Today and Tomorrow" column, despite the acrimony which accompanied its inception, brought him unprecedented reach and respect. His thinking now became known to an estimated eight million readers of two hundred and fifty newspapers across the country and in twenty-five foreign nations. To the dismay of some of his old friends he did begin to associate intimately with men of wealth and power—in the Century and Harvard Clubs in New York City and in the Metropolitan and Cosmos Clubs in Washington, D.C. Yet he did remain a steadfast internationalist and supporter of Franklin Roosevelt's foreign policy of preparedness and assistance to the Allies.

Now Lippmann lost the anonymity he enjoyed behind the unsigned columns of the *World's* editorials, and his judgment was sometimes buffeted by the rising winds of history. It was in "Today and Tomorrow" that he offered his preelection assessment of Roosevelt in 1932 as "a pleasant man who, without any very important qualifications for the office, would very much like to be President." It was in "Today and Tomorrow" that he vigorously attacked the regulatory efforts of the New Deal and endorsed Landon for President in 1936, Dewey in 1948, and Eisenhower in 1952. Yet these positions, disturbing as they were to Liberals at the time, were not based on a time-serving conservatism. Many Liberals shared reservations over the New Deal's pragmatic adventures in regulation. Dewey and Eisenhower appealed to Lippmann as leaders who would reeducate the Republican Party to the mid-century realities of American politics and restore a fully functioning two-party system.[173] Lippmann's criticisms of the New Deal and his support for Republican Presidential candidates led some to denounce him as a pessimist and opportunist who had lost or bartered his Liberal principles. James Reston was nearer the truth when he observed that Lippmann had always remained "an optimistic skeptic," and one who "merely used the news of the day to illustrate his philosophy of the age."[174]

The reserve with which Lippmann guarded his personal life contributed to his reputation for inscrutability. In 1921 he moved to New York to take up his responsibilities with the *World*. Four years earlier he had married Faye Albertson, the daughter of the Christian Socialist Ralph Albertson, in whose home Lippmann and other Harvard undergraduates had enthusiastically discussed social issues in 1910. Near the time of their divorce, he moved back to Washington, and married Helen Byrne Armstrong, in 1938. Their gracious hospitality to young "movers and shakers" in government and academic life was well known, as was their home on Woodley Road, next to Washington Cathedral.

Presidents came calling in the 1960s. After the chill of the Eisenhower years ("Brains, you know, are suspect in the Republican Party," Lippmann told an interviewer), Lippmann, now past seventy, regained warmth and animation with the advent of the New Frontier. His 1955 book, *Essays in the Public Philosophy*, had left its readers with a sharp sense of the impermanent and relative—albeit real—value of representative democracy; and the working title of the manuscript unfinished at his death was, "The Ungovernability of Man."[175]

Yet in the 1960s Lippmann and the America of Liberal hopes seemed to recognize and greet one another anew. In 1958 and in 1962 Lippmann was awarded the Pulitzer Prize for literature, and in 1962 the George Foster Peabody Award for Broadcast Journalism. Later he would agree with the common judgment that Kennedy's thousand days bore more promise than performance. But Lippmann always believed in the importance of symbolic politics, and of the Kennedy legend he wrote in 1967: "I am glad of that legend, and I think it contains that part of the truth which is most worth having.

This is the conviction, for which he set the example, that a new age has begun and that men can become the masters of their fate."[176]

It was Lyndon Johnson's destiny to carry to fruition both the promise and the menace of the Kennedy years, Lippmann found. It was Kennedy who said, "The 'Great Society' asks not how much, but how good; not only how to create wealth but how to use it; not only how fast we are going, but where we are headed." It was Johnson who superintended the enactment of the programs envisioned by Kennedy. (It might be added that it was Kennedy who created the Presidential Medal of Freedom as the highest honor the United States could bestow upon a civilian; and Johnson who awarded it to Lippmann.) Kennedy quoted Lippmann in foreign policy addresses; Johnson inducted Lippmann as a foreign policy speech-writer. Kennedy created the American commitment to combat in Indo-China; and Lippmann broke with Lyndon Johnson over this issue. Branded a "negotiations monger" in the Eisenhower years, Lippmann was convinced that the extension of Communist influence to all of Southeast Asia was inevitable, and that in waging full-scale warfare America was playing the part of a reactionary aggressor against history as well as against the Vietnamese nation. Hence Lippmann spent the closing years of his career as journalist expressing reasoned and cadenced outrage against the course of the country and the office he esteemed above all others. Yet the intersection of history and morality was where he had always tried to stand, and as he had with Theodore Roosevelt, he seemed to find personal vindication as well as sorrow in opposing a President whom he had admired and supported.

Lippmann went into semiretirement and left Washington in 1967 to travel restlessly in Europe for a time, even buying a chateau in France. Then he returned to his native New York City, where he died on December 14, 1974.

CHAPTER 2

War and Diplomacy

I

THE coming of World War I dashed hopes which had become virtually unquestioned for Lippmann, and raised obstacles to progress of which he had never dreamed. Only months before the outbreak of war, he had written with calm assurance that "Patriotism itself has gained a new dignity by its increasing alliance with democratic reform, and there is actually ground for supposing that love of country is coming to mean love of country and not hatred of other countries."[1] Lippmann's hopes could take wing so easily because they had never felt the gravity of international affairs. He had never taken an interest in international politics until after August, 1914. Instead, he had imbibed the easy Progressive faith that democratic reform and domestic politics were controlling, that ". . . the money spent on battleships would be better spent on schoolhouses, and that war was an affair that 'militarists' talked about and not something that seriously-minded progressive democrats paid any attention to."[2]

He had not been prepared to listen when Graham Wallas had warned him four years earlier that a great war might soon break out in Europe, and that if it did, it would smolder on for thirty years. ". . . I had no notion that it would ever touch me or jeopardize the interests of my country," Lippmann confessed later.[3] Thus the war came as a "shock"; he was "not mentally prepared"; and he "struggled with misgiving and reluctance to grasp our interest in the war."[4] He was sufficiently naive that, some days after the assassination of the Archduke Ferdinand, he sailed for England, spent a "delightful" July in London and in the English Lake Country at a Fabian institute with Bernard Shaw and the Webbs, crossed over to Belgium, and was "astonished" and "annoyed" to discover that the German-Belgian border had been closed because of a German ultimatum.[5]

One view of Walter Lippmann's intellectual biography, which has been suggested in fragmentary form by a number of writers, would read something like the following: Lippmann was a bright, but youthful and over-assured writer, whose "dream" was "shattered" by World War I (in his own phrase). The dream was of a world not only free from armed conflict, but in a steady process of pacification through reason, science, and the spread of democratic practices. That dream lost, Lippmann the social theorist sank into a pessimistic decline from which he never recovered. In wartime and the 1920s he debunked public opinion and argued that a posture of Stoic detachment was the best of all possible philosophies. In the 1930s he adopted a policy of noninvolvement and isolation in foreign affairs, shifting drastically to a Machiavellian policy of *Realpolitik* as World War II unfolded. Finally, in the "Ike age" of the Cold War, he developed an illiberal "natural law" philosophy with strong authoritarian overtones, a position which amounted to a confession of the bankruptcy of his youthful Pragmatism and radicalism.

Such an interpretation of Lippmann's intellectual development is certainly credible to some extent—otherwise it would not have been subscribed to, in part, by such distinguished intellectual historians as Charles Forcey, Christopher Lasch, Morton White, and Benjamin Wright.[6] My own reading of Lippmann is that he was a considerably more complex figure, one whose thought possesses moral and theoretical coherence. This coherence contributes to his stature as one of the principal architects of twentieth-century American Liberalism.

It is undeniably true that World War I led to some "hardening" of Lippmann's position and that he now spoke less often as a radical, more often as a Liberal. He now saw Liberals and Progressives arrayed against not only reactionaries on the right but revolutionaries on the left. The coming to power of Bolshevism in Russia had made centrists of the American Progressives overnight. Now Lippmann saw the global alternatives as reaction, reconstruction, or revolution.[7] Now he had a new maxim to defend, one that he had stated prior to 1914 but had not seen as vital: the rule that reform is the antidote to revolution.[8] In 1915, Lippmann could write in a statement with autobiographical overtones that "the moderate radical believes that democratic governments will respond to a majority, that 'capitalist officials' may even be ready to administer socialist policies. It is a difference of opinion [that is, between revolutionary and evolutionary socialists] (based on a difference of temperament and experience) as to whether struggle can be sublimated into politics."[9]

In 1919, in the midst of the Red Scare, Lippmann was still confident that Liberalism was the strongest force in America;[10] and for the overcoming of the panic he placed his hope in "what might be called the latent public, in that community . . . looking for the truth."[11] This faith in the reason of decisive numbers of the public was a steady refrain in Lippmann's wartime writings. The difference for him between the internationalist and the chauvinist lay in "the supremacy of conscious purpose" on the part of the former. Of the internationalist, it could be said, "He is loyal [to his nation] for reasons, not merely by habit. He holds his local patriotism with a sense that it is temporary, knowing that he must be ready to merge it in a larger devotion."[12] Even in what some have held up as Lippmann's most aggressively nationalistic work, *U.S. Foreign Policy: Shield of the Republic* (1934), he presented the hope that ". . . what can prevail everywhere, if the alliance holds together, is the universal law that force must not be arbitrary, but must be exercised in accordance with laws that are open to discussion and are subject to orderly revision."[13]

His Liberal ideal of government by reasoned law was still intact. What the years had washed away was the utopian intimation that government and law could be designed to diminish force and coercion.

II

In 1913, Lippmann had received an invitation to become, with Herbert Croly and Walter Weyl, a member of the editorial board of a new progressive journal Croly was founding, which came to be called the *New Republic*. Lippmann gladly accepted the offer, and it was a happy decision. It afforded him a leading role on one of the most prominent journals of the era. Moreover, when war did come, he was able to extend and deepen his thinking by his close professional association with men who were more advanced than he in years and in their reflection on international affairs.[14]

Thus Lippmann, in concert with the other senior editors of *New Republic*, was able to think through alternatives, adopt positions cautiously, and probe for analogies and illumination from psychology and from history. In 1915, he wrote that "The man who claimed that he was not bewildered would write himself down a fool. We are challenged, every one of us, to think our way out of the terrors amidst which we live."[15] This could stand as a motto for his wartime writing, and for him and his defenders explain many or all of the many shifts of position which were to mark his work over the next sixty years.

The *New Republic* contended that the era of isolation in American foreign policy was at an end, but for many months the editors continued to favor American neutrality between the belligerents. Neither the Atlantic Allies nor the Central Powers could "claim exclusively to represent the interests of a better international order."[16] Moreover, the *New Republic*, attempting to follow a course of tough-minded "realism," pursued a theme hammered home repeatedly by Lippmann—that Americans should be concerned not with the "whence" of the war—uncovering its causes, identifying and branding the aggressor—but its "whither"—its outcome, an outcome which should promote alike the interests of international organization and the interests of the United States, between which the editors saw no conflict.[17] It is noteworthy that as late as December, 1915, the eminent American philosopher Ralph Barton Perry could assail the *New Republic* as pro-German.[18] A survey by the *Literary Digest* of American periodicals concluded that the *New Republic* had made "the strongest denunciation of Great Britain."[19]

The *New Republic's* evenhandedness, however, was a triumph of reasoned restraint over deeper cultural affinities, loyalties, and prejudices. Every senior editor was an Anglophile of one sort or another, and a great many of the contributors to the journal were British, with Norman Angell, Harold Laski, Graham Wallas, Alfred Zimmern, H. G. Wells, Rebecca West, and Bernard Shaw leading the list.[20] If the attitude of Lippmann and of the *New Republic* was never uncritical toward the British, it was always potentially supportive. From the early weeks of the war, there was in the editors' minds a tacit understanding that America would have to intervene should it become necessary to prevent the defeat of France and England. After the sinking by a German submarine of the British passenger liner *Lusitania*, the *New Republic* moved to favor "differential neutrality," a policy of military noninvolvement which would allow the United States to supply the Allies with arms without becoming entangled in their postwar aims.[21]

After long and sometimes agonized consideration, the editors transferred their hopes from the 1916 candidacy of their Progressive hero, Theodore Roosevelt, to Woodrow Wilson. On August 28 of that year, Norman Hapgood wrote President Wilson that "Lippmann is the ablest of the *New Republic* editors and the one who is working to swing the paper openly to you."[22]

The major sticking point in the editors' reluctance to endorse Wilson was their belief that he was an unreconstructed Jeffersonian—literally a reactionary, who did not favor the strong positive use of the government in domestic affairs. "Mastery" was what the times called for, an acceptance of large scale economics and an application to it of the new knowledge of economics and public administration, and such techniques as labor organizing, collective bargaining, progressive taxation, regulatory commissions, and nationalization.

But Wilson courted the *New Republic* editors and his programs and persuasion won them. On one occasion Wilson wrote Hapgood that he had spent "something over an hour and a half with . . . [Lippmann], and enjoyed it greatly."[23] The President also fought to keep Croly's and Weyl's friend, George Rublee, on the Federal Trade Commission. Lippmann, three weeks before the 1916 Presidential election, wrote that he would vote for a President who was "evolving under experience . . . and remaking his philosophy in the light of it." Indeed, Wilson had grown "from a laissez-faire Democrat into a constructive nationalist," one willing to use the national authority of the federal government for national purposes.[24]

Once America entered the war, Lippmann took a leave of absence from the *New Republic* in order to involve himself directly in the war effort. His energies and his enthusiasm ran high. In 1917 and 1918, he served successively in four positions. The first was as Assistant to the Secretary of War, Newton D. Baker, a close friend. Lippmann represented the office of the Secretary on a variety of committees dealing with labor problems as they bore upon war production. Most of these committees involved negotiations with Samuel Gompers, President of the American Federation of Labor. On one of the committees Lippmann served with Assistant Secretary of Navy Franklin D. Roosevelt. In the fall of 1917 Lippmann was appointed Executive Secretary of a secret group of distinguished scholars, known simply as The Inquiry, organized to provide the President with territorial, ethnic, economic, and political information relevant to the organization of the peace, when hostilities should end. The Inquiry prepared a large portion of Wilson's Fourteen Points, the basis of the American terms for a peace settlement.[25]

Lippmann grew restless with research work. It was arranged that he be granted a commission as captain in the Army to establish liaison with the British Propaganda Division, and to direct American propaganda to the German people. The effort was so successful that in one group of German prisoners taken it was found that one out of every three was carrying Allied propaganda, an offense decreed treasonable by the German high command.[26]

Finally, Lippmann was attached to the staff of Colonel House, President Wilson's key confidante and advisor. Since the Germans had agreed to surrender on the basis of the Fourteen Points, the British and Italian leaders demanded a detailed explanation of the meaning of the Fourteen Points. Lippmann wrote explanatory memoranda on thirteen of the fourteen, which were approved by the President and forwarded to the British and Italian governments, which accepted them.[27]

But disillusion set in. Lippmann believed it a mistake for the President, so definitely committed to the Fourteen Points, to head the American delegation. He found the American delegation underinformed, and unequipped to resist the relentless insistence of France and England upon a punitive peace with terms strongly favorable to their national interests. Lippmann was opposed to United States participation in the military expeditionary invasion of the Soviet Union. Dismayed and disheartened, he left the Paris Conference in January, 1919.

He resumed his position on the *New Republic*. One week after the Treaty of Versailles was published, the magazine broke with Wilson and opposed ratification. While Lippmann a decade later related that Croly had taken the lead on the editorial board in opposition to the President, and he had followed Croly, Robert Morss Lovett had a different memory. He dined with the editors on the day of their decision to oppose ratification, and he recalled "Lippmann's vigorous denunciation of the treaty as breaking faith with Germany and a violation of our moral obligations to the world."[28] Soon thereafter Lippmann took a leave of absence from the *New Republic* in order to complete his book, *Public Opinion*. In 1921, he was invited to join the senior editorial staff of the New York *World*, long edited by Joseph Pulitzer, a champion of the interests

represented by the Democratic Party. Following the death of Frank
Cobb in 1923, Lippmann was given charge of the *World*'s editorial
page until the paper ceased to publish in 1932.[29] During the period
1922–1931, he authored five books, none of them on international
affairs. But of the twelve hundred and fifty editorials he wrote for
the *World*, more than one third dealt with international affairs.[30]
Clearly a permanent new dimension had been added to Lippmann's
social and political thought.

III

Lippmann analyzed and wrote and spoke about international affairs for sixty years, under ten Presidents, in a volume reaching into
the millions of words. A corpus of this magnitude cannot be treated
in detail in the scope of a single chapter. But there is a logic to
events, as Lippmann liked to observe, and there is an intellectual
and moral logic to Lippmann's thought. We can examine, then, five
principal categories through which Lippmann structured his
theorizing about international politics: sovereignty and nationalism;
imperialism; war; balance of power; and international organization.
Each of these sets of phenomena represented a moral dilemma for
Lippmann: that is, each represented not only a complex of facts to
be explained, but some opportunity for the constructive use of
American power. It is in the world he desired, as much as in the
world he described, that the unity of Lippmann's thinking upon
international politics is to be found.

Sovereignty and nationalism are customarily considered separate
realities, but Lippmann viewed them as the psychological and jurid-
ical sides of a basic problem: the necessity for national unity in
international affairs. The sinking of the passenger liner *Lusitania*
raised this issue vividly. Americans had always believed they possessed basic democratic control of their nation's foreign policy. Yet
many Eastern urban Progressives, including Lippmann, who were
anxious that peace with Germany not be lost through this single
incident, were also anxious that the President not call Congress into
special session to consider the matter. "To our surprise and humilia-
tion," Lippmann wrote, "some of us discovered that our desire for
peace and our faith in democratic institutions conflicted." He regarded it as an obligation of intellectual self-respect "to search out
the meaning of the discovery that on the issue of our national existence we are not a self-governing people."[31] A further autobio-

graphical aspect to Lippmann's realization of the strength of nationalism lay in his discovery that in time of war, when the need for unity is overriding, "the humane capacity for playing with ideas and speculating freely has almost disappeared."[32]

The requirements of national unity in a lawless world of nation-states, then, presented a problem with two sides: sovereignty, which to Lippmann signified the practical institutional dilemma of submission to nonaccountable leaders; and nationalism, the regressive emotional state of the populace, called up by the need for national unity. It was a practical fact, he acknowledged, that "Danger requires us to be as 'one man.'"[33] The basic reason was obvious—to a Progressive painfully obvious: a single man, or a small number of men acting in concert, could negotiate, while multitudes could not. A large group of persons had an inertia which seemed unavoidable. In part, the inertia was due to outmoded information and ideas, but ignorance was not the crux of the matter: the same sort of inertia would operate among a large number of scientists, for example. What a large group lacked was ". . . quickness of mind, direct contact, adaptiveness, invention, the right proportion of give and take. . . ." The general public, vis-à-vis the sovereign, was something like a customer who could say yes or no to what was offered by a salesman, but could not describe exactly what he wanted.[34]

Thus stated, the problem might simply be one of democracy being incomplete in an imperfect world, a cause for concern for the Liberal, dejection for the radical, but a cause of despair for neither. More ominous implications presented themselves, however, to further reflection.

National unity in wartime ". . . obscures with a horrible shadow the differences of many men out of which is born the curiosity of civilized life," Lippmann reflected. "External danger makes us revert from the democratic to the dynastic conception of the state."[35] In domestic democratic politics, as in the arts and sciences, we come to meet and to know, personally or through publication, those who differ with us. But in foreign politics, within our own borders, we may meet no one who openly disagrees with the sovereign—"politics stops at the water's edge."[36]

The public's thinking on foreign affairs had hardened into the molds of a few slogans—such as No Entangling Alliances, Monroe Doctrine, Open Door—into which patriotism was ready to flow at the behest of the leader. In the United States, Lippmann wrote, "The President has enormous power of directing that flow. His decision as to what shall be published and what concealed is one of the supreme attributes of his office."[37] In 1919, Lippmann did not hesitate to say that the postwar economic recovery of the nation was being hampered by the absence of the President at the Paris Peace Conference, a President who had autocratically centralized in himself decision-making powers: "If he is away the thinking apparatus is away."[38]

Thus the sovereign—in the United States the President—in times of foreign crisis and war had the means to manipulate national sentiment, and he was not likely to lack the will to use that power. The President's decision to do so was likely to be reinforced by his military advisors, who would see the military advantages of a unified, determined population, and swift, concerted action, and who would consequently often be intolerant of Liberal discussion, which would bring delay, and raise qeustions as to whether the chosen course of action was the best course.[39]

But the problem of sovereignty for the Progressive assumed its full grim proportions, according to Lippmann, only when viewed in conjunction with the deep irrational pressures of nationalism. Nationalism was primarily an offensive and defensive reaction to fear.[40] It appeared in time of trouble, and "Like sheep in a shower we huddle about the leader."[41] An upsurge of nationalist sentiment brought with it an eclipse of the critical faculties upon which democratic processes depended, and the result was that the primitive reactions of flight and fight were charged with unconscious emotions, beyond the correction of reason for most persons.[42] In Lippmann's words, " 'Touch me,' says the hero to the Hottentot chief, 'and tomorrow morning you will be looking into the angry eyes of a hundred million American citizens.' No audience within the memory of the oldest theatrical producer has ever failed to respond."[43]

Lippmann's understanding of nationalism, then, was a psychological one, which might be termed a blend of Edmund Burke's theories with those of Sigmund Freud. Nationalism was beyond moderation by reason, an act of corporate regression to origins, in order to find safety and strength for combat. All formal education reflected this: education in school built upon the prerational, tacit education of childhood. "The house, the street, the meadow and hill upon which he first opened his eyes, the reactions to family and

strangers which remain as types of his loves and hates . . . these are
the stuff out of which nationality is made," Lippmann observed. [44]
Later, men come to identify with the larger institutions and symbols
of which the nation was composed, according to Lippmann, and in
dealings with foreign states, they regress from the democratic to the
dynastic conception of the state, are haunted by the ghost of a king,
and rediscover the uses of a monarch. [45] Edmund Burke's notion
that patriotism is nurtured in the "little platoons" in which we live,
ascending step by step to more inclusive associations, is clearly
present in Lippmann's conception of nationalism, as is Sigmund
Freud's "father figure," omnipresent in every authority situation.

Thus to Lippmann it appeared that foreign politics tapped deeper
levels of politics and instinct than those drawn upon, or permitted
play, in domestic parliamentary politics. The sentiments of nationality "blur personality and education, and evoke buried loyalties and
ancient pugnacity." [46] It was on concepts akin to the sociologists'
"reference group" and "negative reference group" that Lippmann
was relying here. Nationalism raised "the old barbaric vanity of a
Chosen People." [47] Nationalism included and excluded other humans with the combined intensity of brother, clansman, neighbor,
and fellow citizen. Because nationalism was so ruthless and indis-
criminating, so intimately linked to birth, childhood, identity, and
survival, "Sympathy for foreigners is the most disinterested and
civilized form of sympathy," Lippmann concluded. [48]

Lippmann conceived each of the principal categories of international politics as presenting some dilemma of public morality and
public policy. He always sought to avoid a priori moral judgments.
He opposed any condemnation of a phenomenon which was based
on a received creed, or an appraisal which failed to show appreciation of the dynamics of the phenomenon under study or of the social
and psychological needs it served. He regarded sovereignty and
nationalism as institutional and psychological aspects of national
unity in an insecure world, rooted in biological nature and personal
identity as well as in the mechanics of leadership and national security. It is equally clear that Lippmann regarded sovereignty as a
dangerous breach of parliamentary politics, and nationalism as a
dangerous collective emotional regression, grounded in fear.

How he believed that nationalism and sovereignty might be re-
formed and surmounted will be seen in greater detail below. But
three observations may be made here. First, Lippmann was con-

vinced that somehow the methods of parliamentary democracy must
be brought to bear on international affairs. He strongly implied that
ultimately either the demands of security and combat would engulf
democratic practice or democratic practice would civilize the conduct of international relations. In 1915, he was still optimistic about
the outcome:[49]

The people have suffered, worked, paid, and perished for ends they did not
understand. They have gone to battle with noble words in their hearts,
ignorant of the true motives and ambitions which arranged the battle. The
great virtue of democracy . . . is that it supplies a method for dragging
realities into the light, of summoning our rulers to declare themselves and
to submit to judgment.[50]

Second, Lippmann was firmly persuaded of the leading role
which education and publicity must play in any major advance in the
conduct of affairs of state. As matters had stood in the modern
world, diplomacy had been the province and prerogative of a small
cultivated elite, among whom rumors and intrigues abounded along
with ceremony and supper parties. Lippmann believed in the "great
healing effect of publicity"[51] and in the vital importance of increasing the number of informed people who could see their own direct
stake in their nation's foreign policy.[52] In part his projected policy
depended on a widening of publicized and regulated economic in-
vestment in the less developed countries. In part, it depended upon
the efforts of editors and educators, whose work was so often per-
verted or suppressed in time of war.[53] The passionate convictions
Lippmann held on this subject were unmistakable: education and
democratic politics are mutually dependent agencies of civility. "In
fact, opposition is about the only incentive we have to practice
reason and tolerance," he wrote. "Unless our ideas are questioned,
they become part of the furniture of eternity. It is only by incessant
criticism, by constant rubbing in of differences, that any of our ideas
remain human and decent."[54]

Third, Lippmann placed some of his hope for the future of humanity in the possibility of enlarging patriotic loyalties beyond national frontiers. Within the past one hundred and twenty-five years,
the United States, Germany, and Italy had been welded into
nation-states out of smaller sovereign entities. Patriotism need not
be exclusively local. If men are capable of attaching their loyalties to

anything so remote and abstract as the British Empire, or even the United States, he claimed, allegiance to some more extensive global union "has ceased to be a psychological impossibility."[55] The examples of Hamilton, Cavour, and Bismarck showed the methods necessary: the creation of a tangible partnership and community of interests, indispensably including economic interests, and an intensive publicity campaign to demonstrate the existence of those shared interests could succeed in creating larger political unities. So Lippmann mused, in 1915, amidst a world sinking steadily deeper into war.[56]

IV

Lippmann observed that once the Western frontier in the United States had closed, a "new nationalism" was evident in America. In part this was due, he believed, to the fact that national consolidation was accompanied by the rise to national power of a variety of middle-class reform movements, claiming to represent American values. But in part it was due to this nation's "entering upon an imperial competition" with the great powers of the Old World. Since then, the Spanish-American War, the construction of the Panama canal, the rise of American naval power, and our growing economic preeminence, had made it evident that America could not, any more than the European powers, evade involvement and responsibility in the affairs of less developed countries.[57] He went so far as to state that "The central motive of a democratic foreign policy must be the modernization of the feeble and distracted nations."[58] Only by the modernization of the less developed countries could the imperial rivalries of the great powers be controlled and finally brought to a halt. Lippmann was convinced that whether a country was subject to imperial exploitation was not a function of its size or the race of its people but of whether it had the administrative capacity and the political development to order its internal affairs and its dealings with outside companies and countries.[59]

In itself, this analysis of imperialism was rather bland and commonplace for an American in 1915. But Lippmann's depiction of imperialism had strands of sterner stuff. He was convinced that citizens of the great powers, "living blindly behind their frontiers," regarded their nation's businessmen abroad virtually as governmental representatives,[60] which, in a perverse way, was not very far from the truth. He wrote: "Free trade may make for the prosperity of the masses, but tariffs, rebates, and monopolies create millionaries. And it is not the masses which control governments; it is certain economic classes, and the colonial governments are very likely to be controlled by colonial capitalists."[61]

Lippmann's principal examination of imperialism, *The Stakes of Diplomacy* (1915), was not tightly knit. At times it was meandering; at times it seemed self-contradictory. One line of argument it took up was the primacy of economic interests in imperialism. "The crux of the problem," Lippmann wrote, "is whether the flag is to follow trade. . . . This is the central nerve of imperialism, and our business is to excise it."[62] Again, he said, "The formula of modern imperialism seems to be that financial groups enter a weak state and create 'national interests,' which then evoke national feeling. The corruption and inefficiency of the weak state 'endanger' the interests; patriotism rises to defend them, and political control follows."[63] Yet only one sentence later came the remark, "I am told that it was the State Department at Washington which in order to secure a diplomatic 'foothold,' invited the American financial group to enter China."[64] A major and grave exception to "the formula of modern imperialism," surely—and yet Lippmann did not even comment upon it.

The most judicious way of summarizing Lippmann's conception of imperialism would be to say that he found it to be due to a combination of causal factors, whose weight would vary from situation to situation. Economic gain appeared to be the most common and durable source of imperialism. But it was often accompanied, sometimes preceded, and on occasion perhaps surpassed, by other factors: the evangelistic work of Christian missionaries; strategic advantage sought by the military; diplomatic prestige desired by the foreign office; bureaucratic challenges or sinecures foreseen by lesser administrators; the unremitting sense of the competitive presence of the other imperial powers, ready to seize any opportunity missed by one of its peers; and the domestic uses of patriotism, to win an election or stifle some socialist agitation for reform at home.[65] Even a nation not initially desiring an imperial enterprise might choose to embark upon it, Lippmann remarked, rather than have another nation close markets and concessions to it.[66]

In this tangled web of interests, any of several factors might serve as the catalyst, activating others in its train, until a nation was committed to an imperial intervention. It was such an undesigned and ungoverned train of events, Lippmann was convinced, that had led to the outbreak of World War I.[67] For the sake of European peace, as well as for the just treatment and well-being of the inhabitants of the less developed nations, he argued, it was imperative that Western Liberalism become "powerful and intelligent [enough] abroad to create a workable organization for the weak states," within which they might modernize and assume their proper status as autonomous nation-states. Such international organization, by lessening the psychological burdens of nationalism and the economic burdens of armaments, would accelerate the development of democratic practices in the domestic politics of the great European powers.[68]

Discussion of multinational protection for the less developed countries was not new, Lippmann pointed out. There had been proposed, with respect to China, the policy of "The Open Door," whereby all industrialized nations might share access to that nation. "Taken at its face value, it meant that modern commerce was to penetrate without destroying the life of the natives and without preempting territory for the business men of any one nationality. The only trouble with the ideal was that it could not be taken at its face value," he concluded.[69] This estimate should scarcely come as a surprise to American Progressives, Lippmann suggested, since the Open Door policy had in effect been tried unsuccessfully on the American frontier—but special privilege, logrolling, corruption, and violence were more evident than any form of equity.[70]

The three basic methods employed in late nineteenth-century imperialism, Lippmann argued, were military conquest; protectorate status, which meant an imposed regimen of finance and police; and the provision of experts in economic development, such as the United States had sent to Persia. All three of these methods failed for essentially the same reason: they involved asymmetrical bilateral relationships, relationships with elements of domination and submission between a single great power and a single developing country. "It is essential to remember," he wrote, "that what turns a territory into a diplomatic 'problem' is the combination of natural resources, cheap labor, markets, defenselessness, corrupt and inefficient government."[71]

Lippmann proposed multinational protectorates, whereby the administration of less developed territories would be placed under the direction of a civil service drawn from several advanced or industrialized nations and accountable to an international conference which would never be permanently adjourned. Ultimately, the administrative functions would be transferred to native officials, he proposed: "There are two great objects to be attained. The first is the creation of efficient authority in the weak states; the second is the development of international political agencies. In these sore parts of the world would arise the beginnings of a world state."[72]

Lippmann believed that there were major advantages to developing international government on such a localized, *ad hoc* basis. First, it would remove the prime "areas of friction" from direct great power contest and thereby lessen the chances of large-scale warfare between the industrialized powers. Second, it would do so without placing the general binding restraints on sovereignty envisioned by the proponents of a universal league of nations to enforce peace. (Lippmann was writing in 1915.) Thus, the industrialized powers would experience no direct restraints upon themselves and their autonomy: there would instead be erected administrative shields around less developed territories. Third, the powerful private interests which wished to invest in less developed territories would learn that they must obey, and negotiate with, the multinational civil service constituted in these regions. By this means, in a Hamiltonian fashion, the most powerful international economic actors would be given a stake in the stability and success of the fledgling outposts of world government. They would soon see that evenhanded enforcement of "the rules of the game" maximized their opportunities for an orderly peaceful return on their investments in such protected territories. Fourth, if this process were in motion, the diplomacy of the industrialized states would be "democratized" as larger and larger numbers of investors, managers, and workers came to see the developing countries as part of an international economy, an international division of labor. Economic interests would be built across national boundaries. Fifth (and it did, quite evidently, rank last in Lippmann's hierarchy of concerns), the plan would provide means for the peaceful and humane development of the resources and capital of the less developed countries.[73]

It was not, Lippmann admitted, a complete plan. He hoped it might be a "compass for democrats out of the maze of imperialism."[74]

V

Lippmann was stunned and shocked by the outbreak of war; but at the same time, he had always been deeply offended by moral indignation unloosed from the bridle of reason. He therefore wrote little about the combat or its horrors directly. He spoke of the war as one "which every well-informed person has been expecting for a decade," though he later confessed he had not been among the ranks of those well-informed persons. [75] He was sure that he spoke for the American people when he said that ". . . they do not want to be told that war is a gymnasium of the virtues; they know it to be the stinking thing that it is." [76] He believed that "Europe, counting its dead, its maimed, its shattered, and its bastards . . . will say that of all the false prophets these [the proponents of racial superiority and warfare] are the most damned." [77] And he expressed alarm that jingoism in America was driving out reasoned argument; and that militarism was threatening to take control of American policy. [78]

However, on most occasions, Lippmann rang themes of restraint and rationality, of the moral as well as the material losses of war, the need to recover and redirect energies to the reform of domestic society. Sometimes he cultivated a resignation to evil in a world where philosophy does not rule: "If the right were so clear that all could see it and accept it gladly, there would be no need of force. It is the obscurity of truth and justice, the finite quality of them, which makes them unable to prevail alone." [79] At other times he criticized the notion that war was the sovereign social scourge. There are horrors of the battlefield, yes; but how many attend the horrors of the slum in time of peace? How many raise the alarm when, in the construction of a skyscraper, it was estimated (in 1914) that the life of one worker was lost for every story raised? How many were willing to publicize, in time of peace, the importance of the fact that the Panama Canal was perhaps the greatest victory ever won by an army?

In fact, Lippmann wrote, we live in an anonymous industrial society where life is cheap, lives are drab and lonely, employments are monotonous, absurd, and demeaning: "You can hire a man to walk up and down the avenue carrying a sign which advertises a quack dentist. You can hire rows of men for the back line of the chorus, just standing there to fill up space. . . . It is possible to hire . . . bellhops to fetch for you, even mourners to mourn for you. [80]

So cry down war, but remember that "The real desire of Americans is to make a civilization in America," [81] and that this can be done only by those who are able and willing "to pay the daily costs of sanity" through reasoning about their world. [82]

Lippmann further sought to clarify his views of war by contending with the pacifist position. The quiet earnestness of his arguments, and their length, indicated the sympathy he felt for the pacifists. He feared their position as a misconception of the program of internationalists. Who might be converted to pacifism? he asked. "The people who are most likely to adopt it are those whose influence is most needed in politics. The half-civilized aggressors will not be converted. The democrats may be. The humane people, the very ones who ought to be influential, are most susceptible to this teaching."[83] But the pacifist, because he is considered by the majority to have become at least a transnationalist, at worst an antipatriot, cuts himself off from the only organization which has any prospect of being effective in the foreseeable future: the nation-state.[84]

Just because coercion and violence are the worst instruments of politics, the control of them should rest, wherever possible, with those who have the least self-interested or malign incentive to use them, he held.[85] Those who favored peace at any price would discover too late that the price was too high. In foreign affairs, it would mean default to the aggressor and the stronger; in domestic affairs it would mean default to the reactionaries. At both levels, Liberals would find themselves diminished by the loss of their more militant allies and cohorts, the pacifists.

Lippmann acknowledged the possibility of co-optation, that the leaders of those militantly seeking peace would become tempted, compromised, and corrupted by the complexities and illicit rewards of politics. But this is the perennial challenge of politics, and if the principles of radicals cannot endure these complexities and temptations, then they are principles too frail to win out in the affairs of men in any event.[86]

To Lippmann, war was a form of flight from reason, a form of madness. Every sane person knew that it was a greater thing to build a city than to destroy one; yet in the grip of martial nationalism, reason lay paralyzed.[87] But Lippmann rarely dwelt upon the horrors of war or the absurdities of jingoism. Such denunciations, he believed, were likely to intensify unreasoning patriotism and to require some new note of shrillness with each repetition. Most of Lippmann's remarks on the subject were indirect and deft. He proposed, for instance, the manner in which all the writings related to the war, "a mountain of evidence on the instability of the human mind," might be classified at some future day. There would be a section devoted to racial theories (a thrust principally at

the Central Powers). There would be a section devoted to "annihilation theories" by authors and spokesmen who supposed that an
enemy nation might be destroyed utterly (a thrust at some British
and Anglophile polemicists). And there would be another section,
cataloging the writings "of sedentary people who enjoyed the war,
who found that it improved their character, gave them purpose in
life, zest in existence, and sound sleep at night. The world will not
laugh at these books. It will put them on the shelf beside the works
of the Marquis de Sade."[88]

How, then, in such an agonized tangle of motives and strivings,
could the realities of war be brought into focus as a dilemma for
policy and social morality? It would do no good, Lippmann was
convinced, to dwell on the wicked folly of war: proponents of peace
might as well paint coal black as insist that war is horrible.[89] To be
approached as a moral and policy dilemma, war must be understood
as a human institution. "It is not a mere release of certain subjective
impulses clamoring for expression," he wrote. "It is also—and, I
think, primarily,—one of the ways by which great human decisions
are made."[90] Lippmann was explicitly seeking to extend the argument put forward by William James in "A Moral Equivalent of
War." War is based on an eruption of aggressive emotion,
Lippmann agreed, and so a psychological understanding of it and
substitute for it are needed. But war is also an ultimate arbiter in the
affairs of nations, and hence for the purposes of social theory it is
important to analyze the social function of warfare, he went on to
say. The moral denunciation of warfare as criminal "is just as likely
as not to make the war seem twice as righteous, and hence twice as
fierce, because it can be said that the enemy is . . . an outlaw."[91]

Reinhold Niebuhr was to make the same point a few years later,
in *Moral Man and Immoral Society*, as James Madison had a century
earlier, in Federalist Number Ten: group aggression is more likely
to be embittered and intense than individual conflict, because the
group can call upon the individual's fellow-feeling and willingness to
sacrifice and bind it to his aggressive urges and behavior.

Thus men err fundamentally in attempting to understand war,
Lippmann argued, unless they "realize that events which lead to
war produce a situation in which war seems less horrible than any
feasible alternative."[92] Going to war is not always viewed by governments as unjust because a present peace is not always viewed as
just, and the future peace not always viewed as assured. Therefore

any effective program for peace must be based on the assumption
that there will be sources of international dispute as far as men can
foresee. What is needed, in a world of finite and nation-bound men,
is a political equivalent for war.[93]

In order to check and supplant the institution of war, Lippmann
called for "a vast network of legislative, judicial, executive, social,
and cultural institutions."[94] More specifically, it should be understood that in the short run the political machinery needed was less
an actual court and law code, or their analogs, than it was institutions to perform the functions of an executive and a party system: to
refine conflict and to give it specific goals and nonviolent modes of
resolution.

VI

Lippmann used the term "balance of power" with different senses
on different occasions, and a reader who found him decrying it at
one point, but declaring it indispensable at another, might reasonably plead confusion. Lippmann's writings were *ad hoc*, addressed
to events, however, and his different uses of the term can easily be
distinguished and reconciled. He used the term in a negative sense
to refer to the old European order, wherein, he believed, international relationships had been structured by bloc diplomacy and
competitive armaments. In this vein he contended that a vindictive
and dictated peace at the close of World War I would leave the
world again at the mercy of an unstable balance of power, which
could never bring a secure peace.[95]

On the other hand, Lippmann could employ the term in a favorable sense: "I realize that this sounds suspiciously like the doctrine
known as the Balance of Power. That is just what it is, and there is
no need to be afraid of a bad name." His meaning here is clinched in
the next sentence: "Where coercive force exists, it must either be
neutralized by force or employed in the interests of what we regard
as civilization."[96] Like his analysis of the Open Door policy, this
favorable sense of "balance of power" was an attempt on Lippmann's
part to project a concept drawn from his understanding of domestic
American politics into international relations. Domestically, business corporations exerted coercive power until they were counterbalanced by reform movements, labor organizing, and legislation.
He saw, or wished to see, a parallel process at work in world affairs.

These two meanings of the term "balance of power," then, though seemingly opposed, were employed by Lippmann to support the same argument: the old European order had broken down, and America in the post-1914 world could no longer stand aloof and isolated from world affairs. (It will be recalled that he held that the United States had not been isolated globally at least since the Spanish-American War.) The old mechanics of balance had broken down.

Lippmann's hope in most general terms was that America could serve as a third force, perhaps in conjunction with other nonaligned powers. "Europe will remain on a predatory basis," he wrote in the *New Republic*, "if it is divided into two well-matched alliances. Only the intervention of the neutral world can give power to the liberals in all countries and make a just peace possible and durable."[97] He tightened this argument by arguing that America's role in the future was to serve as a stabilizing or deterring influence upon the imperial designs of the Allies as well as those of the Central Powers.[98]

At the same time, he did hold, in *The Stakes of Diplomacy* (1915), that France, England, and the United States shared a community of vital interests.[99] These powers, he claimed, though "not saints, . . . have gone so far toward liberalism; and they are so well sated in territory, that they desire a peaceful world."[100] These three powers faced the "nightmare" of a coalition between Germany, Austria, Russia, and Japan.[101] The introduction of two related factors was the best hope for blocking the formation of such a coalition. One would be the emergence of the United States as a powerful, concerned partner of France and England, who remained partly aloof from their claims. The second factor would be the attachment of Germany (which was by geography properly an Atlantic power), to the Western world, by a military defeat, a generous peace, and a revived commerce.[102]

By 1917, with an acute grasp of America's dawning economic preeminence, and its diplomatic and military consequences, Lippmann was exhorting Americans to recognize that "four of the eight or nine centers of decisive authority [in the world] have collapsed . . . hundreds of millions of people have been wrenched from their ancient altars of obedience . . . the necessities of existence [for them] are scarce, and precariously obtained. These people have lost homes, children, fathers . . . they cannot see ahead three weeks. . . ."[103] If an uncertain balance was not to dissolve into still less sure conditions of social chaos and revolution, the United States must assume an active role in European affairs.

Balance of power stood in Lippmann's thought, along with international organization, as one of the two basic means of confining or averting war. By February, 1917, two months before American entry into the war, Lippmann was acknowledging in the *New Republic* that American neutrality had not been impartial but had favored the Allies, since the United States' decision not to break the blockade of Germany was "one of the great strategic facts of the war."[104] The United States was an Atlantic power, and she could not permit the control of that ocean by a hostile Germany. Alliance and intervention were imminent, he argued, but only to prevent the creation of a deadly imbalance: "The world's highway shall not be closed to the Western allies if America has power to prevent it."[105]

Lippmann continued to employ the concept of balance of power in his subsequent writing. He insisted during the 1920s that it was a lie and an illusion to believe the Versailles settlement final; he condemned the "Borahs, Reeds, Hearsts, Coolidges, Mellons [and] Hoovers" for insisting upon strict repayment of war debts to the United States, now a powerful creditor nation; he sought a regularization of international diplomatic conferences; and he even retreated, in the period from 1931 to 1938, to a policy of noninvolvement and isolation.[106]

The two significant additions to Lippmann's theory of balance of power came with his vigorous assertion of the importance of geopolitics during World War II, and his sharp criticism of the Truman Doctrine of containment at the outset of the Cold War. Both of these "additions" were clearly prefigured in Lippmann's writings on foreign policy during World War I, but their amplification in his later work deserves consideration.

The domestic rise and international conquests of Adolf Hitler, along with the armament of Japan, gradually drove Lippmann, often only months ahead of the majority of Americans, out of his isolationist stance. In 1943 he presented a cogent "realist's" geopolitical sketch of the past, present, and future in *U.S. Foreign Policy: Shield of the Republic*. It was widely read and acclaimed, and drew cover stories from *The Saturday Review* and *Time*; but it opened with a confession:

. . . with the advantages of hindsight I am criticizing others for . . . a lack of foresight of which I also was guilty. . . . I should like to make it as plain as possible . . . that nothing could be further from my intention than to say to anyone that I told him so. For the conclusions which I have set down in this book are drawn from experience. I was not born with them. I have come to them slowly over 30 years, and as a result of many false starts and mistaken judgments and serious disappointments.[107]

Borrowing perhaps from William James, who often restorted to commercial metaphors to reach a wide American audience, Lippmann declared that our foreign policy was "insolvent," our former apparent security as a nation "unearned."[108] The founding fathers had understood the hard necessities of international politics, but later generations of Americans had become like the privileged descendants of hardworking successful forbears. According to Lippmann, we first forgot that work is a necessary sacrifice for security, then we came to believe our privileged position was the reward for moral superiority, and finally, like the idle rich, we came to regard foreign exertion as beneath our dignity as idealists.[109] In the nineteenth century, this nation had undertaken extensive foreign commitments; now those obligations, unserviced, were coming due. "The thesis of this book," he wrote, "is that a foreign policy consists in bringing into balance, with a comfortable surplus of power in reserve, the nation's commitments and the nation's power."[110] Any nation's power was composed directly of three factors—its armed strength, its strategic position geographically, and its alliances. Other factors underlay these three, such as morale, and most important, economic capacity, but these three were the front line of any nation's power, he asserted.

Since the proclamation of the Monroe Doctrine in 1823, Lippmann went on to say, Americans had steadily succumbed to an illusion which had brought the nation into mortal peril—that "concern with our frontiers, our armaments, and with alliances, is immoral and reactionary." That illusion would now have to be redeemed with American blood and treasure.[111] Americans had believed our nation, and indeed our entire hemisphere, immunized from attack by expanses of ocean, a fact of nature which we believed had been merely remarked upon by President Monroe.

In point of fact, said Lippmann, an unblinking reading of American history disclosed a quite different set of circumstances. Most Americans seemed to forget that the French, the Spanish, and the Russians had assisted the American colonists in their War for Independence.[112] Most Americans seemed unaware that President Monroe, before proclaiming his doctrine that at risk of war the

United States would resist European imperialism in the Western hemisphere, had obtained the assurance of the British Foreign Secretary that the British Navy would defend the independence of the nations of the New World. The British government went so far as to propose a joint convention and declaration, but since England had not extended diplomatic recognition to the new Latin American states, our government acted alone.[113] Thus the security of the United States, and the hemisphere, was guaranteed by the dominant facts of world politics, as well as of geography: Asia was dormant, Europe divided, and England friendly. But these facts were concealed from American awareness since they were displeasing to our self-esteem.[114]

After Monroe, Lippmann was willing to praise only Theodore Roosevelt for possessing a grasp of America's overseas commitments and vulnerability. Roosevelt had dug the Panama Canal and had enlarged our naval forces so that we might have an effective "two-ocean navy"; and he had seen to it that the United States and England never became estranged.[115] But Wilson and his Republican successors in the White House had reverted to the traditional American frame of reference for foreign affairs—legalistic, moralistic, and idealistic. They did not understand, according to Lippmann, the geopolitical *quid pro quo* that the United States received from England prior to World War I and could have received from the League of Nations thereafter.[116] As a consequence of this long train of events and illusions, Lippmann said, President Franklin Delano Roosevelt had not been able to mount effective rearmament until China and England stood alone against the siege of the Axis powers.

Several factors, then, were necessary for the composition and conduct of a successful foreign policy. One factor was sufficient armaments. The "vicious circle of pacifism," Lippmann argued, spiraled into the unintended consequence of war, because disarmament was never universal, but always one-sided.[117]

Allies were also essential to the foreign policy of a nation. Hamilton and the first five Presidents all understood this fact. The warnings of Washington and Jefferson, for example, had been misread by subsequent generations of Americans. In his Farewell Address, for instance, Washington had actually said, "It is our true policy to steer clear of all permanent alliances with any portion of the foreign world, so far, I mean, as we are now at liberty to do it. . . ."[118] And

Jefferson's admonition, in his First Inaugural Address, read in context, was a warning against *entangling* alliances, not entangling *alliances*.[119]

A further component of a viable foreign policy, according to Lippmann, was recognition by a nation, and its leadership, of the nation-state's "vital interests," those interests which a nation's people may be forced to defend with their lives.[120] In fact, the legal boundaries of the United States had never corresponded to its defensive frontiers, he argued. Those frontiers had included Canada and Latin America and the acquisitions of the United States in the nineteenth century. Our commitments were so extensive in 1943 that they covered two-thirds of the globe, forty per cent of its land surface, and twenty-five percent of its population.[121]

Fully to understand its vital interests, Lippmann declared, a nation must study history carefully. Such a study would show that the United States had been involved in every war since the sixteenth century in which the order of power in the Atlantic or Pacific Oceans was at stake: the wars of 1688–1697, 1701–1714, 1740–1748, 1756–1763, 1812, 1917, and 1941.[122] He went further in underscoring the importance of the study of history, in a revealing passage which could be regarded as an anticipation, in his later work, of a stress upon the importance of uniformities in the past. He wrote, in *Essays in the Public Philosophy*, that

. . . I have written . . . [this book] in the philosophical conviction that the behavior of nations over a long period of time is the most reliable, if not the only, index of their national interest. For though their interests are not eternal they are remarkably persistent. . . . We can best separate appearance from reality, the transient from the permanent, . . . by looking backward whenever we look forward. There is no great mystery why this should be: the facts of geography are permanent, the movement of history is massive . . . ; thus the successive generations of men tend to face the same recurrent problems and to meet them in more or less habitual ways.[123]

The student of history, like the student of geography, would recognize that the two Americas were islands to the Old World, islands to one another, separated by oceans of sea and air, and that the nearest great power neighbors of the United States were England, Russia, and Japan. Lippmann was offering an updated version of the geopolitical writings of the late nineteenth-century American strategist and exponent of American seapower, Admiral Alfred T.

Mahan.[124] History showed, along with geography, that the United States was an island, and that isolation was the worst fate that could befall a nation—a fate that, at best, could be repaired by nothing less than the nation's becoming a garrison state.[125]

At this juncture—1943—Lippmann was no longer expressing, as he had during World War I, concern over democratic control of foreign policy. Instead, he was convinced that "insolvency" was the cause of domestic dissent and division in politics, and that this situation had been markedly evident in the twentieth century in the United States. The statesman intent on upholding peace must give his first attention to the cold calculation of organizing power. If he did so successfully, the people would unite behind him. But in order to succeed, he must act upon the vital interests of the nation, not the short-term readings of the Gallup Poll, Lippmann declared.[126] The grim history of foreign relations in the twentieth century was due to the fact that none of the great powers had been able to shape a solvent foreign policy. They had all—in one way or another—misjudged the equation of their commitments or opportunities and their power, and a cycle of war, unstable peace, and more war had been the result.[127]

In looking toward the possible outlines of a postwar settlement, Lippmann returned to what might be considered the crux in his thinking on balance of power, the intersection of morality and policy: the imperative need for an alliance between the United States and England. During World War I Lippmann had insisted on the common interests shared by the two powers and had proposed that ". . . Anglo-American entente means the substitution of a pool for a balance. . . ." In other words, in 1917 he believed that these two nations as allies would be militarily invulnerable, and that their alliance would be sealed by their joint participation in the League, just as the League's success would be guaranteed by their joint participation.[128]

Frequently during the interwar period he had pointed to the necessity for Anglo-American understanding and cooperation. Only during the deepest days of his isolationist thought did Lippmann concede, in a 1935 essay in *Foreign Affairs*, that the interests of the two powers, while similar, were not identical, and that the United States could not be expected to share fully England's vital interest in maintaining the *status quo* in Europe.[129] Now, in the midst of World War II, he returned to the idea of alliance. The League of

Nations had failed, he said, because the "nuclear alliance" of France, England, and the United States had dissolved.[130] At the same time, he acknowledged that during the quarter century 1914–1939 France had ceased to function as a global power, just as Spain had been conclusively defeated in the sixteenth century. World War II would probably lead to the similar elimination of Germany and Japan as world powers, he thought.[131] It was, therefore, time to renew and deepen our recognition that the United States and the United Kingdom remained indispensable to one another.

One special characteristic of the British-American relationship, in Lippmann's view, was that the British Commonwealth was both inside and outside the American perimeter of commitments and defense.[132] In a deeper sense, however, the community between the two powers was one of shared experiences, common values and institutions, and mingled blood. Two of the errors of President Wilson ironically illuminated the importance and depth of the Anglo-American community. The President, in conceiving of the League, was profoundly influenced by the American idea of consent to memberhip—yet he failed to note that the American federal analogy was not applicable here, because no French or Spanish colony had sought to join the British thirteen. It was English culture which had bound the thirteen together, asserted Lippmann. Second, President Wilson wanted fifty very diverse and unequal nation-states to be juridically equalized by the penstroke of membership in a universal League of Nations. He did not accept the evolutionary alternative, of basing the strength of the League on a "nuclear alliance," akin to the strong principalities which had served as the nuclei of many modern nation-states, including England, France, Germany, Italy, and Russia.[133]

Lippmann evidently hoped and believed—though he did not openly say—that the Anglo-American tradition of the rule of law would provide the best basis, in norm and in historical practice, for a new league of nations. This idea, which fairly bulges between the lines of his writings, took unmistakable expression a decade later in *Essays in the Public Philosophy.* He probably found this theme an impolitic one upon which to dwell in 1943, because the 1917 chances for a Big Two were gone. Instead, Lippmann envisioned a Big Three in the postwar world: ". . . the crucial question of the epoch we are now entering is the relationship between Russia and that Atlantic Community in which Britain and the United States are the leading military powers."[134] Lippmann's 1943 views on a postwar settlement led logically to his 1947 denunciation of the Truman Administration's policy of "containment" of the Soviet Union.

In 1943, Lippmann saw three primary requirements for a peaceful postwar settlement. The first was so important he would call it "our grand objective": a settlement "which does not call for a permanent American military intervention in Europe to maintain it."[135] Any such arrangement would mean an Anglo-American military alliance against Soviet Russia, and this would "set the stage inexorably for a Third World War. . . ."[136]

The second cardinal feature of a durable postwar settlement, following upon the first, was that, as Lippmann had argued in 1917,[137] no attempt to erect a *cordon sanitaire* of anti-Communist states should be made, in an effort to isolate Bolshevism in the Soviet Union. No attempt should be made by the United States and Great Britain, in other words, to reconstitute the governments-in-exile from the prewar states of Eastern Europe. Instead, if at all possible, these states should be neutralized, as a mutual guarantee to the Soviet Union and to the nations of western Europe of their peaceful intentions toward one another, and the best guarantee to the peoples of Eastern Europe that they would not again see their lands become a battleground.[138]

The third feature, most difficult of the three, dependent upon the preceding two, would be the cooperation of the Big Three as the nuclear alliance of a wider association of nations. If the Big Three did not remain united, war would surely follow sooner or later, from their own clashing aims or from a renascent Germany or Japan, whose revival the rivalry of the Big Three would permit or encourage. It was logical, then, that Lippmann strongly endorsed, in December, 1944, the grant of the "veto" to the major powers on the proposed Security Council of the future United Nations Organization.[139]

And what of the threat to the security and well-being of smaller or weaker nations posed by the possibility that the Big Three might seek to become a global triumvirate? No attempt at a collaborative dictatorship could succeed, declared Lippmann. Subject peoples would rebel and the rebellions would open splits among the Big Three. Domination, rebellion, and big-power rivalry would inevitably fuel one another in a vicious circle. The only hope, slender

though it might be, lay in the rule of law. Lippmann could combine
his realism and his humanistic hope in the assertion that "I believe it
can be demonstrated as conclusively as anything can be demonstrated in human affairs that Britain, Russia, America, and China,
as she becomes a great state, cannot remain allies and partners [and
thereby build a durable peace settlement] unless they use their
power, separately and in combination, to maintain liberty through
law."[140]

Given his previous thought on balance of power, it should have
surprised no one that Lippmann sharply attacked the policy of "containment" of the Soviet Union, as that policy was set forth in an
article signed "X," in the July, 1947 issue of the prestigious journal
Foreign Affairs. Mr. X was soon identified as George Kennan, recently appointed Director of the Policy Planning Staff of the Department of State in the Truman Administration. Kennan argued
that "Soviet power . . . bears within itself the seeds of its own
decay," and that if "anything were ever to occur to disrupt the . . .
efficiency of the Party . . . , Soviet Russia might be changed overnight . . . to one of the weakest and most pitiable of national
societies. . . ." The United States, consequently, should adopt a
policy termed containment, confronting Russia with "unalterable
counterforce at every point" where it showed signs of "encroaching
upon the interests of a peaceful and stable world."[141] Writing
twenty years later, Kennan said, "Mr. Lippmann . . . mistook me for
the author of precisely those features of the Truman Doctrine which
I had most vigorously opposed—an assumption to which, I must
say, I led squarely with my chin in the careless and indiscriminate
language of the X-article." Kennan's conception of containment was
neither so bellicose and military, nor so global, as his essay had
made it appear, he said.[142]

Lippmann's response appeared in a series of his "Today and Tomorrow" syndicated columns, collected into a volume entitled *The
Cold War: A Study in U.S. Foreign Policy.* One source of his resistance to the policy of containment could be found in Lippmann's
consistent opposition, for a third of a century, to self-righteous
moralizing, an opposition that reached back to his urbane family's
abhorrence of Bryan and Populism. The policy of containment, as
Lippmann read it, would embark this nation on an "ideological
crusade" to make "Jeffersonian democrats out of . . . peasants . . .
[and] tribal chieftains. . . ."[143]

Moreover, Lippmann warned, the containment policy would imperil American values and institutions. It would require a virtual garrison state. Of the President, Lippmann asked rhetorically, "Is he going to ask Congress for a blank authorization to use the armed forces? Not if the American Constitutional system is to be maintained."[144]

Furthermore, containment must inevitably mean the recruiting and subsidizing of a motley array of "satellites, clients, dependents, and puppets," a policy of ceaseless intervention in the affairs of weak and disorderly nation-states.[145] And should we be unable effectively to impose our will in the internal affairs of these states, should Communist strength threaten them in any fashion, the United States would confront a terrible dilemma. Read in the light of the fires of Vietnam, Lippmann's warning words have an eerie prescience: "We shall have either to disown our puppets, which would be tantamount to appeasement and defeat and loss of face, or we must support them at an incalculable cost on an unintended, unforeseen, and perhaps undesirable issue."[146] (A principal reason Lippmann gave for his support of Richard Nixon for the Presidency in 1968 was his belief that Nixon would deflate our overseas commitments, and in particular swiftly liquidate the war in Vietnam.[147])

What was Lippmann's proposal for policy in the place of containment? First, he would have us recognize that diplomacy is a method of managing relations among rivals, with the goal a condition of balance wherein no power has the prospect of successful aggression.[148] If all nations were friendly partners, there would be no diplomacy, or its nature would be very different. The policy of containment would imply exclusion, the abandonment of diplomacy, and the destruction of the United Nations.[149]

Lippmann would have had United States diplomacy keep open lines of communication to the Soviet Union and seek the withdrawal of American, British, and Russian armed forces from foreign soil in Europe. If Russia demanded a guarantee or ransom for withdrawal, the United States should pay its share.[150] Then the internal affairs of European countries could develop in a more autonomous fashion, and the natural economic interdependence of Eastern and Western Europe could reassert itself through revived trade.[151] Soviet Russia, whatever her professions of ideological fervor, Lippmann was certain, would be guided by her leaders' conception of her national interest.

Finally, Lippmann called upon the American government to develop and pursue the "Marshall line" of commitment to the United Nations, to the autonomy of all nation-states, and to the assistance of the economic reconstruction of Europe, planned and implemented by the European states themselves.[152] The support of national autonomy, "the very thing which only traitors can oppose," would release more energies for peaceful development and resistance to Russian encroachment, Lippmann declared, than any American-orchestrated attempt to direct the affairs of heterogeneous peoples numbering in the scores of millions.[153]

"Containment" continued to draw Lippmann's fire as an aggressive and ideological breach of the principle of balance of power. After the fall of the regime of Chiang Kai-shek in China, and the detonation of a nuclear device by the Soviet Union in 1949, he wrote that the "phantom policy" of containment was utterly defunct and should be replaced by negotiations aimed at reciprocal advantages and stabilizing the international order.[154] To the end of his life, he regretted that the United States had not immediately accorded diplomatic recognition to the People's Republic of China, since the failure to do so for a quarter of a century injected an irresponsible and distorting moralism into the conduct of American foreign policy.[155]

While he initially supported United States military engagement in the Korean "police action" on the grounds that it was multilateral, within a week he expressed misgivings because widespread support from other member states of the United Nations had not been forthcoming, and the Korean conflict would remain an essentially American war.[156] More than twenty years later, he refused in an interview to call the Korean War "justifiable," saying only that it was "certainly explicable."[157]

Much more characteristic of Lippmann's issue positions in the 1950s was his April, 1950, warning, only two months before the outbreak of the Korean War, that America should not overextend herself militarily, should recognize the rising strength of the "nonaligned" powers, and should work to assist their development, both for their interests and our own, in a world order which was passing out of "the nightmare of a two-power world."[158]

Lippmann continued to direct scathing criticism at the doctrine of containment and at what he regarded as the Truman Administration's conduct of foreign policy by manufactured crisis. "Instead of leading the people, the administration spokesmen have relied upon the bastard art of manipulating opinion by sloganeering and shock," he declared.[159]

While he supported Dwight D. Eisenhower in the 1952 Presidential elections, Lippmann was appalled at the doctrine of "brinksmanship," the moralizing, the threat of "massive retaliation," and the proliferation of defense treaty commitments for which President Eisenhower and Secretary of State John Foster Dulles were responsible. Two concerns of Lippmann's during the 1950s were representative, and extensions of his earlier theory of balance of power.

One was presented in a 1958 book, *The Communist World and Ours*, written after he had visited the Soviet Union to interview Chairman Nikita Khrushchev. Lippmann found Khrushchev in agreement with him that neither the United States nor the Soviet Union could "win" in a direct war, in any conventional or meaningful sense of the term victory. Khrushchev told Lippmann that the danger posed by the Soviet Union to the United States lay in the superiority of Soviet ideology for the Third World, and in the rise of Soviet industrial productivity, which would serve to vindicate the ideology and make it possible for Russia to lend important material and technical assistance to the nonaligned nations. Beneath the trappings of utopian rhetoric, Lippmann found Khrushchev to be a practical strategist, who used ideology in service of his nation's interest. Khrushchev recognized the reality of power and of the balance of power. He was a man who could be dealt with through diplomacy.[160] There is no reason to suppose that Lippmann was seduced by Khrushchev into believing in a revival of a collaboration like that of the World War II years. Lippmann had always seen diplomacy as a means of dealing peacefully with adversaries. As he wrote in 1951, "When I speak of a settlement with the Soviet Union I do not mean a marriage. I mean a divorce."[161]

A parallel focus of interest for Lippmann in the 1950s, which carried over into the 1960s, was his belief that the United States must pursue a realistic foreign policy, predicated upon balance of power, in Asia. The alliance with Chiang's Formosa was "a truly entangling alliance." America should not ally itself militarily with weak dictatorships which lay on the perimeter of China, he warned. This was one of the lessons of the Korean War.[162] Lippmann saw that in that war American life and resources had been directly expended, and in great measure, while the Soviet Union remained free of the encounter. The more general lesson was: stay free of ground combat on the Asian mainland. "Where . . . the infantry," he insisted, "is the queen of battles, there the American soldier and statesman must avoid the battle."[163]

Ever since 1943 Lippmann had argued that America's military advantages lay in seapower, airpower, mobility, and firepower. In massive, open, protracted infantry warfare our numbers were no match for those of our potential adversaries. And even such advantages as we possessed had their limits. After the fall of the French forces at Dienbienphu, Lippmann warned that the United States should not intervene to defend the South Vietnam regime with seapower and air strikes: "With almost absolute control of the air over North Korea, we were unable to prevent the Chinese from building up an army that was stronger at the end of the war than at any other time. And against the kind of guerilla warfare that is waged over most of Indo-China, air power is even less likely to be decisive."[164]

Just as he had advised an armistice and negotiation aimed at a political settlement, if possible including neutralization, in Indo-China before the French collapse there, so in 1959 and 1960 he urged that the same course be pursued in Laos. And again with regard to the Laotian conflict, he sounded the alarm against American intervention.[165]

Lippmann denounced Senator Barry Goldwater's campaign in 1964 as that of a man who was likely to put the nation in "the crazy position of risking a very great war while it was disorganizing itself at home."[166] After Lyndon Johnson's landslide victory that year, Lippmann entered one sober warning:

The Johnson conception of the Great Society rests on the two pillars of controlled affluence and of political consensus. If the conception were to fail, it would not be because the conception is false. It would be because of some external cause—possibly because we had become diverted by some entanglement in another continent.[167]

The arrival of additional United States troops in South Vietnam early in 1965 did not distress Lippmann, however. He assumed that they were being used in subordination to diplomacy and the goal of a negotiated political settlement. As he said, "The test of any extension of the war is whether it produces a negotiation."[168]

What we could hope for from negotiations, Lippmann believed, was a truce in what he regarded as a civil war, a truce of sufficient duration to allow Vietnam national reconciliation and to prevent her becoming a direct military outpost of China, although it would be impossible to prevent all of Indo-China from being drawn into China's sphere of influence.[169]

On a television interview, Lippmann complained of the domestic strife being caused in America by the war in Vietnam—a strife which was especially saddening because the war was so unnecessary. "We are not the policemen of mankind," Lippmann said on that occasion. "We are not able to run the world, and we shouldn't pretend that we can." It was the old American moral *hubris*, he argued, to overreach the resources of law, diplomacy, and arms, in an attempt to make a world more to our liking. And the cost was great, he reminded his listeners: "We have neglected our own affairs. Our education is inadequate, our cities are badly built, our social arrangements are unsatisfactory. We can't wait another generation."[170]

As the Johnson Administration continued to escalate the war, Lippmann intensified his criticism of it. The White House sought to woo Lippmann, by inviting him to social functions, for policy consultation, and even for speechwriting. He was also attacked. "God is not dead, he appears twice a week in the Washington Post," was a widely circulated remark attributed to President Johnson. Lippmann was pointedly not invited to a White House dinner for Washington correspondents, where the President referrred to "a political commentator of yesteryear."[171]

Lippmann's criticisms held firm. "It is a naive illusion to think that 1967 is 1939, that Southeast Asia is Western Europe, that Mao Tse-tung is Hitler and that Lyndon Johnson is Churchill," he wrote. And one of his last assessments of the Johnson Administration, made three years after it had ended, was that it had promoted "the greatest disaster that has happened to this country since the Civil War." It was the bitter end of a long period of "inflation of foreign policy commitments" by the United States. Since Lippmann's support of the "peace candidacies" of Eugene McCarthy and Robert Kennedy came to naught, he supported Richard Nixon, one of his least favored figures on the American political stage, as the man to "deflate" our commitments and end the war.[172]

VII

Lippmann, for better and for worse, was himself the idealist he sought to exorcise. When he wrote, "What we project upon the screen of the future is what our hearts desire, not what can be created out of the conflict of desire and reality,"[173] the thoughtful reader cannot help supposing that this was an admonition Lippmann was directing toward himself as well as toward the reader. He was a theorist, and he could not help believing that "the final argument against cannon is ideas."[174] He was a moral philosopher, and he could not refrain from hoping that "hypocrisy continues to be the homage vice plays to virtue."[175]

It can be charged against Lippmann that his idealism was a ruse (possibly self-deceptive): that he "idealized," in the invidious sense, the Monroe Doctrine and the Open Door policy. His concept of "nuclear alliances" within international organizations, one of his critics has charged, allowed him to speak simultaneously of building American military power and international cooperation. Moreover, it permitted him to identify Anglo-American power with the good of the international "community."[176]

Self-serving, self-deceptive, or honestly seeking and imperfect, Lippmann was indisputably an internationalist, from first to last. "'Europe,' as it presented itself to the old-school diplomat, is gone," he observed in 1917.[177] The implication of this fact, Lippmann believed, was that to the victors belong the responsibilities. These responsibilities most Americans had never considered when their nation entered the war.[178] In the wake of World War I there was no chance of restoration. The old imperial powers had been toppled, and politically dormant and submerged nations and classes were experiencing a rising consciousness. The Western hemisphere was no exception, and this fact alone would have made American involvement in international affairs inescapable.[179] He was candid about the doubts and anxieties associated with American entry into world affairs: "That is, I realize, a terrifying programme to most Americans. It terrifies me, and disturbs every prejudice of my training . . . in surrendering our isolation we shall surrender much that is precious to us."[180]

But once again, Lippmann tried with some success to transform his ambivalence into an intellectual resource. His misgivings concerning international involvement enabled him to be coolly realistic about the limits of international organization, even as he embraced its necessity:

... I cannot take seriously any project of peace which does not rest upon ... the premise that the establishment of order in international society depends upon the development of agencies of international government. I can sympathize with those who prefer the liberty of our present international anarchy to the responsibilities of an international society. I am inclined to think that a stable international order would be oppressive and unpleasant in many ways, and I am not wholly sure that I am prepared to pay the price which the establishment of peace on earth would cost. There are many advantages, especially for nations as favorably placed as the United States, in the freedom which this disorganized planet permits us.[181]

Here, in this autobiographical statement, Lippmann may be said to have reached the intersection of morality and policy in his thinking on international organization. Effective international organization, however conceived, would imply losses for the United States and its citizens, perhaps in the form of restraints on liberty, perhaps in the form of resources shared and profits foregone, perhaps in other ways which were unforeseeable. International organization could not rise higher than its source, and it must bear the flaws of the system of nation-states from which it arose.[182]

As he turned over in his mind the possibilities of international organization, Lippmann was torn between the hopeful prospect that American power and values would play a decisive role in any new transnational system and his fear that the old private centers of privilege and power, within America's borders and beyond, would combine to exercise final authority. He was certain that it would be as true for the globe as it had been for nations that "no government had any chance of survival unless it serves the interests of powerful economic groups."[183] How to give these groups legitimate advantages without absolute control, how to keep international government from destroying the liberties and prosperity that were the fruits of the toil of centuries—these were the dilemmas of international organization for policy and morals as Lippmann viewed the world scene.[184]

He had not always considered international organization in such a cool light. During World War I, he had believed, in the flush of youth and the success of American economic and military might, that "danger, hunger, and hope" were driving the nations of the world closer together.[185] A war which grew out of a militaristic nationalism was ending in a collaborative economic and military effort, which could be made the basis of permanent political cooperation.[186] After the Czar was overthrown, Lippmann soared into a euphoria he was soon to lose, and never to regain:

The cause of the Allies is now unmistakably the cause of liberalism and the hope of an enduring peace. . . . Democracy is infectious—the entrance of the Russian and American democracies is sure to be a stimulus to democrats everywhere, and it is now as certain as anything human can be that the war . . . will dissolve into democratic revolution the world over.[187]

The embodiment of Lippmann's hopes—and those of the other editors of the *New Republic* by 1917—was Woodrow Wilson. Through circumstances and genius, President Wilson had created an opportunity without precedent. "He can mean more to the happiness of mankind than any one who ever addressed the world . . . [and] be the first great statesman to begin the better organization of the world," Lippmann wrote.[188] By the time Lippmann left the Versailles Peace Conference, these glowing hopes were ashes. He had been confronted by a diplomat from one of the small powers, who asked concerning the President, "If he knows exactly what he wants, he can get it. Does he know?"[189] A European friend admonished Lippmann that a little of the "everlasting morality of the Fourteen Commandments . . . goes a long way."[190] Soon thereafter Lippmann was warning that unless the American government treated the League of Nations as a vital national interest, the League would be gutted by the fears and ambitions of the contending allies. And he drew the bitter conclusion that the President's program for the peace settlement had been "really nothing more than his gratuitous advice about a situation he did not thoroughly understand."[191]

Earlier, Lippmann had quoted with approval the statement of Jan Christian Smuts that "Europe is being liquidated, and the League of Nations must be heir to the great estate."[192] Lippmann pressed hard with both edges of the blade the argument that the Treaty of

Versailles was imperfect and that its framers had the foresight to create, in the League, a process for continuing face-to-face consultation and revision of the Versailles arrangements. It appealed to his Pragmatism and his vehement opposition to legalism to argue that the reordering of Europe was a historical process, which could not be frozen in a single legal settlement but must be managed by a continuing series of informed and mutual decisions, which the League alone made possible.[193] He could then press home the point that the Versailles conference "is not the Last Judgment. . . . They cannot damn the German people for all time. . . ."[194]

A logical extension of the same argument was his belief that national parliamentary committees (such as the Senate Foreign Relations Committee), including members of the minority party (such as Senator Henry Cabot Lodge), should participate in the deliberations of the League of Nations. Such participation, in fact, was essential to the success of the League, Lippmann argued, for it must become an institution beyond partisan domestic politics, one whose necessity was affirmed by socialists and conservatives alike.[195] Such participation would also deepen the League's reservoir of parliamentary resources, and the "transition from revolution to electioneering is the most radical change which can take place. . . ."[196] Lippmann held to the hope that democratic practices and socioeconomic stability would reinforce one another in a cycle of growth within the proper setting of international organization.[197]

Throughout the 1920s, despite the refusal of the United States to join the League, Lippmann championed cooperation with it and membership for the United States on the World Court.[198] He continued to insist that the attempt to make peace depended "not upon the abolition of force but on bringing the use of force under the dominion of as much law, justice, reason, and good-will as possible."[199] In the 1930s, acknowledging that the League had failed at this task, Lippmann drifted into despair and isolationism.[200] As has been noted above, he continued to espouse the same basic norms for the Allies—and then the United Nations—during and after World War II. He argued that the United Nations—or its "nuclear alliance"—must be willing to exercise force, yet that that "force must not be arbitrary, but must be exercised in accordance with laws that are open to discussion and subject to orderly revision."[201]

Lippmann continued, however, to voice reservations about the League. Lesser powers might fear that through the League they would be drawn into Big Power disputes which otherwise, in the absence of the League, they might have avoided.[202] He was convinced from the first that nations would submit only unimportant problems to binding arbitration.[203] And he developed this argument by suggesting that arbitration of crisis disputes would not work, since the League would always be intervening only when a conflict had reached unmanageable proportions. The League contained "no method for organizing the world, for dealing day by day with the weak spots which are the areas of friction. When the fire is just about to break out," he warned, "arbitration arrives with a teaspoonful of water . . . it merely tries to stop war when the causes have operated to the breaking point."[204]

This observation serves to remind us that Lippmann had proposed in 1915 the creation of institutions of "local internationalism," international conferences to deal with crisis areas, with a multinational civil service administering these territories.[205] His hope was that, permanently convened, these international conferences would gradually gain autonomy for themselves as standing commissions, with the multinational civil service accountable exclusively to the commission. In the course of time, the commission could become the upper house of a bicameral legislature for the territory, with a lower chamber composed of natives. As the natives acquired both parliamentary skills and administrative training, nationhood would be created in graduated legal stages. History had shown the promise of such congresses, Lippmann believed, in the Berlin Conference of 1885 on West Africa, the London Conference after the Balkan Wars, and most notably the Algeciras Conference of 1905 on Morocco, which had proved "the most hopeful effort at world government up to the present [1915]." None of these conferences had succeeded because all had been disbanded after a single session, and the cooperative procedures they had established, lacking authoritative supervision, had been destroyed by national wrangling.[206] But permanent localized international agencies, by supervising and facilitating commerce, could begin the delicate process of transfer of allegiance, by grounding it firmly in the self-interest of powerful economic organizations, Lippmann believed.[207] As more economic interests within the industrialized world gained a stake in these agencies and territories, not only would Great Power rivalry over them be stilled, but an evolutionary growth toward the democratizing of diplomacy would be begun, with a universal world government the ultimate "goal of humane political endeavor."[208]

Lippmann hoped of his proposal that "it grasps the real problems of diplomacy, that it provides not a panacea, but a method and the beginnings of a technique."[209] This statement, expressing concern with the practical and immediate, in an open and tentative spirit, with humanistic objectives, is typical of the tenor and aims of Lippmann's writings on international relations.

CHAPTER 3

Public Opinion

I

WORLD War I left Liberal intellectuals stunned and incredulous—at the scale of destruction of life and property, at the ruthless and random bombardment of civilian populations, at the savage depths of nationalism which had been displayed, at the relentless imperial designs which had been revealed of the Allies as well as of the Central Powers. Science and technology, long hailed as the twin pacific hopes of the future, had demonstrated the demonic powers they could unleash when so directed—a dark possibility which had been foreseen by only a few isolated critics, such as Henry Adams.[1]

So thorough was the intellectual devastation wrought by the war that historians and other thinkers in the English-speaking world abandoned what had stood for two centuries as their guiding principle: the idea that the history of modern Western culture was the progressive history of liberty.[2]

Lippmann must have felt keenly the loss, which Sigmund Freud mourned, of a cosmopolitan European culture. Those with the means and leisure, Freud wrote, had come to regard Europe as "a new and wider fatherland," through which they could travel "without hindrance or suspicion," enjoying the majestic variety of Europe's landscape and history. For the nascent world citizen, this

. . . new fatherland was a museum . . . , too, filled with all the treasures which the artists of civilized humanity had in successive centuries created and left behind. . . . Nor must we forget that each of these citizens of the civilized world had created for himself a "Parnassus" and a "School of Athens" [two great Raphael frescoes] of his own. For among the great thinkers, writers, and artists of all nations he had chosen those to whom he considered he owed the best of what he had been able to achieve in enjoyment and understanding of life, and he had venerated them along with the immortal ancients. . . .[3]

Now, Freud lamented in 1915, "Well may the citizen of the civilized world of whom I have spoken stand helpless . . . his great fatherland disintegrated, its common estates laid waste, his fellow citizens divided and debased."[4]

In one form or another, many observers warned that the war portended the flight of reason from social affairs. The industrialized nations had become, in a bitter remark of Hoffman Nickerson which Lippmann endorsed, "capable of sacrifices so irrationally great that the bleeding victor would faint upon the corpse of his victim."[5]

II

This was a restless and unhappy time for Lippmann. What new form could hope take in this chaotic, degraded, and divided world? He had left the Paris Peace Conference in dismay and disillusion, had briefly resumed editorial responsibilities with the *New Republic*, had seen the ferocity of reaction and the Red Scare, had taken a leave of absence to work on completing the manuscript of *Public Opinion*, continued to write occasional articles, and then, to Herbert Croly's chagrin, had left the *New Republic*, the journal for attentive and committed Liberal intellectuals, to take charge of the editorial page of one of the great Liberal metropolitan daily newspapers, the New York *World*.[6]

Yet in this period of outer and inner turmoil, from 1919 through 1921, Lippmann composed the profoundest and most enduring of all his books. In time, it was to help establish him as one of the principal architects of the neo-Liberal synthesis in twentieth-century American social theory. It marked a tangible maturing of his thinking in a variety of ways. His vigorous style was now in the service of his argument, and not, as it had sometimes seemed in his youthful writings, in command of the argument, leading it over an obstacle course of aphorism, wit, and paradox. *Public Opinion* was also Lippmann's first work which might meaningfully be called universal, catholic in its range of reference and evidence, and treating the dilemma of representative democracy throughout the industrialized world.

The book puzzled many familiar with Lippmann's earlier Progressive and Pragmatic writings, because it seemed to represent a new departure for him, a flight into some sort of Neoplatonism. While Lippmann subscribed to Platonism only partially and qualified it with a heavy infusion of contemporary theory from such sources as Graham Wallas, the Fabian Socialists, and the psychoanalytic followers of Sigmund Freud, Lippmann's own brand of Neoplatonism would remain a constant factor in his studies over the next half-century. *Public Opinion* (1922) was in fact to be the first of what may be regarded as a trilogy, constituting the enduring distinctive structure of Lippmann's thought. The other two fundamental works, which will be dealt with in the chapters which follow, are *A Preface to Morals* (1929) and *Essays in the Public Philosophy* (1955).

III

Public Opinion is a book which would not have been written so soon (Lippmann was barely thirty when he began reflecting on it), so cogently, nor with such a ready readership had it not been for the World War. His study of "power politics" in international relations, his dealings with highly placed officials in the American and Allied governments, his detestation of moralizing, and his consuming humanism, all worked together to make him believe that, as a human phenomenon, war must be understood as an institution in continuity with the "normal" processes of politics. It would do no good for the theorist to pronounce war anathema, or criminal, or insane. Its consequences might be all of these things; but those who waged it, most of them certainly, were none of these things. That it would be understood that he abhorred war, Lippmann took for granted.

He ran the question of the origins of war in the opposite direction, so to speak. Assuming that war is a loathsome institution, does war disclose to us some basic problem in the normal processes of parliamentary government? Lippmann believed that the question could be answered in the affirmative. The World War had revealed, in enlarged and dangerous form, a whole series of problems involving the formation and working of public opinion in the Great Society.

For the term, "the Great Society," and the idea that the problems it generates flow chiefly from its scale and complexity as the civil order of industrialism, Lippmann was indebted to Graham Wallas. In dedicating his 1914 study, *The Great Society*, to Lippmann, Wallas said that it had grown out of the 1910 Harvard seminar in government in which Lippmann had been enrolled. In *The Great Society* Wallas argued that the dominant development of the last century had been the extension of social scale, brought on by inventions in transportation and communications, and that the central source of hope for the guidance of this Great Society lay in the new researches of psychology.[7]

This was the starting point for Lippmann's analysis in *Public Opinion* eight years later. The basic truth which deserved general recognition and further study, Lippmann contended, was that almost no political behavior is a direct response to the social environment. For leaders, as for rank-and-file, the Great Society is remote and invisible. That portion of the social environment which can be known directly in the firsthand experience of a single person, even if he should hold office for a lifetime, is but a tiny fragment of the whole. Virtually all political behavior, whether of a President, a precinct chairman, or a voter, is in response to mediated experience, reported events.

There is in politics normally operating a triangular relationship between event, actor, and response, declared Lippmann. The event is the first point on the triangle; and it occurs objectively, "out there," in the Kremlin, the Congress, or the county courthouse. The second point on the triangle is subjective—the actor's reception of the report-stimulus, and his situating of the report somewhere in the hierarchy of symbols and pictures within his head. If there is a tangible response from the actor, this is the third point on the triangle and it also occurs (if it is an act), "out there." That is why so much political action reminds us of Hamlet, stabbing Polonius through the rustling curtain, mistaking him for the king.[8]

Political behavior so frequently results in conflict because the various actors only seem to share a social environment in common, Lippmann argued. In truth, political actors—from the lowliest soldier or voter to the greatest magistrate—are responding to a pseudoenvironment, a conception of the world subjectively entertained, carried in their heads. Pseudoenvironments clash, not only with one another, but with the objective situation. This is the reason we so commonly experience the tragedy described by Herbert Spencer of a beautiful theory being murdered by a gang of brutal facts.[9] How is the pseudoenvironment formed and sustained? asked Lippmann. How may its structure be better understood and better formed? Lippmann henceforth divides his study into three parts: a consideration of stereotypes, an examination of self-interest and national interest, and an evaluation of the role of the press in relation to government, and public opinion.

IV

Public opinion Lippmann defines as the pictures inside the heads of human beings which are acted upon by groups or by their leaders.[10] These subjective images are not direct and simple reproductions of phenomena in the objective social world. Several telling influences come to play in the formation of stereotypes.

The earliest influence in the formation process is the infant's need, one which continues to develop in the child and adult, for some imposition of order on the "blooming, buzzing confusion" which the world presents to the untutored, drifting senses. Direct exposure to the unstructured ebb and flow of sensation is not a real-life alternative. "For the real environment is altogether too big, too complex, and too fleeting for direct acquaintance. We are not equipped to deal with so much subtlety, so much variety, so many permutations and combinations. And although we have to act in that environment, we have to reconstruct it on a simpler model before we can manage with it," Lippmann writes.[11] This is straight Pragmatism, as is his assertion that "A report is the joint product of knower and known, in which the role of the observer is always selective and usually creative."[12] Drawing upon John Dewey, Lippmann cites the examples of the farm boy in the city, the inexperienced man in the factory, the novice spectator at a ball game, and the alien conversing in a foreign tongue, as examples of the situations in which we must structure and simplify reality in order to cope with it.[13] We should remember, Lippmann admonishes, that while economizing direct experience in this fashion is inescapable, inevitably loss is involved—and when someone else—a correspondent, a news editor, a political leader—"economizes" the experience before it is relayed to us, the process may have some purpose which is not our purpose, or indeed any purpose of which we are aware. Hence we must hold in mind that this process of structuring and simplifying reality is one which occurs at least twice, and very likely several times. The political or military spokesman "briefs" the reporters, whose dispatches may be given to a "rewrite" man, or forced into the mold of editorial opinion, before the reader reprocesses the newspaper's story in his own mind.

Most newspaper readers devote only a few minutes a day to that task, and the privatization of their interests (through advertisements, gossip columns, sports and entertainment features), further diminishes the civic value of this time.[14] The correspondent must severely compress events in the first instance, in reporting them, and in doing so he must employ words which may be taken in different senses by different readers, including mistaken senses.[15] Few adults, in digesting political news, develop very far their powers of lucidity, which Lippmann defines as the "power to dissociate superficial analogies, attend to differences, and appreciate variety."[16] Many persons, groups, and most ominously nations, rarely transcend what the psychoanalyst Sandor Ferenczi termed the magical organization of experience, which characterizes the experience and behavior of the child.[17]

The difficult and demanding task of experiencing the remote and invisible social environment is further compounded by conscious intervention designed to thwart it. This deliberate distortion of social reporting Lippmann placed under the heading of censorship. Censorship depends upon controlled access to the events reported, and therefore it is most readily practiced in time of war.[18] At the same time, censorship, since it is ordinarily an institutional phenomenon, fosters self-deception as well as feeding upon it. In other words, one of the supreme ironies of censorship, which would strain credulity were it not for our experience, is that those wielding the power of censorship come to believe the selective, and hence distorted, conception of reality which they are themselves propagating.[19] Concealment of certain facts, Lippmann believed, is one of the Executive's most powerful instruments; such concealment always is carried out under the protective cloak of "the public interest" or "national security."[20]

The efforts of George Creel and his office, working within the Wilson Administration during World War I, probably constituted, according to Lippmann, "the largest and most intensive effort to carry quickly a fairly uniform set of ideas to all the people of a nation" in recorded history. Creel, in his book, *How We Advertised America*, ticked off his accomplishments: the recruitment of seventy-five thousand orators, who delivered 755,000 speeches to an aggregate audience exceeding three hundred million people (three times the national population at the time); 1,438 designs for posters, cards, buttons, and cartoons; twenty thousand "lantern slides" for illustrated lectures; and the use of the Boy Scouts, fraternal lodges, churches, chambers of commerce, and schools as channels of distribution for printed material.[21] This unparalleled propaganda was made possible by the barriers between the American public and the events of the war.[22]

Culture represents another, more constant and undetectable, form of intervention between event and perceiver. It is the subtlest of all the sources of stereotypes. Lippmann agrees with Graham Wallas that we may have become parasitic upon our social heritage to a dangerous degree.[23] What Wallas's assertion means is that "In the great blooming, buzzing confusion of the outer world we pick out what our culture has already defined for us. . . ."[24] We perceive events through the lenses of the subcultures to which we belong, "through a class, darkly."[25] A man visualizes his social world from "his place on the board in any of the games of life that he is playing," says Lippmann.[26]

The income of the individual and the income of the community determine the amount of communication that is possible within any subculture, or in Lippmann's plainer language, "social set."[27] Ordinarily, the distinguishing mark of a social set is the presumption that the children of the set may intermarry. Relationships, particularly marriage, outside the social set usually involve some doubt, although to be sure there is considerable freedom of movement between sets of the same race in the United States, where economic position is subject to such rapid change.[28] Among all subcultures there is a strong centripetal force at work, a strong pull inward. This is especially remarkable in Lippmann's view, among those with the income, education, and leisure to pursue a serious understanding of the Great Society: "They cannot really be said to suffer from censorship, or secrecy, the high cost or the difficulty of communication. They suffer from anemia, from lack of appetite and curiosity for the human scene. . . . They move, as if on a leash, within a fixed radius of acquaintances according to the law and the gospel of their social set."[29]

Thus the members of a social set regard its limits as their practical human horizon. They convey and reinforce its stereotypes to one another, and to their children. They look up to its opinion leaders, who, so far as the members of the subculture are concerned, are those who share in the running of the world. These social superiors within the set are admired and emulated; and within the national culture certain sets are so advantageously placed that they are admired and believed by most other sets.[30]

A culture as a whole has as one of its sources of unity a moral code, "a scheme of conduct applied to a number of typical instances," according to Lippmann.[31] Subcultures generate subordinate variations on this shared code. The significant aspect of the moral code to which Lippmann wishes to direct attention is that every such code, in order to sustain itself, must generate "a picture of human nature, a map of the universe, and a version of history."[32] In other words, every moral code offers a stereotypically selective view of the facts of human nature and society. "If it has affected human conduct a long time," Lippmann states, "it is almost certain to contain much that is profoundly and importantly true."[33] At the same time, the moral code enforces, under penalty of doing "wrong," and risking rejection, a culture's selective understanding of, and engagement with, the objective world. Conventionally, students of society have held that "a public opinion constitutes a moral judgment on a group of facts." Lippmann wishes to argue instead that "in the present state of education, a public opinion is primarily a moralized and codified version of the facts."[34] Very few codes, under the influence of science, have come to recognize their view of reality as partial and hypothetical.[35] Yet it is only some such recognition of the fragmentary and provisional character of our codes which would enable men to become genuinely tolerant of their political opponents, a prerequisite for the effective play of reason and peace in politics. Without an habitual appreciation that their social knowledge is secondhand and often self-serving, adults remain incompletely socialized to the democratic process. "Without that habit," Lippmann observes, "we believe in the absolutism of our own vision, and consequently in the treacherous character of all opposition."[36]

In each code, in each organized set of stereotypes, there is some "blind spot," some unquestioned premise or premises which secure the system. The blind spot occurs at the point where some ultimate automatism for the cultural code is to be found: providence, the laws of political economy, the dialectic of history, are examples. For most Americans the key blind spot has been "progress." Certainly, the notion of progress, as an undoubtable assumption, "has fitted an extraordinary range of facts in the economic situation and in human nature. It turned an unusual amount of pugnacity, acquisitiveness, and lust of power into productive works," Lippmann concluded.[37]

At the same time, for Americans progress was indeed a blind spot—
"They saw the expansion of cities, but not the accretion of slums;
they cheered the census statistics, but refused to consider over-
crowding. . . . They expanded furiously at reckless cost to their
natural resources. . . ."[38] Thus the blind spot is the area of unexamined faith which stabilizes the code of every culture and subculture and serves as the guarantee of the ultimate rightness of the
social set or of the society.[39]

Lippmann is arguing that without the blind center of progress, a
pluralistic society such as that of America would be in the situation
of the four men allegorically presented by G. K. Chesterton. The
four meet under a lamp post, "one to paint it pea-green as part of a
great municipal reform; one to read his breviary in the light of it;
one to embrace it with accidental ardour in a fit of alcoholic enthusiasm; and the last merely because the pea-green post is a con-
spicuous point of rendezvous with his young lady." Lippmann
agrees with Chesterton's conclusion that "whether this sort of variety is valuable, this sort of unity is shaky. . . . It is not founding
society on a communion, or even on a convention, but rather on a
coincidence."[40] One of the problems with stereotypes, then, is that
they are apt to shatter when they collide with reality.[41] If in fact
links between "reality and human response were direct and immediate, rather than indirect and inferred, indecision and failure
would be unknown," declared Lippmann, and Bernard Shaw would
not have been able to remark tartly that except for the first nine
months of its existence, no human being manages its affairs as well
as a plant does.[42]

Lippmann was also deeply impressed with the role of personal
psychology in the formation of stereotypes. Stereotypes may be the
core of our personal beliefs, and our defense of role and place in
society. Consequently, any attack on one's system of stereotypes is
likely to be perceived as a direct assault on his selfhood. According
to Lippmann, "A world which turns out to be one in which those we
honor are unworthy, and those we despise are noble, is nerve-
wracking."[43] This is because our method of social learning is one in
which we rely upon "certain beloved and authoritative persons.
They are the first bridge to the invisible world."[44] And though we
grow beyond the need for their counsel, parents, teachers, and
masterful friends remain beloved to us, even as we seek to relate to
ever wider environments through a succession of authorities in the

development of our interests. Lippmann points out the richness of the literature of psychoanalysis upon this subject. It is people who join us to the vast realm of unknown things. And we identify with their aims and values as well as with their information.[45] Our needs and our perceptions interpenetrate one another. Our pattern of stereotypes is not neutral, not merely a method of ordering the world for better personal direction and achievement within it. It is highly charged with emotion. Our pattern of stereotypes "is the guarantee of our self-respect; it is the projection upon the world of our own sense of our own value, our own position and our own rights," declares Lippmann.[46] The stereotype becomes the form of our sensation; it "imposes a certain character on the data of our senses before the data reach the intelligence."[47] To some extent stimuli, especially in the printed or spoken word, directly evoke stereotypes, "so that the actual sensation and the preconception occupy consciousness at the same time. The two are blended," says Lippmann, "much as if we looked at red through blue glasses and saw green."[48]

Of course, the social formation of stereotypes must be correlated to the individual's pattern of growth, which nourishes the stereotypes and draws upon them, but which is often idiosyncratic, and sometimes pathological. It is for this reason, according to Lippmann, that "our public opinion is in intermittent contact with complexes of all sorts; with ambition and economic interest, personal animosity, racial prejudice, class feeling and what not."[49]

In general, however, Lippmann seems an environmentalist, impressed with the power of stereotypes to direct the individual's experience and conduct, especially in emergencies, which are likely to be those situations in which the group is most dependent upon its membership for uniformity. Compare, suggests Lippmann, the power of the patriotic and economic codes, which in time of war are simultaneously imposed on separate individuals who may be very close to one another:

There is a war supposed to affect all alike. Two men are partners in business. One enlists, the other takes a war contract. The soldier sacrifices everything, perhaps even his life. He is paid a dollar a day, and no one says, no one believes, that you could make a better soldier out of him by any economic incentive. That motive disappears out of his human nature. The contractor sacrifices very little, is paid a handsome profit over costs, and few say or believe he would produce the munitions if there were no economic incentive.[50]

Such are the anomalies of social codes and of stable patterns of behavior under them. That selves also have profound variations—in relation to personal experience of social situations—Lippmann emphasizes later.

Before turning to Lippmann's treatment of interests and social structure, we must register a word of criticism. Lippmann has, through the first third of his work, developed and consistently employed the terms "stereotype" and "code." But now he begins to make increasing use of terms which he neither adequately defines nor adequately relates to his other terminology. "Fiction," "myth," "symbol," "ideology," require to be defined and distinguished. Lippmann fails to do so. Hence, when it seems reasonable and the best representation of his intent, the earlier terms, "stereotype" and "code," will be used.

V

"The deepest of all the stereotypes is the human stereotype which imputes human nature to inanimate or collective things," says Lippmann.[51] Imputing "selfhood" or "soul" or "geist" to any human association, but especially the state, is mistaken and dangerous from the Liberal point of view. It ascribes some sort of transcendence, or superhuman purpose, to the state. It submerges the individual in this purpose. It subverts the Liberal's view that the state is instrumental, a means to ends which fulfill the claims of persons, claims which are legally recognized as "rights." An "organic" view of the state denies the priority of the person, recognized by the radical assertion of Jesus concerning the law of the sabbath, which may be paraphrased, "The state exists for man, not man for the state." In giving superhuman identity to groups, stereotypes are customarily simplified visual representations—even veritable cartoons—the Russian bear, John Bull, Uncle Sam, or the Republican Party elephant. Conceptual representations of the invisible social world are properly impersonal, abstract, nonvisual. Lippmann advises, "Being flesh and blood we will not feed on words and names and grey theory."[52] These visual representations, to which the multitude respond, nearly always have "identification handles" for hero and villain; the conflict is clear, and it exercises the audience. We identify with the fictional figures portrayed.[53] Evidently Lippmann has the cinema in mind with these remarks, and he generalizes of mass audiences that for them, "a work of art shall be a vehicle with a step where they shall climb aboard, and . . . they shall ride, not according to the contours of the country, but to a land where for an hour there shall be no clocks to punch and no dishes to wash."[54] The popular arts and their stereotypes are designed to represent a simplified version of life, one in which virtue triumphs and an easy pleasure reigns.

We should remember, argrees Lippmann, that "no visual idea is significant to us until it has enveloped some stress of our own personality. Until it releases or resists, depresses or enhances, some craving of our own, it remains one of the objects which do not matter."[55] And in politics, it is not sexuality but pugnacity which is the dominant motif in stereotyping. In order to make politics popular, issues have to be found which can be made to seem to involve fighting, to enlist recruits in a great struggle.[56]

It is at this point that we encounter again the deep, usually hidden, connections between social role and personal characters, according to Lippmann: "For just as psychoanalysis can bring to the surface a buried impulse, so can social situations."[57] When our society or social set demands it of us, we can behave in ways far removed from our accustomed patterns of conduct and indeed release social impulses which are normally considered embarassing or dangerous. Once again, in *Public Opinion*, Lippmann reverts to an example drawn from World War I—the social legitimation of aggression: "The selves which come to the front are those which are attuned to a real love of country [at first]. . . . Gradually [hatred and] the impulse to kill becomes the main business, and all those characters [that is, alternative selves] which might modify it, disintegrate."[58]

This state of affairs points up the dilemma posed by the chasm between our ideals and our institutions. Moral education should prepare the character of citizens for all the situations in which they may reasonably be expected to find themselves. The moralist must choose, says Lippmann: ". . . either he must offer a pattern of conduct for every phase of life, however distasteful some of its phases may be, or he must hope and assume that his pupils will never be confronted by the situations he disapproves. Either he must abolish war [for instance], or he must guarantee that his pupils will never be confronted by the situations he disapproves."[59] Stated in this stark fashion, the limited possibilities presently available to moral education become evident, Lippmann believes. Obviously, the educator cannot determine for each of his students "his place on the board in any of the games of life that he is playing."[60]

What is more, the individual's development is not rigidly and predictably assimilated to the needs of the group, except in severe stress situations, including war. It is more normal that the individual "does not take his personal problems as partial samples of the greater environment," says Lippmann. "He takes his stories of the greater environment as a mimic enlargement of his private life."[61] Unawares, he adapts his character to the stage and props and other characters with whom he must perform.[62] Philosophers and religious sages have always distinguished between polarities within the self—of mind and body, reason and appetite, spirit and carnal self. The modern social psychologist might prefer to say that we have, as individuals, a wardrobe of selves, depending upon how we must behave—for instance, as superior or subordinate, brother or stranger, husband or citizen. At various points in his argument, Lippmann draws upon Freud, Jung, Adler, Ferenczi, Le Bon, McDougall, Jastrow, and other psychologists for illustration and support. One of Lippmann's well-turned conclusions is that

We understand that we see the same body, but often a different man, depending on whether . . . he is making love to a woman he is eligible to marry, or to one whom he is not . . . on whether he is dealing with his children, his partners, his most trusted subordinates, the boss who can make him or break him . . . on whether he is alone in Paris or among his family in Peoria.[63]

The conclusion toward which Lippmann is carrying the argument, and one that will be thoroughly subversive of the old Liberal concept of "self-interest," is that for men as we historically encounter them, in society, there is no single soul readily detectible behind the role, no single unquestionable self. "If the selves are too unrelated," indeed "we distrust the man," says Lippmann; "if they are too inflexibly on one track we find him arid, stubborn, or eccentric." Nonetheless, "In the repertory of characters, meager for the isolated and the self-sufficient, highly varied for the adaptable, there is a whole range of selves, from that one at the top which we should wish God to see, to those at the bottom that we ourselves do not dare to see."[64] "But"—Lippmann drives home the point again—"the characters take their form from a man's conception of the situation in which he finds himself."[65] This, he says, is what sets the concerns of the social analyst apart from those of the psychoanalyst: the psychoanalyst studies the adjustment of the person to a given factor, the environment. The social analyst needs to construct and solve a far more complex equation, in which self and world meld in what Lippmann calls the pseudoenvironment. This is not a "given," but a variable and partially unknown factor, an X for the social scientist. The social scientist must inquire how this X is formed, how it functions, and how it is altered or acted upon.[66]

Under such terms of inquiry, it will be seen that the Liberal concept of "self-interest" is a blind spot, an unilluminating tautology, according to Lippmann.[67] Both "self" and "interest" are constructs from the flux of experience, conceived somehow out of a variety of alternatives; and both are normally conceived with the guidance of culturally inherited stereotypes.[68] Liberalism has neglected to explore either this process of the formation of selfhood or that of the formation of interests.

How does Lippmann propose to examine this dual process? He acknowledges that "The whole structure of human culture is in one respect an elaboration of the stimuli and responses of which the original emotional capacities remain a fairly fixed center."[69] But, he continues, from this relatively stable center, "The cognitive processes, and the actual bodily movements by which the instinct achieves its end may be indefinitely complicated."[70] The arsenal of instincts are "freely attachable to all sorts of objects as stimulus, and to all kinds of objects as gratification."[71] What is in fact experienced as stimulus, and what as gratification, depends in large part on cultural conditioning, which by means of the labile and mobile characteristics of instincts transfers them from childhood objects to adult objects, from facts to slogans, from institutions to leaders, for instance.[72] We may generalize, Lippmann concludes, that "there are many variables in each man's impression of the invisible world. The points of contact vary, the stereotyped expectations vary, the interest enlisted varies most subtly of all."[73]

The community—family, social set, national society—wields heavy advantages. We must, declares Lippmann, from cradle to grave trust others; "complete independence in the universe is simply unthinkable."[74] Unless we could take, as we do, "practically everything for granted, we should spend our lives in utter triviality. The nearest thing to a wholly independent adult is a hermit, and . . . he can act only within a tiny radius and for simple ends."[75] But in the modern Western world, Liberal democrats have never submitted to this commonplace, observes Lippmann, nor to its corollary that the Great Society is governed by an elite, a very small number of men, who are unified by privileges as the rank and file are unified by stereotypes.[76] Liberals have vacillated between two illusions, that of the self-sufficient individual, and that of some sort of Oversoul or invisible hand, which draws order and harmony out of the myriad conflicts between individuals.

In fact, the number of ways in which a multitude can act is severely limited, declares Lippmann: it can strike or boycott or applaud or obstruct, but by collective action nothing can be built, or negotiated, or administered. These activities require organization, and organization brings experts and rulers: "The limit of direct action is for all practical purposes the power to say Yes or No on an issue presented to the mass."[77] Siding with Robert Michels, Lippmann seems to believe the best that can be hoped for is a constructive, representative elitism, in which recruitment into the elites is an open and publicly regulated process.[78]

Lippmann acknowledges the ominous implications of his thinking for democratic Liberalism: the stereotype is both a mechanism of solidarity and a mechanism of exploitation. It immobilizes the personality even as it empowers and activates the group.[79] The official, Lippmann concedes, is likely to find himself more and more frequently choosing the safety of his institution over the value of candor to the public.[80] As a result of modern psychological research, in conjunction with the radical improvement of the means of communications, a revolution in democratic practice is taking place, far more significant than any shift in economic control. The generation of consent, not a new art, is becoming a systematic, self-conscious method and a regular organized practice of government. Under the impact of the new power of propaganda, "the old constants of our thinking have become variables."[81] The old creed of Liberal democracy requires to be reexamined.

The Liberal democrats of the eighteenth century—and it is noteworthy that here real warmth enters Lippmann's writing—"had themselves felt the aspiration of democracy, which is ever so much deeper, more intimate and more important than any theory of government. They were engaged, as against the prejudice of ages, in the assertion of human dignity."[82] Thus the early democrats were not simply propounding an abstract series of propositions: they were locked in a battle of classes, against the hereditary aristocracy. And their political theory, as had every political theory which preceded it, required some blind spot, some assumed "reserve powers of guidance." The Liberal democrats found in the concept "of popular sovereignty . . . the answer to their need of an infallible origin for the new social order," Lippmann declares. "There was the mystery, and only enemies of the people touched it with profane and curious hands."[83] The pioneer democrats could not hesitate to qualify the absoluteness of their assertion. And from the tradition of Western political theory they had inherited "its major premise . . . [that] the art of government . . . [was] a natural endowment."[84] In other words, says Lippmann, just as Aristotle had insisted that the slave was a slave by nature, and the free Athenian self-governing by nature, the Liberal democrats had to insist that the free man generically was a legislator and administrator by nature.[85] Knowledge of the world, and political faculties, were taken for granted by proponents of aristocracy and democracy alike.[86] Public opinion, "a reasoned righteousness," welled up spontaneously out of the people, so far as the Liberal was concerned—he "could not stop to explain that a human soul might not yet have, or indeed might never have, this technical equipment" to legislate and administer.[87] Early democrats put out of their awareness Aristotle's sensible requirement, that "If the citizens of a state are to judge and distribute offices according to merit, then they must know each other's characters. . . ."[88]

Since the period when the pioneer modern democrats had to act out of faith, "the key inventions have been made for bringing the unseen world into the field of judgment"—world wide press services, photography, and experimental psychology as well as statistical sampling techniques.[89] Lippmann contended that the time was in sight when "distant and complicated events . . . [can] be reported, analyzed, and presented in such a form that a really valuable choice . . . [can] be made by an amateur."[90]

Unfortunately, since the eighteenth century, public opinion has remained the grand mystery in Liberal democratic theory. The sources and processes of public opinion remain little studied; politi-

cal organizers have continued to be regarded as "low fellows"; and
not one American political scientist or sociologist had ever, in 1922,
written a book on news-gathering.[91] This was strange treatment for
what was held to be the prime mover of public deliberations and
policy outcomes.

Public opinion is all the more important, Lippmann suggested,
because we do not intuitively sense the need for better ideas nor the
need to prevent the new technical understanding of public opinion
from being used in manipulative ways by the people's leaders.[92]
Instead of giving attention to these problems, most Liberal democratic commentators have been "hypnotized" by the supposed need
to improve methods of balloting and representation. The fighting
gospel of the early democratic Liberals, the Jeffersonians in the
United States, has succeeded so well, in cooperation with the frontier and its isolation, the rural township, and the Protestant ethic,
that it has become an American stereotype that political wisdom
should arise directly from the conscience of the individual.[93] The
principal requirement of applied political science, in the service of
representative government, Liberals have always held, is to find
means of measuring and institutionally registering public opinion
more accurately.

Yet the real lesson of liberal democracy, Lippmann was convinced, pointed in the opposite direction. The real lesson was that in
the absence of education, and of institutions, which so successfully
reported the environment that social realities stood out vividly
against self-centered individual and group stereotypes, common interests would elude public opinion. Instead of effective control by a
shared understanding of the public interest, the affairs of a Great
Society could be effectively managed on a day-to-day basis only by
an elite whose interests were more than transient and local. Since
Lippmann wanted to protect and preserve liberal democracy, it
remained for him to present some program of education and reporting which would convey social realities to the citizens of the Great
Society.

VI

Taking the will of the people, public opinion, as a constant,
operating at all times, Liberal democrats had over time developed
an extensive system of civil liberties. Civil liberties are vital to the
formation of sound public opinion, but they do not guarantee it,

because the truth about distant matters is not always accessible or predictable.[94] Remarkably, right into the twentieth century, Liberals continued to display a neglect of the intelligence-gathering institutions of democracy which seemed to amount to disdain.

For the difficult, often dangerous service performed by the press, American citizens had until most recently expected to pay the smallest coin turned out by the mint.[95] Certainly we should be shocked if we were asked to pay openly for the news of the world the price of a good ice-cream soda, wrote Lippmann.[96] Newspaper circulation, in a competitive commercial field, rests not upon a marriage contract with the readership, but upon free love.[97] The public seemed willing to pay for its news only through a ruse, only so long as the cost was hidden—in the cost of advertising added to commodities which were publicized in the press.[98] The newspaper editor was therefore placed in the difficult position of depending for revenues upon an indirect tax levied upon a group of readers whose loyalties must be held by the editor's skill in serving the readers' stereotyped expectations.[99] Yet newspapers were commonly held ethically accountable to the same standards applied to schools and churches.[100]

At the same time, Lippmann was at pains to rebut Upton Sinclair's charge that the failures of the American press have been due to its corrupt links with the business community. If this relationship actually existed, Lippmann argued, radical newspapers in this country should offer impeccable standards of truth and competence. Instead, their record was so poor that Sinclair, in his book, *The Brass Check*, did not even refer to them.[101]

To advance the discussion, Lippmann proposed, we need to distinguish between "news" and "truth." News is the signalizing of an event, while truth is the statement of hitherto hidden as well as known facts, and an exposition of their relationship, which creates a trustworthy image of reality upon which men may act.[102] The physical scientist had won independence through the use of irresistible methods and proofs—the journalist enjoys neither.[103] But this shortcoming is due to the fact that the press deals with a society in which the controlling forces are very imperfectly recorded. Journalism can normally transmit only what has been recorded for it by the working of institutions.[104] At its best, Lippmann points out, the press is only a servant and guardian of free institutions. The better the institutions, the more accurately they represent the interests they affect, the more accurately they measure and record their own workings, the higher the quality of the news. The press cannot be made to carry, as some democrats have unthinkingly supposed, the full burden of popular sovereignty, and create an effective ruling public opinion by acting on everyone for thirty minutes out of every twenty-four hours.[105] The prime defect of modern representative government, grown far more deadly in the Great Society, as defined by Lippmann, is "the failure of self-governing people to transcend their casual experience and their prejudice, by inventing . . . a machinery of knowledge."[106] People simply have not yet seen "the enormous mischief and casual cruelty" wrought by their uncorrected prejudices.[107]

The breaking down of stereotypes, which bring simplified meaning, and clear moral melodrama, into the quiet lives of millions, would be a painful task. Complex ideas are less interesting than heroic leaders and corrupt villains, just as diplomacy is duller than war, says Lippmann.[108] But the Great Society could be brought under effective human control only by extending to its management the sorts of technology and expertise which brought it into being: the special knowledge of auditors, administrators, engineers— researchers across the spectrum of the physical and social sciences.[109] Lippmann held up "the perfectly sound ideal of an executive who sits before a flat-top desk, one sheet of typewritten paper before him, and decides matters of policy presented in a form ready for his rejection or approval."[110] The separation of expertise from policy could be easily maintained.[111]

Lippmann's grand scheme of reform, then, had an objective and a subjective component, one which was institutional and one which was psychological. The institutional responsibility could be carried out by a reconceived political science and an "intelligence bureau" attached to each cabinet department and major agency of the federal government. These intelligence bureaus, which Lippmann seems to have patterned on the research and reports of the Fabian Socialists in England, must be separately staffed, salaried, accountable, and tenured from the departments to which they would be attached.[112] (This could be read as a direct application of the teachings of James Madison in Federalist Number Ten.) As matters stood, the social scientist was scorned as an outsider who could not produce policies with assured outcomes. The social scientist's own methodological humility, and his lack of access to an adequate factual base, limited and stigmatized his work, said Lippmann:

Imagine medical research conducted by students who could rarely go into a hospital, were deprived of animal experiment, and compelled to draw conclusions from the stories of people who had been ill, the reports of nurses, . . . and the statistics compiled by the Bureau of Internal Revenue on the excess profits of druggists.[113]

That is a rough satirical equivalent of the place and resources of the social scientist. "But the expert who is employed as the mediator among representatives, and as the mirror and measure of administration," Lippmann continued, "has a very different control of facts. . . . he becomes the man who prepares the facts for the man of action."[114] This institutional solution reads like a hopeful generalizing and projecting of his own wartime experience (and even perhaps of his earlier Schenectady experience). The ideal, he says, is the social analyst who can "dip into action and out again whenever it suits him," blending activity and reflection. As a consequence, Lippmann's intelligence bureaus have an academic atmosphere, of impartiality, shared information, tenure, and sabbatical leaves.[115] The function of these bureaus would be addressed primarily to the pressing needs of the legislator and administrator, and only secondarily to the interests of the general voter. Their purpose was not to complicate issues but rather to clarify issues for "insiders," simplify them for "outsiders."[116] The bureaus would meet Lippmann's basic criterion, that "no reform . . . is truly radical, which does not consciously provide a way of overcoming the subjectivism of human opinion based on the limitation of individual experience."[117]

By defining terms, by replacing slogans with concepts, by transforming irreconcilable value conflicts into soluble disagreements over facts, the bureaus would serve the purposes which Fabian socialism had pioneered in contemporary England. They would institute a Socratic interrogation of the facts, and of partisan spokesmen for political programs and legislation.[118] The transformation of stereotypes into concepts is the fundamental Socratic task. And the depth of Lippmann's faith in this task can be found in his assertion that "the difference between the higher and the lower motives is not, as men often assert, a difference between altruism and selfish-

ness. It is a difference between acting for easily [that is, accurately]
understood aims, and for aims that are obscure and vague."[119] To
clarify social aims is to diminish social conflict, says Lippmann:
"here, as in most other matters, 'education' is the supreme remedy," with the proviso that the education be based upon sound clear
knowledge.[120] A basic way to render knowledge sound and clear
(here enters a Pragmatic chord) is to assure that knowledge closely
and normally accompanies action.[121]

As far as the subjective dimension of Lippmann's grand reform is
conceived, he pleads that what is needed is for our minds to "become more deeply aware of their subjectivism,"[122] a process of
"reeducation,"[123] assisted by the teacher.[124] The destruction by
education of a stereotype is at first resisted as painful, because
stereotypes are so often connected to self-esteem. But this demoli-
tion "gives an immense relief and a fine pride when successfully
done. There is a radical enlargement of the range of attention," that
is, of potential experience.[125] This destruction gives the individual
an emotional incentive for a fuller appreciation of scientific method,
which can be used to good advantage by the educator. After criticism, the stereotype "is no longer me, but that."[126] With this kind of
personal awakening of the critical faculties, the student no longer
need view the principles of science as dull and abstruse, declares
Lippmann. They may be taught "as victories over the superstitions
of the mind, and the exhilaration of the chase and of the conquest
may carry the pupil over that hard transition from his own self-
bound experience to the phase where his curiosity has matured, and
his reason has acquired passion."[127] The genuineness of Lippmann's
enthusiasm for education and democracy as reciprocal processes—
an enthusiasm which is authentically Platonic—can scarcely be mistaken, and can scarcely fail to evoke admiration, whether we agree
with Lippmann's faith in this program or not.

"I have written, and then thrown away, several endings to this
book," Lippmann confessed. He would not close without a gentle
rebuke of Plato, for seeming to despair of persuasion after his announcement that "until philosophers are kings, or the kings and
princes of this world have the spirit and power of philosophy, . . .
cities will never cease from ill. . . ." Plato then had Socrates
defiantly add that he would be denounced as a visionary for stating
this position, that the "uselessness" of philosophers is due to the

shortsightedness of the multitude. And with that, Lippmann
remarked ironically, "he hurriedly picked up the tools of reason,
and disappeared into the Academy, leaving the world to
Machiavelli."[128]

Lippmann chose to close on the conciliatory Liberal democratic
note that "it is necessary to live as if good will would work . . . [even
though we] cannot prove in every instance that it will."[129] And then,
at the conclusion of the book, at the end of a decade in which he had
grown to maturity buffeted by conflicts, betrayals, and soul-
wracking violence, Lippmann wrote:

> . . . you cannot despair of the possibilities that could exist by virtue of any
> human quality which a human being has exhibited. And if amidst all the
> evils of this decade, you have not seen men and women, known moments
> that you would like to multiply, the Lord himself cannot help you.[130]

VII

Lippmann dealt with the issues treated in *Public Opinion* in
works other than his 1922 classic. As a journal and newspaper
editor, and then as a syndicated columnist, he had to deal recurrently with the role of the press in American society. A number of
the ideas developed in *Public Opinion* were prefigured in a short
collection of essays published three years earlier under the title
Liberty and the News. In that volume he ventured the judgment
that "in an exact sense the present crisis of western democracy is a
crisis in journalism."[131] Here Lippmann expressed the view that a
concern for objective truth was being overpowered by a concern for
national security, which he found to be just another variation of
the old doctrine that the end justifies the means.[132] Already he
was persuaded that "the protection of the sources of its opinion is
the basic problem of democracy."[133] He argued that "We cannot
fight the untruth which envelops us by parading our opinions. We
can do it only by reporting the facts, and we do not deserve to win if
the facts are against us."[134] At the same time, this book marks the
high-water point of the confluence of Lippmann's earlier radicalism
and his subsequent concern with the structure and functioning of
public opinion. "Change will come only by the drastic competition
of those whose interests are not represented in the existing news-
organization," he wrote aggressively. "It will come only if organized

labor and militant liberalism set a pace which cannot be ignored."
He would rely upon "fearless and relentless exposure conducted by
self-conscious groups that are now in a minority."[135]

Only six years later, in 1925, Lippmann's position could be
characterized as that of a chastened and gloomy Liberalism, verging
at times upon disillusioned conservatism. Public opinion he found,
plausibly enough, to be segmented into attentive special publics.
However, its operation he now held was "partisan, spasmodic,
simple-minded and external."[136] "Only the insider can make decisions," because knowledge exists always in relation to function.[137]
Here Pragmatism was used to justify a conservative stance.

Lippmann was still remote from traditional conservatism, however; one source of the errors of public opinion, he held, was the
ascription by opinion leaders of organic unity and purpose to society.[138] And he was still concerned with the liquidation of "that vast
concentrating of political and economic power in the midst of which
we live."[139] But since Lippmann did not find a party whose interest
could be identified with that of the whole community,[140] he won-
dered aloud whether one might not say that "a nation is politically
stable when nothing of radical consequence is determined by its
elections."[141] In this gloomy and inconclusive work, Lippmann's
best counsel is a skeptical and unsentimental adherence to the usages of Liberal democracy: debate, consent, representation, the
alternation of "ins" and "outs."[142] The specific role of the public
does not include passing upon the intrinsic merits of the question
nor upon the substance of its solution: "What is left for the public is
a judgment as to whether the actors in the controversy are following
a settled rule of behavior or their own arbitrary desires."[143]

Lippmann returned repeatedly to problems associated with public opinion, most notably in *Essays in the Public Philosophy*. The
argument of that book is better considered as an integral whole. It
will be treated in Chapter 5. What remains here is to provide some
critical perspective by examining the basic weakness, and the most
important strength, of *Public Opinion*.

VIII

Lippmann's credulous trust in the power of the expert, the man of
scientific knowledge, is certainly understandable. Some such faith
has bewitched a chorus of American social theorists in the twentieth
century.

Thorstein Veblen introduced a number of concepts which implied recognition of what C. Wright Mills was to call the Marxist theme (it was also Pragmatic, a theme that Lippmann shared) "that those who are functionally indispensable to the community are the men who count. . . ."[144] Veblen's beliefs in a growing split between technological industry and nonproductive ownership, in an "instinct of workmanship," in "the discipline of the machine," would all be familiar to readers of Lippmann. Max Lerner summed up Veblen's conception of the role of the men of applied science in a sentence: "The engineer holds the key to the whole structure of production, but he holds the key as a hireling who has not yet learned that he can run the machine for himself and his kind rather than for his masters."[145]

C. Wright Mills argued in his famous letter to "The New Left" that the agency of reform in the latter twentieth century could be neither the bourgeoisie nor the proletariat, but the intellectuals, "because that is what we are, and where we stand"—in a position to understand injustice, to conceive alternative policies, and to persuade majorities to act upon them.[146]

The economist Robert Heilbroner, while acknowledging that scientists have no social program of their own at the present, has urged that "In the long run, the ascendant [scientific and technological] elites within capitalism are not themselves capitalist in mentality, and will slowly incline society toward that deliberate application of intelligence to social problems that is characteristic of their professional commitment."[147]

John Kenneth Galbraith has proposed to call the organization formed by all who participate in corporate decision-making the "Technostructure." "It embraces all who bring specialized knowledge, talent, or experience to group decision-making," says Galbraith. "This, not the management, is the guiding intelligence—the brain—of the enterprise." To it, in partnership with the state, the future belongs.[148]

Don Price, Peter Drucker, Daniel Bell, and numerous other social commentators have voiced similar judgments.[149] For American writers, working in the world center of technology and prosperity, it is natural enough to turn to the men of science and learning, as an agency of peaceful change, or as a means of apologizing for existing patterns of power, income distribution, and social growth. But to many of Lippmann's critics it seemed hard to tell whether he favored the progressive or the conservative uses of the scientific-technological community. Many of his critics would agree with Heywood Broun, who (in another connection) said of Lippmann that he was the greatest carrier of water on both shoulders since Rebecca at the well.

The basic weakness in Lippmann's thinking on public opinion, however, reaches deeper. It lies in his supposition that knowledge and policy could be divorced. It is this supposition that causes Lippmann's hope for the future sovereignty of public opinion, based on intelligence bureaus, to ring hollow. The *Pentagon Papers* and Watergate episodes reinforce the judgment of the Platonist that knowledge is directly translatable into profit and office, economic and military and political power. As a consequence, sensitive information will never be candidly and freely surrendered by its possessors. On the contrary, sensitive information will always be jealously guarded, from superiors and inferiors within the organization, from bureaucratic adversaries who could exploit such information to their own advantage.

Neil Sheehan, writing the introduction to the *New York Times'* abridged edition of the *Pentagon Papers,* used words which might easily have appeared in *The Phantom Public:* "The guarded world of the government insider and the public world are like two intersecting circles. Only a small portion of the government circle is perceived from the public domain. . . ." Sheehan's conclusion, however, is diametrically opposed to Lippmann's conception of the socially beneficial consequences which would flow from allowing the "insider" freedom of action:

The segments of the public world—Congress, the news media, the citizenry, even international opinion as a whole—are regarded from within the world of the government insider as elements to be influenced. The policy memorandums [in the *Pentagon Papers*] repeatedly discuss ways to move these "audiences" in the desired direction, through such techniques as the controlled release of information and appeals to patriotic stereotypes.[150]

While much of what Sheehan says—and the *Pentagon Papers* demonstrate—could be taken as confirmation of Lippmann's works of 1922 and 1926, Lippmann could scarcely have approved, for instance, of the fact that for six months prior to the Tonkin Gulf incident in August, 1964, the United States government had engaged in clandestine military attacks upon North Vietnam while planning to obtain a congressional resolution which the administration planned to employ as a virtual declaration of war.[151]

Daniel Ellsberg, who released the *Pentagon Papers* to the public, wrote of the self-deception which the Executive Branch had practiced upon itself, again in terms reminiscent of Lippmann's *Public Opinion*. One of the broad lessons of Vietnam, he wrote, was that there were situations

. . . in which the U.S. Government, starting ignorant, did not, would not, *learn*. There was a whole set of what amounted to institutional "anti-learning" mechanisms working to preserve and guarantee unadaptive and unsuccessful behavior: the fast turnover in personnel; the lack of institutional memory at any level; the failure to study history, to analyze or even record operational experience or mistakes; the effective pressures for optimistically false reporting at every level, for describing "progress" rather than problems or failure. . . .[152]

The great struggle between the Legislative and Executive branches of the federal government in 1973–1974, usually called simply Watergate, was a struggle for possession and control of information. That information was so important that once it changed hands and was made public, it brought the first resignation from the office of President in American history. Obviously such information, directly implicating the President in the commission of felonies, was not to be surrendered lightly. On its possession depended the holding of what is often called the most powerful office in the world. Here was knowledge directly redeemable in power of the greatest magnitude. The President's dismissal of the Special Prosecutor when the latter insisted upon access to some of the information, and of two Attorneys General who supported the Special Prosecutor, is convincing evidence of how quixotic it would be to expect that any nonpartisan "intelligence bureau" could obtain such sensitive information.

From another perspective, it could be maintained that the *Pentagon Papers* and Watergate support the argument of *Public Opinion* that "open government," with a free flow of information to Congress, the media, and the people is vital to the preservation of representative government. It could be argued as well that the passage of an expanded Freedom of Information Act in 1974, with tougher enforcement provisions, by margins of ten-to-one in both houses of Congress over the veto of President Ford, showed that Congress is aware of the importance of public access to government information.[153]

But however extensively Vietnam or Watergate may be read as confirming the main thrust of *Public Opinion*, the critical objection remains: since knowledge can be directly transformed into profit or power, there is no warrant for supposing that it would be fully and candidly shared with any "outsider," such as an agency representing the media or the public.

Further light is shed on Lippmann's naiveté in this matter by his assertion that knowledge and policy are readily separable, conjuring up the image of an executive seated at a bare desk, reaching a decision on the basis of the data on a single sheet of paper before him. Few if any students of public administration, nor anyone with experience in government, would endorse this view. John Kenneth Galbraith has discussed how he, as head of the World War II Office of Price Administration, often found that he had been locked into a course of action by the information supplied him by attorneys and economists who were his subordinates, before an issue ever reached his desk.[154] Some twenty years ago Henry Kissinger complained, after serving as a consultant to the National Security Council, that the adoption of policy positions on the basis of short "briefings" by relatively junior officers of the National Security Council or of Cabinet departments amounted to a delegation of authority by the President and his top advisors. The power to define a problem, to control the flow of information concerning it, was the effective power to dictate the solution or policy adopted.[155]

Richard Neustadt, Theodore Sorensen, and numerous other students of the Presidency have agreed upon the vital need of the Chief Executive for information from a variety of sources and interests if he is to reserve to himself the genuine authority to make decisions.[156]

Of course, Lippmann recognized that selection and valuation are wedded to perception, that opinion is a codified version of the facts, that one's opinions will depend upon where he is placed on the board of the game he is playing. But Lippmann's rationalism and hopefulness overpowered the gloomy consequences for representative government to which these valuable insights pointed.

The strength of Lippmann's *Public Opinion* lay not in the reforms he proposed but in his analysis of the functioning of public opinion in modern representative democracy. The significance of the work is to be found in its disclosure of the epistemological fragility of modern democracy. Epistemology concerns itself with how knowledge is obtained and verified; Lippmann demonstrated that our methods of knowing social reality are slender and frail when measured against the speed, scale, and power of technological civilization and the limited role reason has to play in human affairs.

Hannah Arendt has pointed out that the traditional antidote for the ancient political art of lying—the inconsistency between the lie and reality which time discloses—may be obsolescent. Military policies, for instance, can be set in motion so swiftly that there is no time for reality to come into play against the falsehood and permit the public or its representatives to cope with it.[157]

The scale of the Great Society, emphasized by Graham Wallas, made it necessary that political action be based upon mediated knowledge, reports which the public had few or no means of independently verifying. Lippmann could not foresee the extent to which the manufacture of history would be developed under totalitarian regimes, but he recognized that even during World War I "ministries of befuddlement" had sprung up in every nation at war. After all, he had held office in one of them.

It was the Pragmatists and Sigmund Freud who allowed Lippmann to see that not only was "interest" a transient thing, defined rather arbitrarily under the changing pressures of perceived events, but that the self too was to some extent socially constructed. That reason was by no means supreme within the self was a truth acknowledged by the founding philosophers of Liberalism in the seventeenth and eighteenth centuries; but it was a truth gradually glossed over and lost in the spread of capitalism and parliamentary democracy, each of which explained human behavior by means of a supposed rational calculus of self-interest.

Lippmann, following Wallas, wanted to return human nature to the center of the study of politics and to assess it unsentimentally with the aid of depth psychology. To do so would be to reveal a political animal who was rational and sociable, but also emotional, pugnacious, in conflict with himself and capable of dangerous regressive behavior.

It was appropriate that Lippmann should predicate his criticism of the optimistic received Liberalism on the question of epistemology. For epistemology was the arm of philosophy used by the founding generation of Liberal theorists to challenge and break the supremacy of theology in Western thought. John Locke, to take the most prominent example, had argued that men could not presume to knowledge of things ultimate: that was the proper province of faith. What could be known by men was to be found through the senses and reflection upon sensory data. This knowledge was sufficient for human needs. Although the parallel is not a complete one, Lippmann too was jousting against what had become a deductive psychology and against any pretension to knowledge which could justify coercion against the private moral behavior of individuals.

Lippmann's blend of skepticism and humane hope, his sense that reason was under siege and must be rescued and restored to authority, was much closer to Enlightenment Liberalism than he acknowledged. He was helping to forge a tempered neo-Liberalism which would be more able to withstand the hammer blows of the twentieth century: two world wars and two totalitarian systems with designs of global domination.

CHAPTER 4

The New Morality

THE 1920s were a decade of disenchantment for those who had been Progressives. The hopes for the League of Nations lay blasted. The regulatory agencies of Roosevelt and Wilson were gutted by the Harding and Coolidge Administrations. The spirit of Progressivism within the Republican Party had expired. For America the decade was culturally vulgar, economically frenetic, and politically inert. Drift was king, having deposed mastery. For Lippmann it was a time of reassessment and career change, as he passed from high government advisory responsibility, to the measured cadences of the *New Republic's* editorial board, to seclusion as an author, and finally to the hurly-burly of headlines and deadlines at the editorial desk of the New York *World*.

I

In 1929 appeared *A Preface to Morals,* one of Lippmann's best received and most widely read books. It would be easy to conclude that this book represented a search for another role, a burrowing underground for Lippmann in a time of political blight. That may be taken as a partial explanation of the book, but it is not the most important part of the truth.

In the first place, it should be remembered that Lippmann had always been attracted to politics by its moral dilemmas and possibilities. From the pathetic slums of Chelsea to the magnificient corridors of Versailles, he had held in steady view the ethical dimensions of politics.

From one perspective, all political theory can be understood as a secular reworking of the ancient problem of theodicy. "Theodicy" is the justifying of God's ways to man—the problem of reconciling the presence in the world of a God whose power, knowledge, and goodness admit of no limit, with the obvious presence in the world of

123

evil, in the form of cruelty and innocent suffering, for example. Political theory may be viewed as theodicy brought down to earth. This is because political theory must struggle with the analogous secular problem of how to explain or defend might (that is, political power) in societies where might so often violates right (justice), either inadvertently or by design. One of the oldest answers to this central dilemma of political theory is supplied by Plato, when he asserts that justice will not be secure until philosophers are kings, or princes pursue philosophy. Elusive and paradoxical as Plato's solution was, Lippmann strongly sympathized with it. Indeed, in *Public Opinion*, Lippmann had rebuked Plato for advancing the philosopher-king in a half-apologetic, half-defiant fashion. In *A Preface to Morals*, he stated his conclusion bluntly: "The ultimate question [that is, the prior and controlling question] is not how the populace is to be ruled, but what the teachers are to think: That . . . is the preface to everything else."[1] Politics was the royal science, but true educators, those with a *philo-sophia*, a love-of-wisdom, were the true royalty.

Lippmann's Neoplatonism, however incomplete, was evident enough to be attacked from two sides. More thoroughgoing Platonists could wonder whether Lippmann's position was not too eclectic. Had he really grasped or expressed the Platonic sense of "knowledge," or was not knowledge for Lippmann really only an elevated version of American "know-how," the very technical knowledge which Socrates had scorned? The answer to this challenge depended, of course, upon the purity and intensity of the critic's Platonism. I believe this is a fair objection to Lippmann's work in his Progressive phase, prior to World War I. But in the third of a century from 1922 to 1955, from the appearance of *Public Opinion* to the publication of *Essays in the Public Philosophy*, Lippmann's conception of "knowledge" much more closely approached that of "orthodox" Neoplatonists. (By orthodox Neoplatonists, I mean simply those who believe Plato came as close to full human wisdom as anyone ever has, or could.) In other words, Lippmann's conception of knowledge moved away from the position that knowledge is sensory data, temporarily structured for problem-solving, toward the position that knowledge is an understanding of a changeless moral order, which can be won only through a discipline of renunciation or strict limitation of the operation of the senses and appetites. Lippmann refers to Plato and

Platonists some two dozen times in *A Preface to Morals*, invariably in a favorable manner.

From an opposite vantage point, Lippmann's works on public opinion and public morals in the 1920s were criticized for being too Platonic, too elitist and antidemocratic. Lippmann, it was said, had beaten a hasty and reactionary retreat from his earlier radicalism and Pragmatism. In practice, the royal rule of reason meant the rule of economic royalists. Lippmann's philosopher-king was a Harvard man in an executive office where he was effectively immune from popular scrutiny or removal from office.

A variation on this latter objection was that the ethic of "indifference" Lippmann advocated was an aristocratic Stoicism, at the opposite pole from his earlier championing of full and direct representation of all those groups with interests at stake in the resolution of an issue. The imperturbable, well-lettered Lippmann had found the prototype of the philosopher-statesman in his own personality, or in that of his teacher George Santayana. Santayana, personally cool and aloof, was certainly a striking outsider: a Roman Catholic, a Spaniard by birth, a student of American philosophy in relation to the Western philosophic tradition, he had left the United States soon after Lippmann's departure from Harvard, and lived in England, Paris, and Rome, until his death in 1952 at the age of ninety.

Santayana was invited by *The Saturday Review of Literature* in 1929 to review *A Preface to Morals*. He wrote an elliptical review, generally skeptical of Lippmann's approach. Santayana dubiously regarded his former student as still a dewy-eyed democrat, still dreaming of a progressively enlightened and humane social order. Lippmann was a "brave" philosopher, one who believed "mankind can endure the truth." "It would be interesting to hear," Santayana wrote with cutting irony, what Lippmann "forsees will be the ruling passions, favorite pleasures, and dominant beliefs of mankind when the hitherto adventurous selfish human animal has become thoroughly socialized, mechanized, hygienic, and irreligious."[2] If these mocking comments were too general for the reader, Santayana further sharpened his pen and aimed it directly at Lippmann:

. . . I believe even moralists might easily endure the truth about morals if they would only face it. . . . The virility and chivalry of virtue lies precisely in being inflexibly true to oneself, although all other people may be different and one might have been different too. I commend this reflexion to those who feel safe in their ethics and politics if they think they are swimming with the tide—a form of cowardice peculiarly modern and peculiarly short-sighted.[3]

Thus so far as Santayana was concerned, Lippmann was too oriented to America, to the people, to historical developments—he was not sufficiently the royal moralist.

A professional philosopher raised the further point that Lippmann's advocacy of "disinterest" made him (and Santayana) Epicurean, not Stoic, since the Stoics had believed in a cosmos which was a community of gods and men, that is, a universe in which the highest human purposes were supported and fulfilled by divine purpose. This minor point is worth mentioning because it highlights the fashion in which Lippmann's work defied classification. He avoided school-thought of any kind, I believe, as a deliberate tactic in order better to serve what he conceived to be his larger office as a widely heard social theorist in a representative democracy. *A Preface to Morals* cites no Stoics, it is true; neither does it cite any Epicureans. It is the case that Lippmann wrote, as had the Epicureans centuries earlier, of an "indifferent universe"; and it is also the case that Lippmann totally avoided the central Epicurean doctrine of balancing and managing the appetites so that pain could be minimized and pleasure stabilized at some optimal and secure level. Lippmann's familiarity with Freudianism, as well as his acquaintance with ancient philosophy, would have made him doubly aware of the arguments for this position; and he was seeking a convergence of the ancients and the moderns in *A Preface to Morals*. This sort of naturalistic humanism evidently did not provide the synthesis he was seeking.

Such a wide variety of interpretations of a book often suggests that none of the critics has wholly captured the structure and intent of the author's argument, and I believe this was the case with *A Preface to Morals*.

II

The purpose of Lippmann's essay was to gain understanding of the breakdown of the old moral code—political, economic, and sexual—which had been grounded in religious belief. Further, the essay proposed to search for some equivalent for the old moral order. Lippmann said he was addressing himself to unbelievers who were experiencing distress and a sense of emptiness at their loss of belief. He acknowledged that there were many in American society who remained devout believers, and he said he had no wish to disturb their faith. There were others who professed defiance or exhilaration at the decline of Christianity, and again, Lippmann's counsels were not intended for them.

But Lippmann was unabashedly autobiographical when he presented the essay as an attempt of one of the perplexed to reason his way out of the "blank misgivings," the loss of assurance that life had meaning, the pall of routinized work and routinized pleasure, the dizzy sense that "Aristophanes must have been thinking of him," contemporary man supposed, when he had written, "Whirl is king, having driven out Zeus."[4]

The devastating loss of the religious understanding of life had been hidden in the nineteenth century by the orthodox pieties and hopes of the Liberalism of that time, "which begat us," declared Lippmann. But now that freedom was no longer an unattained goal, it was a problem. The old orthodoxies of Liberalism now seemed "pleasant fantasies which concealed the greater difficulties that confront men, when . . . [they have] won the freedom to do what they wish. . . ."[5] Lippmann was hearkening back to the argument with which he had introduced *Drift and Mastery* fifteen years earlier: "The battle for us, in short, does not lie against crusted prejudice, but against the chaos of a new freedom."[6] The idea that freedom could be dizzying and threatening, that men could in large numbers prefer to regress to autocracy, was an old conservative motif, which was to become a cornerstone of the neo-Liberal synthesis in twentieth-century thought. The most famous elaboration of the argument was provided by Erich Fromm in his arresting book, *Escape From Freedom*, first published in the United States in 1940. Lippmann saw the peril, "the impulse to turn back from his freedom,"[7] clearly in 1929 and he was not the first to do so, as was noted above in Chapter 3. The successful rebel, Lippmann wrote, is as disoriented as a released prisoner. He "ought to be very happy"; for there are "no conventions, no taboos, no gods, priests, or princes," to bind men and women in contemporary Western society. "The prison door is wide open," yet the inmates "stagger out into trackless space in a blinding sun."[8]

To repeat, there were of course men and women who did not experience the anxiety of freedom so keenly: ties of family, of faith, of career and material success, suffice for a great many. Yet for numberless others, and among these some of the most sensitive, the most active in the earlier struggles for liberty, life had come to seem a confused scene of "unsanctified compulsions." The compulsions of fashion, of majority rule, of supply and demand, seem "painful and, as it were, accidental, wanton, and full of mockery."[9] For a person with these experiences, "pursuing his casual ambitions, satisfying his hungers, and for the rest accepting destiny as an idiot's tale" was an almost unbearable experience.[10] The 1920s, Lippmann had found, were a surreal social and psychological landscape, in which lost dreams and abandoned causes stood in vivid detail, huge, grotesque and lifeless, on the desert of prosperity. In such an age of postbelief, where political hope had died more abruptly and publicly than religious hope, the Liberal was undergoing a sort of crucifixion. Lippmann visualized his plight as follows: "For the modern man who has ceased to believe, without ceasing to be credulous, hangs, as it were, between heaven and earth, and is at rest nowhere."[11] Thus the starting point of Lippmann's analysis of morals was anxiety and alienation: social institutions, social codes, social movements were collapsing; and psychological homelessness was affecting increasing numbers of men and women in advanced industrial society.

Could understanding the situation create any hope? At least it could be said, Lippmann believed, that the curse of modernity kept visible, albeit in negative form, the goal toward which men wished to be in motion: "to be wholly alive." That goal was barred for many a man now because "that depends upon his sense of being completely engaged with the world, with all his passions and all his faculties in rich harmonies with one another, and in deep rhythm with the nature of things."[12]

Furthermore, there were historical parallels to be found with the contemporary situation, its confusion of authority, its conflict between science and religion. "Plato was born into such an age," said Lippmann.[13] The Greek philosophers appeal to us as at once so fresh and so profound because they were confronted with a historical situation in many respects remarkably similar to our own.[14] And we might anticipate that in basic ways the response of our culture would be parallel to the response of Athenian culture: "humanism arises in complex and changing societies. . . ."[15]

But there was a difference between the American era and earlier ages of stressful social change, which threatened to cancel out any hopeful parallel. According to Lippmann, "The earlier rebels summoned men from one allegiance to another. . . ."[16] This had been true of rebellious institutions from Plato's Academy to the Lutheran Church. Luther believed in "Protestantism for good Catholics." Enlightenment Liberalism had drawn heavily upon the deference, decorum, and civility associated with what had been for generations an aristocratic parliamentary regime.[17]

What we were embarked upon now, in the twentieth century, was something utterly novel (so new that Lippmann had to adopt the phrase itself from the historian Charles Beard): "a technological civilization."[18] Contemporary Western society, with America in the vanguard, had succeeded in harnessing together three forms of social activity which had been quite separate: "pure" scientific research and theory, invention, and the corporate quest for profit. The impact upon society and its mores was genuinely revolutionary. We had institutionalized, in Alfred North Whitehead's telling phrase, "the invention of invention." As a consequence, Lippmann was deeply concerned that "The acids of modernity are so powerful that they do not tolerate a crystallization of ideas which will serve as a new orthodoxy into which men can retreat."[19]

Thus, unlike previous ages of social change and disorder, contemporary industrial society was dissolving not only the morality of the old order but the social institutions and habits which had supported the religious morality. The transformation of machine society promised to be more rapid and more nearly total than anything hitherto recorded in history. Lippmann set out to examine the web of dilemmas resulting by studying the past, to analyze how religious morality had functioned in earlier ages; and by studying the present, to discern more exactly what were the novel factors in our situation and how the materials of the problems might be used to construct a solution.

III

Lippmann argued that historically the Christian religious tradition—and others as well—had been a dual tradition. Two levels of religious experience and practice had been intertwined. Lippmann called them simply "popular religion" and "high religion."

He did not refer openly to the distinction he was making as one of "double truth"—that there is a higher form of religious knowledge

for the sophisticated and initiated and a lower legendary truth for
the multitude. The idea is an ancient one in philosophy and religion.
It is most commonly associated with the name of Averroes, a
twelfth-century Islamic commentator on Aristotle, who subscribed
to Greek philosophy so wholly that some defenders of the Christian
faith charged him with propagating a doctrine of "double truth,"
whereby revelation and human philosophy could hold opposing positions on a question, and yet both be true. It is hardly surprising
that Lippmann refrained from referring to this ancient controversy,
which might have led critics to classify him as an eccentric contemporary exponent of a long-dead heresy. Lippmann wished to write
for his own times, to appeal, as he explicitly said, to his readers'
experience, not to metaphysics,[20] and to avoid being pigeonholed as
any sort of schoolman or doctrinalist.

Popular religion understands religious phenomena to exist as factual realities exist. Adherents of popular religion "do not distinguish
two planes of reality and two orders of certainty."[21] God is supreme
ruler of all the world just as tangibly, certainly, and specifically as
the Emperor Charlemagne was once supreme earthly ruler of much
of Europe. As William James had pointed out, religion does not
simply interpret accepted faith; it postulates new facts as well.[22] The
Christian church had always sought to instil a new life in its members not by appealing to their will, but by telling a story, narrating a
sequence of events.[23]

Popular religion, which could for most purposes be equated with
the institutional church and its ties with the bulk of its membership,
was a system of commandment and obedience, reward and punishment.[24] It could be said, stated Lippmann, that "fundamentally the
great churches are secular institutions; they are governments preoc-
cupied inevitably with the regulation of the unregenerate appetites
of mankind."[25]

It is a defining characteristic of adherents of popular religion,
Lippmann continued, that they suppose that "their wishes are of
more than human significance."[26] The great moral sages have been
worshipped by the multitudes as gods.[27] The multitudes supposed
that adherence to these teachings in simple form would evoke a
reciprocal loyalty and love from God.[28] While renunciation of desire
is accepted by the popular tradition as well as by the high tradition
as the path to salvation,[29] popular religion betrays its repressed

infantilism in its imagery of heaven, where all human desires are fulfilled.[30]

High religion embraces a very different religious psychology, declares Lippmann. For it, the problem of evil—"sin, sorrow, crime, fear, frustration, pain, and emptiness"—can be overcome only by so disciplining human desires that we have ceased to covet, ceased to desire anything evil, ceased to desire anything which is out of accord with the possibilities allowed by the structure of reality.[31] He who subscribes to high religion realizes that there is not space enough, time enough, objects enough, to satisfy all human desires.[32] He regards salvation not as a condition to be won after this mortal life, but rather within it, "as a condition of the soul which is reached only by some kind of self-discipline."[33]

Thus the adherent of high religion does not regard asceticism as a means to an end, but one form of the goal itself. Lippmann quotes Spinoza with approval: "Blessedness is not the reward of virtue, but virtue itself; nor should we rejoice in it that we restrain our lusts, but, on the contrary, because we rejoice therein we can restrain our lusts."[34]

High religion is at variance with popular religion on a number of questions which the proponents of popular religion would take to be vital, but the understanding of renunciation is the crux of the matter. Immortality, for example, is understood by popular religion in a very plain and unadorned fashion: it is the continuation of personality, and probably of personal relationships, after the close of mortal life. While the believer in popular religion insists that if we are immortal we shall meet our friend again, and have our blisss amplified by continuing the friendship, "the platonist loves the memory of his friend after death as he loved an ideal image of him during his life." Lippmann continues, with evident feeling:

For not even the gods, says Homer, can undo the past; no accident of mortality can destroy anything which can be represented in the mind. Heroes die, but that such heroic deeds were done is a chapter forever, as Mr. Santayana says, in any complete history of the universe. The thinker dies, but his thoughts are beyond the reach of destruction. Men are mortal, but ideas are immortal.[35]

Thus even this difference between popular religion and high religion on the subject of immortality can be seen to hinge on the issue of renunciation of desire. For desires must be authentically surrendered, high religion insists, not simply deferred in the expectation that they will be gratified later and elsewhere on a grander scale. Once naive desire is surrendered ("I shall meet my friend again . . ."), the individual is placed in a radically different relationship to those beautiful persons and objects in his world. First the desires must be disciplined effectively. Lippmann points out that the original Greek meaning of our word "asceticism" is "I practice," a reference to the training of the athlete.[36] Once a command over the desires, and hence their harmony with one another and with the world, is achieved, epistemological and moral transformation have been won. In entering what Lippmann calls this platonic world, the individual is surrendering "the very desires of which his hope of immortality is the expression. He must detach himself from his wish to acquire and possess objects that die; he must learn what it means to possess things not by holding them, but by understanding them, and to enjoy them as objects of reflection."[37] He understands phenomena "in the light of their origin and destiny, with sympathy for their own logic and their own purposes. . . ."[38]

Life is no longer a succession of objects at which the person grasps and is frustrated by losing or gratified by holding. He is most truly at home in the world, and most fully the possessor of it, because his vision has enlarged in proportion to the manner in which his desires have been subdued to a fitting human scale. This has been the highest wisdom, Lippmann is convinced, of the great sages of all cultures and epochs—Socrates, Plato, Ptolemy, Origen, Jesus, the author of the Fourth Gospel, Buddha, Confucius, Augustine and Luther in phases of their thought, Eckhart and Erasmus and Spinoza. He compares this wisdom with innocence:

To be able, as Confucious indicates, to follow what the heart desires without coming into collision with the stubborn facts of life is the privilege of the utterly innocent and the utterly wise. It is the privilege of the infant and of the sage who stand at the two poles of experience; of the infant because the world ministers to his heart's desire and of the sage because he has learned what to desire.[39]

IV

Lippmann's preference for high religion was unmistakable. What was surprising was that he went on to argue that "The real effect of modernity upon religion . . . is to make the religion which once was the possession of an aristocracy of the spirit the only possible kind of religion for all modern men."[40] To rework Santayana's metaphor so that it agrees with Lippmann's perception, the tide of history had turned so that it was moving with the moralist-swimmer in the direction he had originally chosen.

High religion was the only practical alternative for modern man because of novel elements in contemporary industrial society, particularly in its science and politics, which will be explored below. But the passing of popular religion was also made inevitable by the collapse of the old institutional superstructure which had cooperated with and supported popular religion. In simple terms, religion provided most men with an imagery of how the universe is governed and these images of God's rulership changed as the empirical political experience of the community changed, declared Lippmann:

Thus . . . Yahweh, as he appears in many famous portraits in the Old Testament, is very evidently an Oriental monarch. . . . He governs as he chooses, constrained by no law. . . . The God of medieval Christianity, on the other hand, is more like a great feudal lord, supreme and yet bound by covenants to treat his vassals on earth according to a well-established system of reciprocal rights and duties. The God of the Enlightenment in the Eighteenth Century is a constitutional monarch who reigns but does not govern.[41]

The God of modernity, who is variously depicted as the motive force of evolution, or the sum of the laws of physical nature, "is really a kind of constitutionalism deified."[42] In other words, the complexity of modern society and its pluralism have splintered sovereignty and diffused it so that the old aristocratic systems no longer provide credible analogies for the divine government of the universe.

It remains for Lippmann to explain how the novel elements in our social situation are working toward the establishment of high religion on the ruins of the collapsing morality. While he devotes attention to a variety of factors, there are three principal ones: politics, experimental science, and industrial organization.

V

Lippmann had contended that the divine government of the world had been understood by the masses on the basis of "credible analogies" with monarchy and lordship.[43] Further, he had argued that the church itself had historically been, in a manner of speaking, an agency of the state—an institution to govern the inordinate desires of its only partially pacified subjects.[44] The coming of constitutionalism had subverted the older credible metaphors of autocracy. And the church had subverted itself—and thereby the unquestioning obedience upon which the Christian polity drew.

The subversive process was lengthy and complex, but its essentials may be swiftly sketched. "What Luther did," Lippmann summed up, "was to destroy the pretensions not only of the Roman Catholic Church, but of any church and of any priestly class to administer God's government on earth."[45] What Luther brought on was a revolution which ever thereafter divided Christendom, and its power to limit or to sanctify political rule.[46] Toleration breached the logic of the Reformers as surely as it did the logic of the Papacy, but civil peace demanded toleration.[47] No longer would debates about election and predestination carry for the whole community the same weight of meaning of eternal citizenship.[48] Indeed, the modern nation-state began to draw into itself much of the loyalty which the church universal had once commanded.[49] The sovereignty of religion in the larger sense of its authoritative moral regulation of all essential human activities, was set on a course of irreversible decline. Today, Lippmann observed, "Each activity has its own ideal. . . . Each ideal is supreme within a sphere of its own . . . ideals are no longer in a hierarchy under one lordly [religious] ideal. They are free and they are incommensurable."[50]

Another name for the advanced stages of this process is moral relativism, and nowhere has it advanced further than in America, concluded Lippmann. Americans have crossed an ocean, crossed countless frontiers en route to the Pacific, passed into the family of nations, as individuals have passed—usually upward—into different social classes, have passed into mechanical culture, have passed in growing numbers from the countryside to the city.[51] The farmer's dependence upon the seasons, the soil, the rain and sun, have been largely lost. The son's dependence upon the father for apprenticeship and livelihood has been lost. The continuity of the generations—the tie of family to place—has been lost. And with all this movement, change, unfamiliarity, and material improvement, religious and political certitudes alike have been lost—not defied so much as forgotten. William Graham Sumner once remarked of his religious beliefs that he had not deliberately discarded them—he had put them in a drawer, and one day he opened the drawer and found it empty. This is what Lippmann means by asserting that "the sense of authority is not established by argument":

It is acquired by deep familiarity and indurated association. The ancient authorities were blended with the ancient landmarks, with fields and vine-yards and patriarchal trees, with ancient houses and chests full of heirlooms, with churchyards near at hand and their ancestral graves, with old men who remembered wise sayings they heard from wise old men.[52]

The most important political "added factor" in modernization, pregnant with constructive consequences, has been complexity. Again and again Lippmann returned to the theme of the benefits of complexity, in *A Preface to Morals* and in earlier and later works. It must have left many of his readers baffled and disappointed, if not angry. Of what worth was sheer complexity in itself? What had become of the young Progressive, who insisted that interests must be clarified, represented, and their conflicts fought through to an open and majoritarian resolution? Wasn't "complexity" one of those "blind spots" Lippmann had warned against in *Public Opinion?* Wasn't it another form of automatism, like Adam Smith's "obvious and simple system of natural liberty," "which establishes itself of its own accord"—which Lippmann derided in *A Preface to Morals?*[53] The objections are understandable. Complexity, to understate the matter, is an improbable rallying cry for moral reform or social hope. To many it appeared that Brer Lippmann was disappearing into the briar patch. Whether Lippmann's conceptualization of complexity met these objections fully is doubtful. But it was more than praise of the maze of modernity by one lost within it.

What specific advantages did Lippmann see flowing from com-plexity? Several can be distinguished. Since complexity develops in urban settings, it is inherent in this contemporary complexity that men must behave moderately in order to preserve social peace. Their ancient enemies—ethnic, racial, religious, political—are their neighbors and interdependent workmates.[54]

The intricacy of modern urban life also reinforces both its durabil-ity and its responsiveness, Lippmann contended: "Its strength lies in its sensitiveness. The effect of bad decisions is so quickly felt, the consequences are so inescapably serious, that corrective action is

almost immediately set in motion."[55] The human and economic
costs of dislocation and bad policy so swiftly and visibly ramify
through society that incentives to reform are quickly generated.

What is more, added Lippmann, as social relations become more
complex, the division of labor proceeds, and an undesigned cos-
mopolitanism arises, habits of obedience and dependence are
weakened, as are the centralization of authority and leadership.
Decentralization is the ironic and unforseen consequence of urban
complexity he continued: "it diffuses the experience of responsible
leadership throughout the population, compelling each man to acquire the habit of making judgments instead of . . . trusting to
custom and organic loyalties."[56]

By the same token, governmental authority is exerted less unilat-
erally and more reciprocally, through consultation, persuasion, and
the necessary employ of expertise. "What the government really
does," Lippmann wrote, "is not to rule men, but to add overwhelm-
ing force to men when they rule their [own] affairs."[57] What he was
proposing, in the midst of the disastrous experiment of Prohibition,
was that any law depends upon community acquiescence and
affirmative support and that no law can ever be enforced more than
selectively.

The momentum of this line of argument impelled Lippmann away
from his position of three years earlier in *The Phantom Public*, that
public opinion is so episodic that it is necessarily ineffectual. Public
opinion, Lippmann argued now, in 1929, is neither mysterious and
ineffable nor hopelessly fragmented and discontinuous: "The
naively democratic theory was that out of the mass of the voters
there arose a cloud of wills which ascended to heaven, condensed
into a thunderbolt, and then smote the people [not, note, the gov-
ernors]."[58] Now Lippmann saw public opinion as a continuous process, operative through private institutions as well as public, in a
reciprocal manner, being shaped by government, as well as em-
powering it.[59] "The real law in the modern state," he argues, "is the
multitude of little decisions made daily by millions of men."[60] The
reader who is surprised by statements such as these, and more
drastic equivalents, such as "Government is in the people, and stays
there," need not suppose that Lippmann has forgotten *Public Opinion* or is repudiating it. The difference is more sensibly accounted
for by the fact that in *Public Opinion* Lippmann was dealing within
the more limited scope of political science, narrowly construed:

opinion formation and expression as they had a direct bearing on government action. Here, in *A Preface to Morals,* Lippmann is concerned with a far wider range of belief and authority, of values, mores, and usages. That is the reason he finds the workings of public opinion more variegated and freely ranging, more continuous and inescapable.

Finally, it is complexity which allows Lippmann to bring onto the stage the character who might be called the hero of his entire lifework: the man of reason. In *A Preface to Morals* the hero has three costumes to wear—that of the moral philosopher, whom we shall meet in the next section of this chapter; the civil servant; and the statesman.

The ideal of the civil service, Lippmann held, was an acknowledgment by society that many of the affairs of its government must be carried out by "a class of men who have no personal and no party allegiance, who are in fact neutral in politics and concerned only with the execution of a task." The civil service was certainly in an early and imperfect stage of development, but it was standing institutional proof of how imperative disinterested judgment is to the functioning of our complicated contemporary society.

The politician Lippmann viewed as one who profited from serving a part of the community at the expense of other parts: he was the leader of what Madison had named a faction. The statesman "reeducates desire by confronting it with the reality"[61]—an apt description of the teacher and the moral philosopher as well. To see "high politics," like "high religion," as inherently and ultimately an educational respor.sibility, is a characteristically platonic position. The task of the statesman for Lippmann was to "clarify the wants" of the people and "to act upon the hidden realities of a situation in spite of appearances. . . ."[62] Statesmanship thus might require acting against the wishes of the people. It called for courage and the willingness to surrender office if need be. It was based not only upon the knowledge of the leader but of his character. It required "a high and imperturable disinterestedness."[63]

Another fundamental novel element in contemporary society was science. The term "science," as Lippmann used it, was a spacious one, allowing room for a variety of related meanings. It was a vocation, a body of knowledge, a method of inquiry, a means of arriving at judgments and guiding public policy, the framework for a world view, and more besides.

Science has been understood as hostile to popular religion because science does not serve the layman's need to believe. He requires ultimate, immutable, invincible truths; science can provide
only partial, tentative, contingent truths, Lippmann declared.[64] Indeed, the reconciliation or synthesis between science and religion
which some theologians were trying to work out was impossible
because one of the elements to be reconciled—scientific
knowledge—is subject to such continual change that a stable accommodation with it and some other body of fixed truth (such as
religious dogma) is inherently impossible.[65] Another bar to accommodation between science and religion, Lippmann observed, lay in
the fact that scientists true to their profession could never accept
jurisdictional limits on the boundaries of their inquiry. To them all
phenomena, natural, social, and psychological, are subject to the
interrogation of science.[66]

A second source of the adversary relationship between science
and popular religion, Lippmann suggested, was that science presented a world which does not subserve human hope and divine
purpose, a world which is "utterly indifferent to our personal
fate."[67] The science of Aristotle and Thomas Aquinas had been a
popular science in that it was teleological and discovered purpose in
infrahuman nature which could be aligned with man's desires and
God's will. According to Lippmann, "The radical novelty of modern
science lies precisely in the rejection of the belief, which is at the
heart of all popular religion, that the forces which move the stars
and atoms are contingent upon the preferences of the human
heart"—or more exactly, that the phenomena of nature and the
phenomena of human life are both grounded in the same divine
substratum.[68]

Another source of the opposition between science and religion,
Lippmann implied, without saying so directly, might have positive
consequences. It was that science, not the churches, had become
the provider of miracles for modern man. Lippmann referred to the
marvels of exploration and engineering which science had wrought,
particularly in the last century. The fact that theologians and scientists would agree that radios and vaccines, airplanes and skyscrapers
are not "miraculous" is beside the point, he believed. The point is
that these are practical marvels which arrest the attention, and in-
spire the awe, of the multitude and often confer real benefits or
enjoyments as well. Such developments not only generate and rein-

force humanistic self-confidence, but they increase the flow of intellectual authority away from the churchmen and to the scientists. The awe in which science is held, however superstitious it may be in its early popular form, declared Lippmann, might prepare a later shared understanding that science holds the keys to the kingdom of the humanly possible, that the habits of the scientific mind may open the gates to a new moral and social order as well as to an improved human niche within nature. This brings us to the crux of Lippmann's understanding of the import for morals of modern science.

As Lippmann envisioned it, the most distinctive and revolutionary fact about contemporary society was that disinterested knowledge of the world was for the first time in history the basis of the entire material organization of the world, of power and profit. Three statements summarize Lippmann's sweeping view of the importance of science for society and for the future of morals:

. . . whatever the motives which cause men to endow laboratories, to work patiently in laboratories or to buy the products, the fact remains that inside the laboratory, at the heart of this whole business, the habit of disinterested realism in dealing with the data is the indispensable habit of mind.[69]

Scientific method can be learned. The learning of it matures the human character.[70]

It is no exaggeration to say that pure science is high religion incarnate.[71]

These statements might cause many scientists to blush. The question of immediate interest here is, Why didn't Lippmann blush?

Why did he seriously make these propositions? There are two possible answers: the first is that Lippmann was writing as an apologist for what might be called the dynamic status quo of American industrialism, in which both corporate profits and power were pyramiding. The second possibility, which I believe is the correct one, is that Lippmann's hopes seized control of his reason and repatterned the facts. He made too much trenchant criticism of American capitalism in other works, in his newspaper writings of the 1920s, and in *A Preface to Morals* itself, to allow us to view him as a serious apologist for the new American corporate order. It can be said by critics that his position was privileged and secure, that his criticisms of American capitalism were not original, that they were not sufficiently sustained or systematic. But all of these criticisms, which have real merit, do not amount to convicting Lippmann of being an apologist for corporate capitalism. How much his argument excludes or minimizes is evident—the importance of profits, the close-range direction of research, the role of advertising in inducing "artificial needs." These omissions are all the more glaring since Lippmann was familiar with such objections through the writings of Thorstein Veblen, for instance, for whom Lippmann often professed admiration.

But Lippmann did not want to surrender the vision—in part because it would appear so improbable to others—of a grand new entrance and role for the man of reason. At least it might be coming to pass that disinterested, analytic reason—which had so long been Lippmann's vocation and ideal in public affairs—was gaining an institutional base from which it could not be dislodged. And his arguments on the subject do not altogether lose their cutting edge and persuasive power.

Because science "is the ultimate source of profit and of power, . . . therefore it is assured of protection and encouragement by those who rule the modern state," Lippmann concluded.[72] Whether planning for prosperity or for war, no advanced nation could afford to fall back in technological and industrial capacity, nor in scientific research. (Einstein and Fermi, after all, did not disconfirm this argument.)

Capitalism, Lippmann went on to argue, was indeed an "infantile" way of life, oriented to grasping and gratification.[73] But it was in fact set on a course of self-liquidation. Because there was under "naive" (Manchester) capitalism, no system of reciprocal rights and duties, the contemporary American business society was, properly speaking, "not a social order at all, as the Greek city-state or the feudal society was a social order. It is rather a field for careers, an arena of talents. . . ."[74] Nor would the "sop," the "ostentatious benevolence" of "corporate responsibility" save the present business society. Perhaps the deepest flaw of "naive capitalism" would turn out to be the disabling flaw Lippmann had found seven years earlier in "naive Liberalism." It was the defect, it will be recalled, of uninformed perception and self-centered motivation reinforcing each other. It was a flaw which could be remedied only by a platonic reconstruction of society. The error in naive capitalism, Lippmann asserted, "which renders it utterly meaningless," is the assumption that "each man knows his own interest and can therefore pursue it. But that is precisely what no man is certain to know, and what few men can possibly know if they consult only their own impulses."[75]

Progressivism and Socialism had simply reframed and repeated the naive bourgeois error, Lippmann believed, by adopting a single-factor psychological explanation of social behavior and development. They were utopian because they assumed acquisitiveness was the sole source of moral error, and that it could be corrected by regulating or replacing the capitalist leadership.[76]

In fact, what was required was subtler, more difficult, and far more time-consuming. It was nothing less, Lippmann declared, than the reeducation of the corporate and political leadership to the discipline of reality. As the businessman, in an increasingly complex, remote, and invisible social environment, came gradually to realize that he was no longer the monarch of all he surveyed, that his hard-won experience was less and less adequate to the constantly expanding web of social relationships and economic imperatives, he would come to rely more upon expert advice. He would come more and more to submit his impulses to the collected disciplines of knowledge in which his corporation shared; he would become less dominated by immature acquisitiveness; and he would increasingly play the part of the disinterested administrator. Finally, as "the old distinction between public and private interest becomes very dim," said Lippmann, he would, even if insensibly, take on some of the attributes and attitudes of the public servant.[77] The disfranchisement of the legal owner of the corporation, the shareholder; the rise of professionals with a sense of accountability to their professional standards and colleagues; the steadily growing demand for expertise; all led Lippmann to subscribe to John Maynard Keynes' hopeful assessment that "the battle of socialism against unlimited private profit is being won in detail hour by hour."[78]

VI

If Lippmann's hopes and prescriptions for society seem far too assured and sweeping to us today, they were nicely counterbalanced by the humility and sensitivity he brought to his description of the role of the modern moralist—his own role. The moral philosopher in the American age found himself beset and bewildered.[79] He was no longer certain that he was right, said Lippmann.[80] He was no longer the spokesman and enforcer of a respected received moral code.[81]

He felt trapped between the pharisee and the hedonist. The pharisees consisted largely of unreconstructed churchmen who regarded contemporary moral standards and behavior as a willful rebellion against God, a rebellion to be put down with exhortation if possible, and with coercion if necessary.[82] It was entirely appropriate, Lippman agreed, that one of the most widely known and respected of American pharisees, William Jennings Bryan, should expend his strength in the last fight of his life in an attempt to ban the teaching of the scientific hypothesis of evolution in the public schools of Tennessee.[83] The hedonist, on the other side, trusts "immature desire, disregards intelligence, and damns the consequences."[84] According to Lippmann, those who invoked Freud on the one hand insisted upon sexuality as "casual," while at the same time they would undergo elaborate and costly psychoanalysis to free themselves of the burden of apparently trivial sexual episodes, especially those of childhood.[85] The hedonist really labored under the futile but painful burden of shrinking his "human desire to its primary physiological satisfaction."[86] Small wonder that one of the latter hedonists of antiquity, Hegesias, was called the "persuader to die."[87]

As Lippmann viewed the matter, the moralist's loss of command was confirmed, if he needed further confirmation, by modern depth psychology, which found the life of the modern man is "a play of many characters within a single body," a cast of characters lacking in direction and in distinction between the heroic and the villainous.[88] We had apparently reached the stage described in Plato's satire of democracy in the *Republic,* where the constitutional form of the individual's mental life is republican, with no hierarchy or controlling "form of the good."[89] The moralist must then rediscover with Aristophanes that "Whirl is King, having driven out Zeus."[90]

Yet amidst all the confusion, the moralist was able to see that with theism gone, his task is that of the humanist. "Happiness cannot be the reward of virtue; it must be the intelligible consequence of it. . . . Such a morality may properly be called humanism, for it is centered not in superhuman but in human nature. When men can no longer be theists, they must, if they are civilized, become humanists," concluded Lippmann.[91]

How was the task of the modern humanist to be defined and pursued, Lippmann asked? First of all, the humanist moralist must recognize the "radical displacement" of moral authority from the tradition and institution to the individual. The humanist would then recognize that contemporary man, in his adulthood, is autonomous, literally self-lawed, or self-ruling.[92]

To be autonomous is to have responsibility for recognizing, to the fullest extent possible, all of the moral dimensions of the situation in which one finds oneself, and for anticipating so far as possible all the consequences of one's actions. Nowhere, Lippmann believed, was the burden of autonomy more keenly or intimately felt than in the realm of sexual behavior: "It is in the hidden issues between lovers, more than anywhere else, that modern men and women are compelled, by personal anguish rather than by laws and preachments . . . . to transcend naive desire and to reach out towards a mature and disinterested partnership with their world."[93]

Disinterest, as difficult as the term or the concept might be for members of a culture which had glorified self-interest into the cardinal rule of politics and economics, was the central goal of the education offered by the humanist moralist. "An emotion," Spinoza said, "which is a passion ceases to be a passion as soon as we form a clear and distinct idea of it."[94] This discovery, Lippmann contended, is equivalent to the central insight of Freud's psychoanalysis that "To become detached from one's passions and to understand them consciously is to render them disinterested. . . . This is the principle by which a humanistic culture becomes bearable."[95] Disinterest is the equivalent of innocence; disinterest allows us to say, Lippmann asserted, that a "man has virtue insofar as he can respond to a larger situation. . . . He is just if he acknowledges the interests of all concerned . . . and not merely his own."[96] Disinterest allows the person to respond to experience in successively larger wholes, over more space and time, with more reflection, and more comprehension of, and sympathy for, the consequences of his actions for others.[97]

But in teaching disinterest, Lippmann continued, the modern moralist must rely on persuasion, clarification, inducement. He can no longer command or coerce. He "strives to give a true account, imaginatively conceived, of that which experience would show is desirable among the choices that are possible and necessary."[98]

Persuasion in the modern world would mean that the moral philosopher would not codify. He would not compile inventories of good and bad desires or good and bad objects. His approach should rather deal with behavior and psychodynamics, showing that "the quality of good and evil lies not in impulses as such, nor in objects as such, but in the relationship between impulses and objects."[99] Here Lippmann's Pragmatism reappeared in the functional and relational conception of good and evil, terms which he normally shrank from using.

The moralist might also seek to persuade by appealing to the individual's highest aspirations, learned earlier in formative experiences. While he did not openly invoke the platonic doctrine of anamnesis, Lippmann remarked that "Were the nature of good and evil really made plain by moralists, their teachings would appear to the modern listener not like exhortations from without, but as Keats said of poetry: 'a wording of his own highest thoughts and . . . almost a remembrance.' "[100]

The modern moralist might also point to the convergence in conclusions between the sages of high religion and the pioneers of modern depth psychology, reminded Lippmann. The model of personal growth presented by psychoanalysts such as Ferenczi was "the matrix of humanism," tracing as it did the career of the self, from hallucinatory omnipotence to a sympathetic acceptance of an ever-widening range of reality and relationship.[101] These were the "poles of development" of infant and sage.

The contemporary moralist, then, would have a vital role to play in enlarging the humanistic resources of the individual and of the community, Lippmann declared. He could enable the individual to substitute cognitive appreciation of, and partnership with, others, with nature, and with artifacts, for seizure, domination, and possession of them. He could humanize relationships by enabling individuals "to draw the sting of possessiveness out of their passions. . . ."[102] He might help dispel the "aura of dread" which was inevitable so long as good and evil remain entangled with a theory of divine government of the world. To be able to achieve detachment from our passions, to understand their origins and their higher possibilities, would be to rob the passions of their unacknowledged domineering authority in our lives, declared Lippmann. It would mean achieving the self-knowledge for which the dialectic of Socrates had been designed.[103] The moralist's task was incomplete; perhaps it would always remain unfinished. But in modern industrial society it had an unprecedented pressure of institutional necessity behind it.[104] Now, said Lippmann, "the religion which was once the possession of an aristocracy of the spirit [is] the only possible kind of religion for all modern men."[105] The ideal was implicit in events; it was necessary; the task of the moral philosopher was to make it visible, and successful.

VII

Much of Lippmann's writing on morality seems commonplace because so much of the work he wrung out of research and reflection has passed into the domain of "common knowledge." No book of Lippmann's was more thoroughly researched than the *Preface*. That he had struck close to the popular understanding of current moral issues—while not merely restating that understanding—is attested by the fact that the book passed through fourteen hardcover editions.

Yet how successful had he been in *A Preface to Morals*? The Christian as opposed to the humanist, the Marxist as opposed to the Liberal, the academic specialist as opposed to the widely read educated man: each has an Archimedian point from which to judge, if not to budge, the world. In this book Lippmann's strengths as a humanist, Liberal, and generally educated man are also his weaknesses. In the realm of morality, where men and women crave certitude and must make judgments, he was counseling calm recognition of the impossibility of certitude and the necessity of keeping judgments open to revision or reversal.

In a society in which self-interest had always been regarded as the compass of social behavior, he was proposing "disinterestedness" as the polestar for conduct. Whether this ideal would ever have appealed to more than a tiny cerebral elite of Americans is doubtful. For his confident assertion of the rising importance of the scientist-engineer, he offered no empirical evidence. Recent studies indicate that two generations later, only some 1.2 million Americans can be classified as scientists or technologists; and of these a mere one thousand wield any real policy influence, with perhaps four hundred actively engaged in doing so.[106] Much of Lippmann's faith in the ideals of disinterestedness and the scientist-technologist may be reduced to his belief in the continuing introduction of novelty into American society, or, in other words, to the idea of progress.

But it should also be remembered that *A Preface to Morals* was less an attempt to present a matured solution to current moral dilemmas (which Lippmann believed was inherently impossible), than to explore and clarify these dilemmas. His invocation of the Socratic method of questioning—others and oneself—on moral issues was sound in an age when the dissolution of the received morality was becoming abruptly evident through the uses of affluence and the development of mass media of communications. The codified morality of the pharisee had always been distressing to Lippmann; and by opposing the hedonist to the pharisee, he was able to create a plausible median type in the form of the Socratic humanist. This process allowed Lippmann—and his readers—to believe that in an age of expanding scale and a diminished sense of individual efficacy, morality was more vitally personal than ever. The convergence he saw between the "high religion" of the sages and modern depth psychology lent some cultural and scientific credence to this hope.

Working out a twentieth-century moral orientation free from formal religion may have had deep personal significance for Lippmann as well. Born a Jew, raised in the Hebrew faith, he had dissociated himself from Judaism as a college student and never thereafter showed any special interest in the Jewish religion or people. In speaking of extreme nationalism, he had deplored the ancient barbaric vanity of the idea of a chosen people, evidently identifying it with pharisaism and the exaltation of the group over the individual as well as over other groups. His own morality, of course, was cosmopolitan, with the humanist's insistence upon toleration. He wrote at one point that every man must come to terms with his origins. Perhaps it was peculiarly difficult for him to do so, and *A Preface to Morals* can be seen as a definitive stage of his personal effort to "be at peace with the sources of his life."

A Preface to Morals stood at a juncture between *Public Opinion* and *Essays in the Public Philosophy.* As in the earlier work, he was arguing for epistemological modesty and caution, for close scrutiny of what we know and what we have received from others. A viable morality could be based only upon the suasion generated by shared experience. The interrogation of experience of self and the world in order to determine rules of conduct was the task of the Socratic moralist.

At the same time, *A Preface to Morals* pointed forward to *Essays in the Public Philosophy.* Lippmann was acknowledging that no society could hold together and function without a core of moral imperatives. He was acknowledging that politics, itself intrinsically a moral enterprise, is set in a wider cultural matrix. And he was strongly implying that there is a unity to human nature which underlies all historical change and cultural diversity. The modern Western world could find the highest wisdom not only in the Hellenic, Hebraic, Christian, and humanist moralists of earlier times, but in the sages of other cultures—such as Buddha and Confucius.

CHAPTER 5

The Public Philosophy

I

*T*HE *Good Society* appeared in 1937 and provoked considerable excitement as a repudiation of the New Deal by America's leading Liberal analyst of current affairs. It has been interpreted in that way by recent critics of Lippmann's work as well, who have found it a startling departure from the warm support he had given to President Franklin Roosevelt's legislative programs as late as 1935.[1]

Lippmann's explanation of the book and its content contradict such interpretations. He recounted in an introduction to the 1943 edition of the book that he had begun work on it a decade earlier, in the late summer of 1933, when Franklin Roosevelt had been in office scarcely six months. The New Deal is not mentioned in this explanation and is referred to infrequently in the lengthy text. Instead, Lippmann relates that he commenced, continued, and finished the book under the mental pressure of international developments, particularly the rise of Hitler and Japanese aggression in the Far East.

The book was designed to advance, or rather to reaffirm, two propositions. The first, which he believed to be the more fundamental, was that morality, law, and politics in Western culture have developed upon the assumption (derived from religion) that all humans are equal and inviolable in their personhood. He concluded that this intuition of inviolable selfhood had issued in the logic of Liberalism, that all men are bound by a supreme law in their dealings with one another, kings as much as commoners. The essence of this higher law lay in the denial that men may be arbitrary in their transactions with one another, and in their affirmative obligation to deal justly with one another. This moral law had been unfortunately debased in the latter nineteenth century into the absolute right of property, admitted Lippmann. Liberals consequently abandoned "the dogmatic absolutism of this counterfeit natural law—which judges made and then found," and opposed to it the equally spurious absolute of popular sovereignty.[2]

The second basic proposition was that the industrial revolution

. . . which still engages the whole of mankind and poses all the great social issues of the epoch in which we live, arises primarily from the increasing division of labor in ever-widening markets; the machine, the corporation, the concentration of economic control and mass production, are secondary phenomena.[3]

This had been a central understanding of Liberalism, he maintained, but since classical economics and Supreme Court decisions had corrupted Liberal logic into ideological apologetics for the defense of corporate capitalism, and progressive Liberals had rebelled with the counterdogma of absolute majoritarianism, Liberalism had been divided against itself. Since 1870, the weakness of the Liberal heritage had been compounded by the assaults of aggressive nationalism, and since 1917, by Bolshevism, fascism, and Nazism. State capitalism and state socialism were the current forms assumed by left-Liberalism, including the New Deal, and Lippmann termed them "gradual collectivism," pragmatic forms of collectivism which were less militant and martial than communism or fascism, but ultimately no less erroneous.[4]

All forms of collectivism together constituted a reaction or counterrevolution against the Liberal genius of modern social economy, which had been a respect for an international division of labor, a global economic Great Society.[5] In adopting this view of the importance of the market as an allocator of resources, labor, and capital, Lippmann felt required to abandon the beliefs of his Progressive days that economic concentration was inevitable, and that a union of science and political authority was the best hope for a humane future.

He was laboring under anxious doubts about his own earlier adherence to a species of collectivism and wondering whether all forms of state-directed economic endeavor were not tending toward the grim totalitarian practices of Russia, Italy, Germany, and Japan. In fact, he affirmed that "Collectivists have no stopping place short of the totalitarian state."[6] The issue was the reciprocity entailed by the supremacy of law versus the "overhead" or authoritarian determination of legality by a central authority in the furtherance of economic planning. [7]

Lippmann's analysis of "gradual collectivism" is strikingly similar to that made by several distinguished students of American politics in the 1960s, particularly to that of "interest group liberalism" by Professor Theodore Lowi in his 1969 work, *The End of Liberalism.* Lippmann was concerned that "The gradual collectivist has to believe that a mass of special privileges can be distributed among interested groups in such a way as to raise the general standard of life." In fact, however, as the programs of the New Deal demonstrated, the most disadvantaged groups in the community—such as farm workers and sharecroppers—lacked the resources and leadership even to gain inclusion under the "reform" laws, such as the National Labor Relations Act and the Agricultural Adjustment Act. The effect was to give protection to those "interests capable of bringing influence to bear upon the government," "making privilege universal."[8] Ultimately, such laws operated to

. . . sanctify the self-regarding purposes and do nothing to subdue them. For many particular interests do not in any conceivable combination constitute the general interest; to entrust the government of a nation to such a body would be to turn the sovereign power over to a coalition of its most powerful interests.[9]

Americans were entering a "polity of pressure groups" in which there were rising expectations of increased wealth because of the conferring of privileges by the government. Lippmann feared that some equivalent of the corporate state of fascist Italy was the logical outcome of such expectations and policies.[10]

The quest for the public interest, for an agreed-upon language of discourse in the natural law tradition which stood behind and beyond contemporary Liberalism, was the goal which animated Lippmann's inquiries thereafter. The year following the appearance of *The Good Society,* he carried his studies into a working manuscript for *Essays in the Public Philosophy.*

II

The argument of *Essays in the Public Philosophy* opens with the proposition that during the years between 1900 and 1920, the Western democracies began to go into decline. Although they possessed superior material resources, they proved unable to prevent two world wars. Prior to 1914, in the 1930s, and again following 1945 they had been unable to construct and manage a durable peace. Their decline could also be reckoned by the spread of a "counter-revolution" against Liberal democracy, in the multiple guises of Bolshevism, fascism, and Nazism. These totalitarian creeds agreed in rejecting Liberalism as a system of undirected compromise, unable to provide peace and prosperity.

Lippmann had come to the conclusion that the Liberal democracies were ill rather than wounded. They were suffering from an institutional disorder in which their respective executives had lost effective control of critical policy decisions in foreign and domestic affairs. The executive had been eclipsed by the representative assembly, which in turn was subject to manipulation and control by power brokers, special interests, the mass media, and, episodically, by convulsions of public opinion.

At the level of ideology and social theory, Liberalism had been assailed by variants of what Lippmann called the "Jacobin heresy," the ideas of an extremist faction in the French Revolution. The Jacobins, Lippmann held, asserted that all injustice could be overcome by social revolution. They promised a collective regeneration of human nature in the act of violent revolution: for this superhuman goal, inhumane methods were necessary and justified.

The neglected resource of Liberalism was the idea that politics was a *res publica*, a public thing, a common realm in which differences could be overcome by reasoned discussion. Instead of absolute rights and irremediable conflict, a renewed appreciation of the natural law tradition would restore respect for shared authority and hope for the future. Properly applied, the canons of the natural law tradition or the public philosophy would provide standards to guide the resolution of important civic disputes, such as those concerning private property and freedom of speech. An understanding of the public philosophy would also reestablish the truth that every enlightened person lives in two realms, a realm of concepts and ideals in addition to the realm of nature and history. The balancing of these two realms, it would then be seen, is the task not only of professional philosophers and theologians but of every citizen living in liberty.

Essays in the Public Philosophy was greeted by many Liberal critics with dismay and derision. The book was called antidemocratic and anachronistic. Its author was said to be a "tired Liberal," a "futilitarian," who had suffered a collapse of courage, an old man in reaction against his own youth. Some of the ablest objections to the book will be considered below, in section VII; but my own understanding of *Essays in the Public Philosophy* is quite different.

An appreciation of the book is greatly enhanced by a study of Lippmann's thinking over the forty years prior to the appearance of this book. When it is read in this way, it does stand as an appropriate summation of, and crown to, his lifework. Once again, the continuities and consistencies are most illuminating.

The book is almost universally known by the shortened title *The Public Philosophy*, and this in itself is a minor misfortune. "Essays in" denotes a tentativeness, a hypothetical character, which Lippmann intended the work to have. To "essay," after all, is an old verb meaning to attempt. It is all the more important that the book be regarded as a collection of papers, since the manuscript represents a composite of his thought at two different times, separated by an interval of sixteen years. He opens the book, characteristically, with an autobiographical remark upon its origins. The work was begun in 1938, when he was living in Paris, "filled with foreboding" that the nations of the Atlantic community would prove unequal to Hitler's challenge and that "we should lose our great traditions of civility." He continues, "I began writing, impelled by the need to make more intelligible to myself the alarming failure of the Western liberal democracies to cope with the realities of this century."[11] He had finished a draft of the book when the fall of France intervened, and with Pearl Harbor he had put the manuscript away and deferred the project indefinitely.[12] But the military victory of the Allies did not banish the theme from his mind or restore his confidence in the vitality of the institutions of the liberal democracies. He continued to muse upon the historical developments which had taken place in the span of his lifetime. ". . . the more I have brooded upon the events which I have lived through myself, the more astounding and significant does it seem that the decline of the power and influence and self-confidence of the Western democracies has been so steep and so sudden."[13]

The sections which follow examine in order the parallels with Lippmann's earlier work which show that the origins of the *Essays* are to be found in his earlier thinking as a Progressive, as an analyst of foreign affairs, as a theorist of public opinion, and as a proponent of a modern moral philosophy.

III

Lippmann's 1955 work was, as we have noted, received by a large number of American commentators as a retreat from Liberalism, a "failure of nerve." Lippmann was set down as part of the "new conservativism" of the Eisenhower years.[14] We should not expect, following this interpretation, to find more than faint traces of the young Lippmann, the ardent Progressive of *A Preface to Politics* and *Drift and Mastery*.

Yet some of the central ideas of *Essays*, and a good deal of its tone, can be found directly connected to his theorizing as a Progressive. First, let us admit his own testimony on his views, which should of course be set aside if it is contradicted by the substance of his argument. He acknowledges that his views have evolved, have undergone change when he writes of his belief in the public philosophy: "It is a conviction which I have acquired gradually, not so much from a theoretical education, but rather from the practical experience of seeing how hard it is for our generation to make democracy work."[15] But he insists that the fact that he ascribes harmful consequences to the "enfranchisement, emancipation, and secularization" of the last one hundred years does not mean that he is illiberal, or opposed to popular rule. ". . . I should say that I am a liberal democrat, with no wish to disenfranchise my fellow citizens."[16] On the contrary, he pleads, "It did not come easily to one who, like myself, had known the soft air of the world before the wars to recognize and acknowledge the sickness of the Western liberal democracies."[17] Lippmann's concern was to restore and preserve the vitality of Liberal institutions. But he did believe that to do so required of the theorist that he expose to scrutiny his own first assumptions: ". . . we must be uninhibited in our examination of our condition."[18] He believed that in fact he had argued "hopefully and wishfully" in contending that Western institutions could be restored to full vigor, under contemporary conditions. For he still recognized, as he had as a young Progressive, that "We cannot rub out the modern age, we cannot roll back the history that has made us what we are."[19] He was as undaunted in maturity during the frigid years of the Cold War as he had been as a youth in the soft air of peace and strongly believed that "Rational procedure is the ark of the covenant." He could now add, "of the public philosophy."[20]

Lippmann returned, in the *Essays*, to his early appreciation (never renounced) of the importance of Graham Wallas' conception of the Great Society, although in the *Essays* the term took on two added meanings. It still represented, as it had in Lippmann's Progressive work, "a general change in social scale," to use the words of Wallas.[21] This change was brought about by the great expansion of wealth, technological capacity, and hence of population in the societies of Western Europe and North America. Between 1870 and 1914 the world's population had grown by almost the total increase of all the generations between Adam and Newton. While working hours were reduced, the real income per person gainfully employed had risen seventy-five percent or more.[22]

And yet these changes in social magnitude bore destructive as well as constructive potentialities. Now Europe could finance huge armies and could reman and resupply them while fighting continued. High explosives, long-range artillery, armored automotive vehicles, and aircraft, coupled with the urban basis of economy and state, made attacks upon civilian centers far more "logical" militarily than such attacks had been for centuries.[23] The means of growth, both in population and in wealth, was technology, and technology had a demonic side which would bring Graham Wallas' forecast of a thirty years' war to terrifying life.

The second new meaning, or new emphasis, which Lippmann attached to the term "Great Society," involved pluralism. He argued that natural law theorizing in the past had been occasioned by the rise of pluralistic social orders. Such a polycentric society had been created by the conquests of Alexander the Great, who rejected Aristotle's advice that Greeks and barbarians could not live under a common system of law and justice. Instead he sought an empire which embraced Greeks and Persians alike. In "refusing to agree with men who divided mankind into Greeks and barbarians," as one Alexandrian scholar put it, Alexander "declared that it was better to divide men simply into the good and bad."[24] It was also true under the Roman Empire that the cultural diversity of Rome's subject peoples led the Roman lawyers to distinguish between civil law, applicable only to Roman citizens; commercial law enforced in commercial disputes throughout the empire and known as the law of the peoples; and natural law, described by Ernest Barker as "the law imposed on mankind by common human nature, that is, by reason in response to human needs and instincts."[25] The work of the Roman lawyers was reinforced by the teachings of the Stoics and absorbed into the writings of the Church Fathers and canon lawyers. Lippmann draws the inference that these historical experiences demonstrate that the idea of a higher law, or rational order, ". . . is not only an attractive and a sublime conception but that it is a necessary assumption in the government of large and heterogeneous states."[26]

Lippmann was persuaded that there was a "modern revival" of natural law theorizing in the period 1500–1800, induced by the cultural diversity released by the Reformation and Renaissance and by the rise of a system of nation-states whose boundaries did not correspond with the demographic contours of religious faith and cultural ferment. In the nineteenth century, the combined impact of the industrial revolution, the end of slavery, mass enfranchisement, and skepticism served to snuff out a belief in higher law, declared Lippmann. The absolute sovereignty of the secular state (and of electoral majorities within the Liberal democracies) was accepted. In fact, the acceleration of the centrifugal tendencies in nineteenth-century culture actually intensified the need for acknowledgment of shared ethical principles and political procedures grounded in reason. Great Societies—those which are culturally diverse—are those which most strongly require recognition of the public philosophy. Lippmann concluded that the successful Great Society was that of Zeno, the cosmopolis, in which the polity took its laws from the cosmos, the order of nature.[27]

As he had as a young Progressive, the Lippmann of the *Essays* felt that governments could master events. Foresight, plan, and choice could direct the course of history in vitally important ways. The disorder in the Western Liberal societies came not "from the machinations of our enemies and the adversities of the human condition," he argued, but from mistaken choices by leaders and peoples. The Liberal societies had the physical resources to prevail—the question was whether they could analyze their malady in public discussion, and then exert the will to master it.[28]

One of the historical sources of the problem was the long period of social peace during which Liberalism had established itself. It was, said Lippmann, a time of "expansion, development, and liberation." Even in America, where the greatest war took place within the century after Waterloo, emancipation of slaves and accelerated economic growth had been the outcomes, and a half-century of peace (1865–1917) had followed. During this time, Liberals became imbued with the idea that in a free society government should be weak. Their belief was that in the ordinary course of affairs governments need not enter into conflicts of interests and values but could stand above the social contest as morally neutral referees. If the economy continued to expand, everyone could enjoy more of its fruits. The deserving poor could work their way upward and out of poverty, while the deserving rich had their reward. Justice would be a by-product of economic growth, group conflict, and restrained government. Then, added Lippmann, ". . . public good could be thought of as being immanent in the aggregate of private transactions."[29]

The elder Lippmann was convinced, as he had been in his youth, that this "Manchester Liberal" conception of government was mistaken. Governments must be empowered to govern. They must be capable of dealing with the "hard issues" of "war and peace, of security and solvency, of constitutional order and revolution." This requirement meant in turn that governments must be able, particularly over the short run, to enforce unpopular policies—to tax, conscript, command, and prohibit. "If they are to do their duty," he wrote, perhaps unconsciously summoning up the metaphor which Santayana had hurled at him twenty-five years earlier, "they must often swim against the tides of private feeling."[30]

Because of the need for difficult and sometimes unpopular decisions, Lippmann favored now, as he had in 1914, a strong executive. At one level, the institutional meaning of the disorder of the democracies was a devitalization of the executive, which he referred to as "the derangement of powers."[31] The Founding Fathers had seen the risk of vesting too little power in the executive, as over against the people and the representative assembly.[32] In the twentieth century, the problem that was potential in 1787 had become actual. Because of the new importance of public expenditures and the dissolution of the aura of authority which had protected kings in earlier times, representative assemblies had come to be dominant within the government; and public opinion, its spokesmen and manipulators, now exercised a power beyond government.

In one sense, indeed, Lippmann was persuaded that the representative assembly was not part of the government at all. He wrote that "representation must not be confused with governing."[33] The representative is closely bound, and properly so, to his constituents and their interests and to their view of their interests. The executive owes his basic allegiance to the constitution and the laws, to his office, and to his highest understanding of the objective requirements of the public interest. On this view of the matter, "government" is identified with "public administration," the executive branch. The people and the representative assembly form a conjoint popular power; the legislative branch, Lippmann wrote, is an agency "to represent them [the people] to the government"; "the governors themselves" are the Chief Executive and his subordinates.[34] "The executive is the active power in the state [that is, the populace politically organized: not a term identical with "government"], the asking and the proposing power. The representative assembly is the consenting power, the petitioning, the approving and the criticizing, the accepting and the refusing power."[35] Thus while on the one hand Lippmann sees the will of the people as more and more intimately assimilated into the political process, on the other hand he believes the popular will must be checked, informed, and led by the executive. Each power "must be true to its own nature, each limiting and complementing the other. . . . If either absorbs or destroys the functions of the other power, the constitution is deranged."[36]

Lippmann's view of government as administration perhaps derived from his own practical experience, which had been, in Schenectady, Washington, and Versailles, with the executive and not with the legislative branch. Certainly it was a steady refrain in the writings of his Progressive period. But in any event, he vigorously defended the position that this was no more than the traditional Liberal concept of the "consent of the governed." "What then are the true boundaries of the people's power?" he asked: "The answer cannot be simple. But for a rough beginning let us say that the people are able to give and to withhold their consent to being governed. . . . They can elect the government. They can remove it. . . . But they cannot administer the government." Thus wrote Lippmann in 1955, citing Thomas Jefferson as one of his authorities.[37]

Even in arguing for the power of intangible ideas, Lippmann emphasizes in the *Essays,* as he did in his first books, practice and the practical. There is no escaping, he wrote, "the indubitable fact of experience that we are often mistaken, that it makes a difference to have been wrong."[38] Ideas exert a radical power in every person's life because of their power to organize experience, and ultimately the organization of experience results in the formation of character.[39] These are arguments which might mark a Pragmatist, and in fact he does draw heavily and explicitly upon his youthful grounding in the teachings of William James and Charles S. Peirce and others.

For instance, Lippmann, recognizing the diversity within the natural law tradition itself, holds that "none of the main ideas of our civilization has a single meaning," but instead, multiple meanings.[40] As illustration, he used the idea of freedom. The definitions of liberty proposed by Thomas Hobbes, John Locke, and the Baron de Montesquieu, while differing, present "different facets of a complex idea." They supplement, and thereby relativize, one another. Any one definition might be deemed best for a given set of circumstances. Each has its proper use, like garments in a wardrobe.[41] Lippmann draws upon James' words to make the point that in the flux of life, "things are off their balance. Whatever equilibriums our finite experiences attain to are but provisional. . . ." Our ideas are at once packaged past experience and instruments to structure the experiences of the future. As James put it, "the essence of life is its continually changing character . . . [while] our concepts are discontinuous and fixed."[42]

Aristotle was right, Lippmann suggests, when he asserted that the tasks of the theologian and the philosopher are to set forth doctrines, with the difference that theologians do so in mythical form, and philosophers with the use of concepts. This recognition of the need for plural interpretations may be called "the language of accommodation," Lippmann proposes, using the phrase of a Cambridge Neoplatonist. For the "language of accommodation" to be meaningful, however, there must be an ultimate accommodation or agreement upon first principles which are more basic than immediate differences at hand. These must be a shared universe of rational discourse, a public philosophy.[43]

In an attempt to show the practical applicability of the public philosophy—an aim that any Pragmatist would sooner or later insist upon—Lippmann took up the issues of private property and freedom of speech, arguing that the concepts associated with natural law would bring order to conflict on both questions. In dealing with these subjects, he wrote in language which might have been taken directly from his Progressive days.

Of property, he argued that "In the public philosophy an absolute right to property, or to anything else that affects other men, cannot be entertained. To claim it is to be outside the law and the bounds of civility."[44] A rational justification of property would necessarily be one in which the rights of property were relativized by the recognition that private property is a creation of the laws of the state, the recognition that in any sphere of social life the erection of absolute rights for some would mean the invasion of the rights of others, recognition that rights and duties must correspond to one another in a reciprocal fashion if a social order is to approach justice. There are in Western society well-accepted rights to use, enjoy, and dispose of property. But these rights should not be absolutized, or divorced from their duties, or the overarching protection of the legal order. If these rights of property are absolutized, wrote Lippmann, as they were in much nineteenth-century Liberal theory and policy, abuses inevitably follow, as they did in that period:

Absolute owners did grave damage to their neighbors and to their descendants: they ruined the fertility of the land, they exploited destructively the minerals under the surface, they burned and cut forests, they destroyed the wild life, they polluted streams, they cornered supplies and formed monopolies, they held land and resources out of use, they exploited the feeble bargaining power of wage earners.[45]

Because Liberal theorists had abandoned the natural law tradition, they could find no remedy for these ills, Lippmann argued. They no longer could resort to the idea that the sovereign, or the strongest power within the state, is bound by a higher law and that private property is the creation of civil law for social purposes. As a consequence, the exclusion of workers from social benefits proceeded rapidly, and the counterexclusionary force of revolutionary Marxism arose. With no bonds of common interest, tradition, and discourse to bind them to the owners, the workers could indeed believe that they had nothing to lose but their chains, and a world to gain. This was social division of the gravest magnitude, "the ominous phenomenon of the 'two nations,' "[46] which Progressivism had striven to avoid.

When he came to the subject of freedom of speech, Lippmann was equally insistent upon reciprocity of rights and duties, a principle employed to sustain community by maintaining commensurability between contending interests. Freedom of speech has become a protected practice in Western societies, Lippmann asserted, because of the discovery among the Greeks, preserved in the Socratic dialogues, of the value of dialectic as a method of attaining truth, especially moral and political truth. Once again, the conception is one of a partnership of separate or opposed parties, in the interest of the higher common good. The "dispute must not be treated as a trial of strength. . . . In a Socratic dialogue the disputants are arguing co-operatively in order to acquire more wisdom than either of them had when he began."[47]

During the late 1960s, Lippmann refused to attack in print the tactics of antiwar demonstrators or to endorse the argument of President Johnson, the columnist James Reston, and other commentators, that domestic divisions in the United States over the war were giving aid and comfort to the enemy. Demonstrations, draft-card burnings, even disruptions of public addresses, drew no condemnation from Lippmann. Instead, he contended that "free debate" was not possible when the "government turns upon its weakest opponents; it is destroying the process by which a free people ascertain what is true and agree upon what is right."[48] Had Lippmann's critics paid closer attention to the argument of the *Essays*, a decade earlier, they would have spared themselves the need to fault Lippmann as an inconsistent Liberal, or one fearful of facing down a defiant radical minority. In the *Essays*, he had written that the dividing line between liberty and license is to be found where freedom of speech is no longer respected as a means of attaining truth, and becomes instead the cloak for exploiting the unawareness of the people, and manipulating their passions.[49] These were exactly the terms on which the administration of Lyndon Johnson was indicted by its critics. Under conditions of exploitation, Lippmann had written in 1955, freedom becomes the pretext for "a hullabaloo of sophistry, propaganda . . . and salesmanship. . . ."[50] Clearly, in the *Essays*, he was concerned about the advantages of access and credibility which possession of political office confers. "Rarely, and on very few public issues," he wrote, "does the mass audience have the benefit of the process by which truth is sifted from error—the dialectic of debate in which there is immediate challenge, reply, cross-examination, and rebuttal."[51] Yet this was the principle which regulated and justified freedom of speech under natural law. Hence the people and all their spokesmen should remain vigilant, remembering that

. . . the right to freedom of speech is no license to deceive, and willful misrepresentation is a violation of its principles. It is sophistry to pretend that in a free country a man has some sort of inalienable or constitutional right to deceive his fellow men. There is no more right to deceive than there is a right to swindle, to cheat or to pick pockets . . . there can be no immunity for lying in any of its protean forms.[52]

It would be well to remember that the antiwar dissidents had launched their movement with the most scrupulous regard for debate, evidence, and logic, in a series of "teach-ins" staged at colleges and universities across the country. Moreover, during this whole unhappy period there was only one candidate for highest office—the 1968 nominee of the Democratic Party for Vice President, Senator Edmund Muskie—who regularly offered his opponents in the audience access to his microphone, and this practice almost without fail silenced hecklers and halted disruption of his speeches. He was meeting—as high officers in the Johnson Administration had not— Lippmann's test of the duties attaching to freedom of speech. One was candor and truthfulness. The other was that, under the public philosophy, "the right to speak is protected by a willingness to debate."[53] Lippmann the Progressive and Liberal was not a dim shade but alive and well in many of the arguments of the *Essays in the Public Philosophy*.

IV

There are several important respects in which the *Essays* represent a restatement or reworking of Lippmann's theories concerning foreign affairs. In the first place, the prelude to the argument is the proposition that the Western parliamentary democracies are unable to organize and maintain a durable peace. It was their failure at this critical task which drew Lippmann to study afresh the nature of the ideology and institutions of the Liberal countries.

He chose to specify the year 1917 as the watershed which worked the breakdown of the Western constitutional order. The "system of executive responsibility broke down during the war, and from 1917 on the conduct of the war and then the conditions of the armistice and the peace were subjected to the dominating impact of mass opinions."[54] In the year 1917 the American system for dealing with foreign affairs was drawn into a general European war. It was the year which marked the injection of Wilsonian idealism, as well as American military force, into the conflict. And it was the year in which Lippmann lost his Progressive innocence about the unimportance of foreign affairs to the American republic. He makes a satirical commentary on his own earlier text, when he writes caustically of the inflated hopes that accompanied American entry into the war: "This last war would make the world safe for democracy. This crusade would make the whole world a democracy."[55] The parallel is too close, and Lippmann's sensitive memory too strong, for it to be a coincidence that in 1955 he nearly paraphrases his oft-criticized statement in the *New Republic* of April 7, 1917: "It is now as certain as anything human can be that the war which started as a clash of empires in the Balkans will dissolve into democratic revolution the world over."[56]

The choice of the year 1917 also allows Lippmann to reintroduce the idea that the missteps of President Woodrow Wilson had led the nation down the treacherous slope to ultimate disaster. "It was not for want of power but for want of statesmanship that the liberal democracies failed," he wrote.[57] It was not mere chance nor of little moment that Wilsonian ideals accompanied American armies into battle. For what happened at this juncture of the war was that the western Allies found their nations near exhaustion yet their terms for peace beyond reach by negotiation. So the Allied governments turned to the dark arts of propaganda. With the assistance of Wilsonian idealism, the goals of the Allies were absolutized. According to Lippmann, greater sacrifices were obtained "by 'democratizing' the conduct and the aims of the war: by pursuing total victory and by promising total peace."[58] What happened was that the war was raised, in the propaganda of the Allies and the belief of their peoples, into a conflict that might more accurately be called religious than military-diplomatic—the conflict was given a transcendent meaning. The ". . . enemy had to be portrayed as evil incarnate, as absolute and congenital wickedness. The people wanted to

be told that when this particular enemy had been forced to uncondi-
tional surrender, they would re-enter the golden age. This unique
war would end all wars."[59]

Undoubtedly, part of the intensity of Lippmann's feeling on this
point issued from his personal involvement with, and ambivalence
over, America's entry into the war. While he had articulated the
extreme and groundless hope that the war would dissolve into global
democratic revolution, he had also been steadfast in insisting upon
restraint, negotiation, and ultimate reconciliation as the only rational means to wage and end war. He had insisted from 1917 on, as
he did in the *Essays,* that the goal of statecraft in the real world must
be "to wage war for rational ends and to make a peace which would
be observed or could be enforced."[60]

Nationalism he feared and opposed, during the Cold War as during World War I, as a regressive phenomenon, socially and
psychologically. In the 1950s, the added peril was that of totalitarianism atop nationalism. Lippmann argued that the theoretical and ideological root of totalitarianism was Jacobinism, the theory
which had flourished at the radical left of the French Revolution,
and had been inherited and adapted by the Bolsheviks and Fascists
alike. Just as Plato had done, Lippmann drew a parallel between the
good life for the individual—which he equated with the rule of
reason over appetite in the individual's life—and the common good
or public interest of society—which he identified as consisting of the
rule of those who are knowledgeable and informed over those, but
with the consent of those, who are uninformed and who will appeti-
tively choose "the soft side of the equations of reality."[61] In the
parliamentary democracies, responsible officials had been made by
public opinion to resemble "the ministers of an opinionated and
willful despot."[62] The disorder of the democracies was the principle
of their adversaries. Liberalism would founder in discussion and
compromise, the Many should rule through the Vanguard or the
Leader, the Party or the Fuhrer, a grand revolution would establish
a New Order, the thousand-year Third Reich, or the Dictatorship of
the Proletariat. Both totalitarian systems, the Communist on the
Left and the Fascist on the Right, promised that a peaceful and
stable social order, based on bonds deeper than Liberals had ever
foreseen, would issue from a great convulsion of violence.[63]
Lippmann's answer to this challenge is examined more extensively
below, in section VI.

V

One of the thematic arguments of the *Essays*, for which Lippmann was roundly criticized, was that "Mass opinion has acquired mounting power in this century. It has shown itself to be a dangerous master of decisions when the stakes are life and death."[64] He was seeking to exclude public opinion from playing a role in the vital decisions of state, his critics charged. Once again they found him inconsistent. Once again they appealed from the new reactionary Lippmann to the old Progressive Lippmann. He was now working in the clumsy apparatus of the "new conservatism" of the 1950s, they charged, revealing his disdain for the people, for democratically accountable government, for the ability of the common man to make meaningful and effective political decisions. There was much in the *Essays* to lend substance to these criticisms. Lippmann declared flatly that

Strategic and diplomatic decisions call for a kind of knowledge—not to speak of an experience and a seasoned judgment—which cannot be had by glancing at newspapers, listening to snatches of radio comment, watching politicians perform on television, hearing occasional lectures, and reading a few books. It would not make a man competent to decide whether to amputate a leg, and it is not enough to qualify him to choose war or peace, to arm or not to arm, to intervene or to withdraw, to fight on or to negotiate.[65]

Public opinion imposes a "compulsion to make mistakes," particularly in foreign affairs, because the movement of opinion is much slower than the pace of events. "It takes much longer to change many minds than to change a few," he argued. "It takes time to inform and to persuade and to arouse large scattered varied multitudes of persons."[66] As a result, public opinion has at critical junctures been out of phase with the development of events, and public opinion has set the boundaries of the possible for public policy in the parliamentary democracies. The operation of public opinion has been discontinuous; and because of its inertia, it has served to block policy changes at critical points when war might have been averted by preparedness, or shortened by negotiation. Public opinion has interjected into the decision-making process a massive veto which has disabled the statesman of the parliamentary democracies.[67] The intervention of public opinion could be conceived of as a series of simple, inconsistent negatives to vital questions:

Prepare for war in time of peace? No. It is bad to raise taxes, to unbalance the budget, to take men away from their schools or their jobs, to provoke the enemy. Intervene in a developing conflict? No. Avoid the risk of war. Withdraw from the area of conflict? No. The adversary must not be appeased. Reduce your claims on the area? No. Righteousness cannot be compromised. Negotiate a compromise peace as soon as the opportunity presents itself? No. The aggressor must be punished. Remain armed to enforce the dictated settlement? No. The war is over.[68]

Lippmann further angered his Liberal critics by insisting that a distinction must be drawn between the voters and the people, "as a community of the entire living population, with their predecessors and successors"—an inclusive community over time as well as space, embracing prior generations and generations unborn as well as the living. We must adopt the habit of thinking plainly about the sovereign people, Lippmann argued, and with this his Liberal critics could agree.[69] "No more than the kings before them should the people be hedged with divinity," Lippmann wrote. "Like all princes and rulers, like all sovereigns, they are ill-served by flattery and . . . they are betrayed by the servile hypocrisy which tells them that what is true and what is false, what is right and what is wrong, can be determined by their votes."[70]

With the argument developed in this fashion, the Liberal becomes uncomfortable. Of course it is true that a majority vote cannot determine an issue of a factual nature, in the sense that it cannot generate or negate facts. An election, many would agree, cannot change the intrinsic nature of an action from bad to good or good to bad, but who, or what agency, is to determine the intrinsic goodness or badness of an action? If elections cannot in an ultimate sense "legislate morality," they can assuredly determine the limits of the publicly permissible on morally arguable issues. Shall the state impose capital punishment? Shall public monies be expended for a war? For making available abortions at the individual's discretion? This kind of question has been settled historically if not directly out of election returns, at least indirectly by the working of public mores in conjunction with the judgment of elected officials, or magistrates appointed by elected officials. Lippmann, his critics pointed out, did not descend to making distinctions of this sort in the *Essays*.

Moreover, the critics urged, if it was plain thinking about the people that Lippmann wanted, why did he resort to a flight into the mysticism of Edmund Burke's conception of the people as a corporate entity? How, apart from an autocrat's seance, are we supposed to consult the interests of those dead and those as yet unborn? Lippmann might have answered that it is possible to consult both those deceased and those unborn through conceiving of ourselves in any single generation as trustees, as men and women who are heirs to the achievements and resources of a tradition in which our ancestors participated, and men and women who shall prove themselves to be benefactors or malefactors to those who are to follow us. Certainly he believed that we often behave in this fashion, even if we are unaware of any conception of trusteeship. There are many situations in which we acknowledge by our behavior some more extensive understanding of community, and of the public interest, than the immediate advantage of those living. "That is why young men die in battle for their country's sake and why old men plant trees they will never sit under," Lippmann argued.[71] It is this more extended, largely invisible, community which "gives rational meaning to the necessary objectives of government."[72]

Liberals have traditionally distrusted this sort of organic language about community because it seems to lend strength and credence to the claims of institutions over against the claims of individuals. Conceiving the state as an organism seems to subordinate the aims and purposes of individual persons to those of the society or state, and moreover to political purposes which are not clearly experienced or understood by the individual. So to diminish the claims or rights of the individual upon the institutions within which he lives is to demean the dignity of the person, Liberals believe. It serves to weaken the restraints of popular will upon the powerful, and to permit a conservative authoritarianism wherein the favored few will divine and announce the public interest, or ideological mass movements which give the individual a sense of participation and meaning at the cost of surrendering his liberties and ultimately his identity. Following this line of criticism, Liberal critics could plausibly see Lippmann's position as self-contradictory, as an appeal for the kind of individual submission and discipline which could bring about the very kind of illiberal counterrevolution which he opposed.

Lippmann himself did not see the historical situation or his analysis in this light, of course. He insisted that he was giving full recognition to the Liberal principle of the consent of the governed.[73] He did not wish to exclude the people from the policy process but rather to argue that "the statistical sum of their opinions is not the final verdict on an issue. It is, rather, the beginning of the argument"; "In that argument their opinions need to be confronted by the views of the executive, defending and promoting the public interest. In the accommodation reached between the two views lies practical public policy."[74]

However unsure or unsatisfying Lippmann's thought on these questions may be, he was not seeking an elitist transfer of authority to some controlling minority, nor was he ascribing all responsibility for error to public opinion. Because so many of his critics have read him in this simplistic fashion, it is necessary to examine the evidence to the contrary.

What he understood to be taking place in present-day parliamentary politics was a process of mutual manipulation in which candid public debate and understanding of the issues was made difficult. On the one hand, democratic politicians sought to manipulate, to wheedle and cajole, public opinion for their own purposes, which might or might not include some higher conception of the public good. On the other hand, democratic officeholders often found themselves caught in a vise between the demands of public opinion and the pressure of events. Consequently, public officials sensed that they were unable to lead, unable to initiate policy, but consigned to the role of attempting to harmonize social reality with public opinion. Most winning democratic politicians, Lippmann contended, were intimidated men: "They advance politically only as they placate, appease, bribe, seduce, bamboozle, or otherwise manage to manipulate the demanding and threatening elements in their constituencies."[75] In such an insecure environment, truth is the first casualty. A degree of self-deception becomes the price of self-respect. Since not telling the truth, "though prudent, is uncomfortable, they [the leaders] find it easier if they themselves do not have to hear too often too much of the sour truth. The men under them who report and collect the news come to realize in their turn that it is safer to be wrong before it has become fashionable to be right."[76] What we now know of official self-deception—as evidenced by the wishes of superiors being reflected back to them in the reports of their junior officers during the American combat involvement in Indo-China—lends support to Lippmann's analysis.

An important factor in magnifying and distorting the proper role of public opinion in the political process, Lippmann was convinced, was the rise of the mass media. The mass media had made possible the swift and simultaneous communication of events to all parts of a highly diversified society. Experience had demonstrated that "public opinion becomes less realistic as the mass to whom information must be conveyed, and argument must be addressed, grows larger and more heterogeneous."[77] In the press, radio, and television, the bulletin supersedes the older report, the headline overshadows the story, the sensational displaces the complex, the fleeting image comes to stand for the invisible reality.

It was also true, he believed, that there was an interplay between the rise of the mass media, the rise of the dominance of public opinion, and the rise of moralism in public policy. The media, like the moralist, tend to turn "the hypothetical into the dogmatic, and the relative into the absolute."[78] This was an added sense in which the manipulation of leaders and led was a mutual one, asserted Lippmann: both leaders and led were apt to be ensnared in the web of ideology which the leaders—such as Woodrow Wilson—had woven out of popular ideals, hopes, and fears.[79]

Most of the critics of the *Essays* left the book with the impression that it was an antidemocratic tract, a polemic against popular rule. Lippmann was arguing that the increased role of public opinion in the political process must be resisted by officeholders, and that mass opinion bore sole responsibility for the "disorder of the democracies," many critics held. The fact that these critics failed to see that his analysis was more complex and subtle was probably due to the unclarity and uncertainty of Lippmann's argument on the matter, central though it was to his entire thesis. The source of our difficulties, he suggested, was a "devitalization of the executive." This in turn could be traced to the dominance of government by public opinion and to the dominance within the government of the elected legislature. But, he urged, power could not be effectively wielded by the people. If this were true, more specific agencies must be at fault; but what were they? More than once in the *Essays* Lippmann takes up the question, only to discard it. He offers suggestions but not analysis, on this point, and hence the suggestions were overlooked. Some of them are to be found in the following passages:

In substance they [the parliamentary governments of the Allies in World War I] ceded the executive power of decision over the strategical and the political conditions for ending the war. . . . This revolution appeared to be a cession of power to the representative assemblies. . . . In fact, the powers which were ceded by the executive passed through the assemblies, which could not exercise them, to the mass of voters who, though unable also to exercise them, passed them on to the party bosses, the agents of pressure groups, and the magnates of the new media of mass communications.[80]

. . . the executives become highly susceptible to encroachment and usurpation by elected assemblies; they are pressed and harassed by the higgling of parties, by the agents of organized interests, and by the spokesmen of sectarians and ideologues.[81]

. . . [the executives] are . . . swollen rather than strong, being too weak to resist the pressure of special interests and of departmental bureaucracies.[82]

This derangement of the governing power . . . has also transformed the assemblies in most, perhaps not in all, democratic states from the defenders of local and personal rights into boss-ridden oligarchies.[83]

Thus the recovery of leadership, so far as Lippmann was concerned, would require much more than (perhaps even something quite different from) a transfer "up" of responsibility and authority from the people to their political officers. More democracy within political parties and within elected legislatures would be necessary. Somehow the interchange of information and inducements between private institutions and elected officials would need to be made more open, more subject to public scrutiny and to legal regulation. Concentrated private control of the mass media was highly undesirable and should presumably be checked by governmental regulation.

Had Lippmann made these proposals affirmatively, rather than stating the negative conditions which made them necessary, his *Essays* might have received a much different reading from the left-Liberal critics. That he failed to do so was not a sign that he was illiberal, elitist, or reactionary, but rather a symptom of his peculiar disinterest in the functioning and reform of institutions, and of his conviction that in the final analysis politics is a moral drama, to be understood as part of intellectual history, with the assistance of modern psychology.

VI

When Lippmann took up the conception of the Great Society from Graham Wallas forty years earlier, he had been immediately struck by the importance of how knowledge is gathered, ordered, and communicated in large-scale industrial society. His systematic treatment in *Public Opinion* dealt with how the invisible realities of remote events were censored and distorted, unknowingly by individuals and deliberately by governments intent on promoting their own policies. The filter of selectively received and stored experience constitutes a set of "pictures in our heads," he had concluded, a "pseudoenvironment" to which our behavior responds. Now in the *Essays* he proceeded to enlarge the conception of the pseudoenvironment, equating it with the individual's "cultural environment," the mentally transmitted world of shared experience and values which is interposed between the individual as a biological organism and empirical reality.[84]

This thinking moved Lippmann further toward Platonism, since he was asserting that ideas are supremely important, the substratum of culture. His concern with the invisible world beyond the horizons of the senses had expanded beyond the spatial and geographic dimensions which absorbed him in *Public Opinion*, to the temporal dimensions of social and personal development. "Because ideas have the power to organize human behavior, their efficacy can be radical," he wrote. "They are indeed radical when, as the image of what a man should be, they govern the formation of his character and so imprint a lasting organization on his behavior."[85]

Accepting a dualism similar to Plato's, and using concepts similar to those of his teacher Santayana, Lippmann laid it down that there are two "realms of being":

As a man awakens from his primordial condition where, as Bacon said, custom is the principal magistrate of his life, he finds himself living in two worlds and subject to two allegiances. There is the familiar world which he knows through his senses and there is a world of which he has only intimations and knows only through the eyes of his mind. He is drawn between the two disparate realms of being, and the tension within [that is, between] them is the inexhaustible theme of human discourse. To neither can he give his whole allegiance. Their prevailing contrasts are his wretchedness. Their occasional harmonies in the lives of saints and the deeds of heroes and the excellence of genius are his glory. In the traditions of civility, the prevailing view has been that the two realms are inseparable but disparate, and that man must work out his destiny in the balance, which is never fixed finally between the two.[87]

The awakening described is platonic. It is a turning inward of the self through discipline of the senses and development of the individual's capacity to grasp the moral and intellectual meaning of ideas by engaging in philosophic reasoning. Lippmann might better be described as holding a Socratic position or that of the young Plato. In his mature writings Plato ascribed final reality to the realm of forms or ideas. Human happiness, he correspondingly held, lies in attaining contemplative access to the ideal realm: the goal was a form of beatific vision of the unity of being and goodness. By contrast, Lippmann finds that human destiny is achieved not by departing from one realm to the other but by balancing the two. He leaves the clear impression that there is no single method for reaching this balance but rather a variety of culturally relative possibilities, in the lives of men of sanctity, courage, and genius. Hence, while critics of Plato have accused him of favoring an ascetic regimen which would stifle individuality—and he does seem to seek a happiness in which the self is surpassed and forgotten in a mystical communion with the invisible realm of being itself—Lippmann's aim would foster a heightened sense of selfhood. The individual experiences the exhilaration of being freed from bondage to merely customary, conventional knowing and doing, and experiences an obligation and a fulfillment in maintaining a tension between the actual and ideal realms in his own life. Like Socrates, Lippmann has no final substantive truth (no Form of the Good, no God) to reveal, no single path to the truth, and no final deliverance to promise. Lippmann confirms this view of his intentions by declaring that Socrates is the classic example of the civilized man. His image, in the writings of Plato,

. . . is the image of a man who has become fit to rule. He is ruled within by his second and civilized nature. For it is the true person who has qualified as proprietor of the laws and institutions of Athens and of the ideal of life which they serve. The necessities and the purposes of Athenian life are not something outside of Socrates, something alien, extraneous, imposed and only reluctantly conformed with. They are the ends of his own true character, established in that part of his being which he calls himself.[87]

This view of Socrates, as one who has disclosed "the inwardness of
the ruling man," is not, Lippmann observes, a counsel of servility or
conformism.[88] On the contrary, what he endorses in Socrates as a
moral model is his freedom from unreflective acquiescence, his
inner deliberation and conferring of consent. Socrates has grasped
and inwardly consented to the moral purpose of the laws of Athens.
Hence he will not flee an unjust penalty of death even though the
opportunity is presented to him. Individuality, consent—these are
Liberal concerns.

Lippmann uses the ideal of Socrates to advance the notion that
there is an objective moral order, while at the same time implicitly
disavowing any assumption that there is a single guaranteed route to
that order through creed or institution. Indeed, each of these reciprocal propositions requires examination: There is an objective moral
order. The moral order cannot be completely realized, by an individual, institution, or society.

There is an objective moral order. No other proposition advanced
in the *Essays* drew so much consternation and opposition from the
book's reviewers as this one, and we shall turn to the critics' arguments below. First let us consider the position which Lippmann
developed.

The "objectivity" of the moral order is the critical question for
modern society, he maintained. The issue is whether men recognize
that in moral affairs "beyond our private worlds there is a public
world to which we belong."[89] The reality of the moral order—
beyond human wishes—is the truth which must be accepted if a
politics of representation and deliberation is to succeed. Exactly
how the moral order is conceived is a secondary question. There is a
variety of images of God, for example, but this is understandable; it
is the correlate of the truth that "there can be no image [of God or of
the moral order] which has concreteness to our sense perceptions."[90] It is not critical to determine whether the moral order is
given by God or is inherent in the constitution of nature, with no
God necessary. The natural law tradition has included both orthodox religious thinkers and nondeistic naturalists. Of overriding
importance has been their agreement that the moral order does not
issue from human invention. As Lippmann states, "It was not someone's fancy, someone's prejudice, someone's wish or rationalization,
a psychological experience and no more."[91] Lippmann remained

convinced that human subjectivity was not an arbitrary accident of nature, with no necessary connection with outer reality, but the key to the comprehension of the human situation, capable of disclosing its objective constitution.

In practical terms, the discovery of natural law depended upon prudence, detachment, and reflection. It required of the individual that he raise his line of vision beyond his own immediate desires and interests. In this sense, natural law could be understood as synonymous with the public interest. The public interest could be "presumed to be what men would choose if they saw clearly, thought rationally, acted disinterestedly and benevolently."[92]

This is an ideal, to be sure, but it has been one of the recurrent ideals of Western culture. An ideal of such magnitude and duration inevitably has arisen in a variety of historical situations and therefore has taken on a variety of emphases and meanings.[93] The conception was anticipated in the practice of Alexander the Great, formulated by the Stoics, taken over by the Roman jurists, adopted by the Church fathers, recaptured with force and clarity in the work of the Scholastic theologians, and revived in modern form in the period 1500–1800. In all of these situations, the core meaning of the concept was the same: there is, beyond positive or man-made customs or enactments, a moral constitution to human life and affairs which is constant beneath the accidents of time and place—this standard, recurrently plumbed in the depths of social experience, has usually been identified by the term natural law.[94]

VII

The criticisms which were made of Lippmann's renewed use of natural law theory help illuminate the boundaries and the resources of that school of thought and of Lippmann's argument in the *Essays*. Two principal lines of disagreement were developed by the critics. The first was that natural law depends upon an elitist epistemology. Most persons have never experienced or encountered natural law. How then are its contents and directives to be discovered? Evidently by some elite of seers. But who shall oversee the seers? Surely not the sightless majority. Therefore natural law is a pretext for illiberal and reactionary practices, since it does not permit, much less require, democratic accountability for those who exercise authority. This is the line of reasoning developed by Morton White, who contended that the concept of "self-evident truth" is the crux of natural law theory, and that when examined, it is an empty category of an invalid deductive rationalism.

. . . Lippmann and his cohorts must show that a belief in self-evident principles of natural law is *necessary*. . . . Does Lippmann suppose that he is likely to persuade . . . a doubtful man that there are essences or notions which, if properly unpacked, make the truth of moral principles evident? I submit that . . . even if the public should be persuaded of the existence of Lippmann's essences—he will fail to show them, really, that the principles of political morality are either self-evident statements about men in which, as Aquinas says, "the predicate is contained in the notion of the subject," or [is] logically deducible therefrom.[95]

White argued that Lippmann deserves to be dismissed summarily because the logical defects of the natural law argument can be traced to a psychological deficiency: "Lippmann and his cohorts lack courage . . . all of this philosophical machinery is not so much an effective instrument of rational persuasion as [it is] a kind of self-encouragement, useful for philosophical whistling in the dark . . . the weak man needs support."[96] White's position implies that natural law contains a double fault: it represents an imposition of personal preferences upon others, and a surrender to the fantasy that no imposition has taken place, that the others already subscribed to this position (or were morally refractory for not having done so). And this is not mere idle fantasizing; it contains a hidden antidemocratic agenda, according to White:[97]

Lippmann speaks of the principles of natural law as those which all men, "when they are sincerely and lucidly rational," will regard as self-evident. But who are the wise and the sincerely and lucidly rational? In practice the devotees of natural law identify them by their willingness to say that certain specific moral principles are self-evident. It is not as though partisans of natural law identify wise or rational men on the basis of a clear criterion which is independent of the specific principles that are said to be self-evident.[98]

Natural law theory is unable to convert skeptics, and Lippmann and his cohorts are correspondingly ready to resort to antidemocratic arguments and methods. This morally tainted motivation is so intrinsic to the advocacy of natural law that White seems uncertain whether it is cause or effect: the important point is that the two are certainly found together in the thought of Lippmann. The *Essays* stress "human deficiency, selfishness, and ineptitude," White says, and are "eager to revive this notion [of natural law] and to put it in the hands of wise statesmen who will not be so tied to the demands of the people."[99] In terms of institutional practice, this is the ultimate import of Lippmann's entire argument for the public philosophy.

A second line of criticism of the *Essays* was that natural law philosophy encourages a rejection of the achievements and benefits of the contemporary Liberal social order in favor of some previous cultural epoch in which natural law was a guiding force in social theory. According to this analysis, proponents of natural law are susceptible to a sort of epistemological nostalgia, a yearning for some bygone society in which the validity of the law of nature was recognized, at least by an influential intellectual minority.

Benjamin F. Wright developed this critique of the *Essays* in his 1973 study entitled *Five Public Philosophies of Walter Lippmann.*[100] Wright has a scholarly interest in the natural law tradition, and his remarks are more tempered than those of White sixteen years earlier. But Wright's criticisms are no less severe in intention and in fact bear one striking resemblance to White's indictment. Both men insist that Lippmann has evidently experienced what Gilbert Murray called a "failure of nerve." Wright's final judgment upon Lippmann is that he lacked the courage and intellectual stamina "to face the very real difficulties of his own stage in history and attempt to propose a philosophy of politics that might aid in bringing about a method or principle for dealing with them."[101] Lippmann blinded himself to the achievements of Liberal society and entered a "romantic" plea for a renaissance of only the golden features of an age that was past.[102]

Lippmann could arrive at this position then, only by a strained misreading of history, which ignored the accomplishments of the contemporary Liberal democracies over both their present adversaries and their own earlier internal injustices. The Western democracies had made

. . . grave and costly errors, but compared with the suicidal mistakes of the old regimes in Russia and China or the weakness and instability of democracies in Italy and Spain, their record is one of remarkable consistency, though it doubtless lacks much of the wisdom of the kind yearned for by perfectionists, particularly by those having the advantage of 20–20 hindsight.[103]

Conversely, Lippmann surveys the historical development "of the doctrine of a natural law that provided a standard by which the actions and legislation of men could be judged." He omits reference to the hideous injustices of slavery, peonage, serfdom, and religious persecution and warfare.[104] It is true that Lippmann never specified a preference for any given prior age or nation, but the general atavistic thrust of his thought is clear. In substance, he was not extending but retracting faith in reason. The rationality he prescribed was circumscribed by nonrational religious faith and political fealty. Wright concluded: ". . . I think he discarded both science and the democratic society, as he now saw it, as instruments. It is almost a call for a retreat to the cloisters, to the life of contemplation and faith. . . . Despair had succeeded hope."[105]

In the final analysis, then, said Wright, Lippmann lacked the earthly confidence which had characterized Liberal political theory —indeed, the theory of the same early modern constitutionalists for whom he expressed admiration:

Madison and his fellows of the first great age of constitution-making were building for the future, employing all the learning and experience they had, not longing for the past. Lippmann, in a less troubled age (for the West was certainly stronger and even less divided than were the colonies and states in 1776–1788), despairs of the time of his maturity. . . .[106]

Other scholars have analyzed and criticized Lippmann's work in impressive fashion, most notably David Spitz and Heinz Eulau.[107] But I believe the criticisms of White and Wright have been the most penetrating, and it is not incidental to the incisiveness of their studies that they joined issue with Lippmann on the question of natural law. It would be appropriate to observe, before I attempt to construct a rejoinder from the *Essays*, that Lippmann's argument does provide grounds for serious misgivings by Liberal critics. The book seems to invite, or even guarantee, objections of the kind considered above. Even Lippmann's choice of words evokes resistance, Wright protests:

It is interesting to speculate on the reason why Lippmann chose the word *civility* instead of such possibilities as *humanity*, *dignity*, even *liberty*, or such traditional phrases as *equal justice under law*. . . . Is it incorrect or unfair to him to say that in making this choice of words he was expressing a long-standing, though not always expressed, longing for aristocracy?[108]

Lippmann does give expression to his admiration for aristocracy and tradition. He points out that the civil liberties of the people were not enacted by popular vote, that in fact civil liberties were instituted before general enfranchisement, making no mention of the social struggles which accompanied the rise of universal suffrage.[109] Instead, he emphasizes the distinction between the British and the French aristocracies as being of controlling importance. In England, there was a gradual process of "enfranchisement by assimilation" into the governing class; in France, the impermeability of class boundaries led to enfranchisement through violent revolution.[110]

A yearning for an aristocratic past might also be inferred from his almost plaintive question, "Could modern men again make vital contact with the traditions of civility?"[111] Clearly, something had been lost in Liberal civic culture, in Lippmann's judgment, and the loss, which he called "the rupture [of the natural law tradition] in modern times," derived from a break in the continuity of generations. The art of ". . . governing well has to be learned," he wrote. "If it is to be learned, it has to be transmitted from the old to the young, and the habits and the ideas must be maintained as a seamless web of memory among the bearers of the tradition, generation after generation."[112] It is in "the mirror of history" that a person sees the image of his "second nature," what he is living for and should become—the image of his inner potentialities as a creature of civility. "This second nature, which rules over the natural man, is at home in the good society," Lippmann wrote. "This second nature is no proletarian but feels itself to be a rightful proprietor and ruler of the community."[113]

Left-of-center readers of the *Essays* are likely to be even more disturbed by the way in which the argument of the *Essays* shuttles back and forth between "aristocracy" as a social class and the political institution of the "executive," as though they were somehow equivalent. Lippmann quotes with approval Henry Maine's statement that there is no essential difference between monarchy and democracy since, in Maine's words, "the tests of success in the performance of the necessary and natural duties of a government are precisely the same in both cases." These duties for Lippmann concern ". . . the defense and advancement abroad of the vital interests of the state and . . . its order, security, and solvency at home."[114] Liberties and representation are not mentioned at this point as duties or tests of government. As we have seen earlier, Lippmann speaks of "the governing or executive power" as contradistinguished from "the elected assembly and the voters." Governing and government are closely identified with the executive, whose primary allegiance should be to his office, the laws, the criteria of truth and professional conduct, and, through conscience, the natural law. The primary responsibility of the assembly (Lippmann avoids—because the implications of the word might contradict his argument?—the word "legislature") is to represent faithfully the opinions and interests of the people.[115]

The substance of Lippmann's linkage of executive and aristocracy is to be found in three propositions. The first is that due to Liberal attachment to the legislative function, the executive function has been constricted and crippled in Liberal states in the past century (1850–1950).[116] The second is that "in the white light of the enlightenment and the secularization of men's minds," the republican executive has lost the prestige and hence some of the authority which monarchs commanded as executives.[117] This loss of psychological responsiveness to political authority, then, is closely related to the wider loss of faith which has characterized modern Western culture, to the fact that "Modern men . . . have a low capacity to believe in the invisible, the intangible, and the imponderable."[118] The third proposition is that the preponderance of society at all times has required a vulgarized, mythologized, materialized version of intangible moral truth. "The multitudes of men everywhere and always have demanded detailed codes of conduct. They are necessary to their comfort, their convenience and their peace of mind . . . ," Lippmann writes:

Without the casuists, who legislate the specific rules, translating and transmitting the inspired words into an intelligible system of ceremonial and legal precepts, the vision of the seer could not make much contact with the existential world.[119]

If there is strong evidence of an irreducible aristocratic bias in the *Essays*, however, it is also true that the nature of that aristocracy is not fully recognized by the critics. Lippmann does hold that the public philosophy can never be popular, because it is ". . . addressed to the government of our appetites and passions by the reasons of a second, civilized, and . . . acquired nature."[120] Thus the public philosophy is aristocratic in the sense that it will presumably never be wholly understood and adopted by a majority. But he is speaking of what Calvin called the "invisible church," what Jefferson termed the "aristocracy of talent and virtue." It has no necessary or assured socioeconomic base, or institutional home, except that it is positively correlated with education. It is an aristocracy of character. The aristocratic code ". . . is not inherent in prerogative and birth":

It is functional to the capacity to rule. It is because aristocrats have been rulers, and not because they were born into the aristocracy, that they have held themselves to the aristocratic virtues. When, like the French nobles on the eve of the Revolution, they have lost the self-mastery which is the principle of the ruling man, they are unable to rule.[121]

This line of reasoning impels Lippmann to say that ". . . the public philosophy of a free society cannot be restored by fiat and by force."[122] It is not the outer compulsion of law but the inner imperatives of conviction and conscience, anchored in character, which enforce and implement the public philosophy.

Lippmann's departure from received Liberalism here is in the sphere of psychology. He breaks with Liberals in denying, as Plato had denied, the possibility of an alliance between appetite and reason. The philosophical psychology of the modern middle classes, whether addressed to politics, economics, or social behavior generally, had held that an alliance of reason and appetite was not only possible but normal. This was the view of John Locke, of Adam Smith, of Jeremy Bentham. Lippmann held that one or the other must rule: "When reason no longer represents society within the human psyche, then it becomes the instrument of appetite, desire, and passion."[123]

The same emphasis upon interiority suffuses Lippmann's understanding of natural law: "The first principle of a civilized state is that power is legitimate only when it is under contract."[124] In other words, inner consent, express or implied, is the cornerstone of constitutionalism and the law-state. It is perhaps unfortunate that Lippmann did not state in more detail his conception of natural law. Quite possibly he refrained from doing so because he wished in a slender volume of one hundred and twenty-eight pages to reach as wide an audience, and foreclose as few questions, as possible. He was familiar with the large scholarly literature on the subject and was not seeking entry to it. But it is wrongheaded and unfair to describe Lippmann as either a reactionary or an arid deductive rationalist, as Morton White has done.

There is nothing inherent in natural law philosophy which renders it politically conservative. Lippmann deplores the fact that in the nineteenth century Liberal reformers "abandoned to the reactionaries" the natural law tradition.[125] And he definitely asserts that this abandonment was not a necessary course of action. Lippmann believed that natural law had played a significant role of theoretical guidance in the English and American Revolutions, in the founding and development of modern constitutional republicanism and its dedication to civil liberties. Historically, it had been conditions of diversity and pluralism which elicited affirmation of a universal rational order. He found no contradiction—but instead numerous reinforcing connections of circumstance and logic—between liberty and natural law.[126]

If ratification is asked for Lippmann's understanding that natural law is not inherently conservative, it can be found in the work of Herbert Marcuse, a political philosopher of impeccably radical credentials. Acknowledging that the term "natural law" is no longer in general use (a fact to which Lippmann responded by coining the term, "the public philosophy"), Marcuse finds the theory valid and necessary for proponents of radical social change:

> The doctrine of the right of resistance has always asserted that appealing to the right of resistance is an appeal to a higher law, which has universal validity, that is, which goes beyond the self-defined right and privilege of a particular group. And there really is a close connection between the right of resistance and natural law. Now you will say that such a universal higher law simply does not exist. I believe that it does exist. . . .[127]

The rationality which Lippmann identifies with natural law is not a series of logical exercises undertaken *a priori*, apart from experience. "Rational *procedure* is the ark of the covenant of the public philosophy," he wrote.[128] It is a faith in the efficacy of practical reason, applied to circumstances through self-conscious detachment and dialogue, which he offers. He states: "To expect to be given—to expect not to have to judge and find—the fixed points which are the

mean in each particular case is, says Aristotle, to ask for more preci-
sion than can be given to this subject."[129] To determine the requirements of justice in a given situation it is necessary that the men
concerned reach for the meaning of a universal rational ideal; they
must also understand it and apply it within the limits of a given set of
historical circumstances. Implementing natural law is a proceeding
in which an ideal and a situation must be fitted to one another. The
"fit" is usually imperfect, and always temporary.[130] Surely, this is
not the approach of a doctrinaire rationalist.

It is difficult to understand how critics such as White could have
been unaware of the complexity of Lippmann's understanding of
natural law, especially since the *Essays* appeared at a time when this
very complexity of natural law was being asserted by its foremost
contemporary proponents, such as the political philosopher Jacques
Maritain.[131] Paul Ramsey, reviewing the work of Maritain and of
Edmond Cahn, concludes that the view of natural law as something
deduced logically from prior abstract principles must be rejected as
a stereotype. Maritain had thoroughly argued that knowledge of
natural justice is gained gradually, through natural inclination, and
in the form of judgments ". . . rendered in the context of particular
cases or in the midst of concrete affairs."[132] Ramsey further con-
tends that Edmond Cahn, in his 1949 essay, *The Sense of Injustice*,[133]
and in his 1955 book, *The Moral Decision: Right and Wrong in
the Light of American Law*,[134] had emphasized that determining
what natural justice requires is a process in which personal responsibility must be accepted. A "free verdict" could be reached only
"through unlimited discussion with decision-makers of the past and
present who have been confronted by similar or related cases."[135]
Lippmann wrote of the public philosophy:

These issues arise concretely in the fixing of public policy. . . . There is in
truth no final word. Instead there are the provisional points of equilibrium
of an unending tension among variable elements. Where exactly the point
of equilibrium will be in a particular place and at a particular time cannot be
defined *a priori*. It must be judged empirically within the postulates of the
public philosophy.[136]

The question of Lippmann's attachment to executive authority
troubled many readers of the *Essays*. No simple explanation of his
views suggests itself, but two points may be used to keep the question in perspective. The first is that Lippmann may have not in-

tended to speak as one-sidedly on behalf of executive power as he in fact appeared to do. In his discussion of constitutional law, as already noted, he emphasizes the significance of consent being given; and it is true that the natural law must be inwardly received also. The sophisticated will understand, he hints, that the authority of natural justice does not emanate from a law-giver: "There were some who could not conceive of binding laws which had to be obeyed unless there was a lawgiver made in the image of the human lawgivers. . . . There were others to whose capacity it was not necessary to condescend with quite that much materialization."[137]

The second point has to do with the historical situation in which the *Essays* were published. Lippmann had been discouraged, as other Liberals had been, by the congressional confinement and defiance of the Presidency in domestic affairs in the years following the death of Franklin Roosevelt. And he was dismayed by the diminished Presidency of Dwight Eisenhower, who turned away from moral leadership on the issue of racial desegration and failed to use the resource of his popularity in any sustained fashion to help the Republican Party reconstruct itself as a competitive electoral alternative to the Democratic Party. Five years after the *Essays*, Richard Neustadt's book, *Presidential Power: The Politics of Leadership*,[138] appeared. It was a scathing critique of the acquiescent style of leadership pursued by President Eisenhower, and an emphatic call for a more vigorous executive, and was only the best known of several works making a similar appeal.

It is surely ironic that if Lippmann had hailed the chief executive as the advocate of the interests of the disadvantaged and condemned Congress and the state legislatures as preserves of special privilege, his work would have been received as congenial and timely by Liberals. This was not the central thrust of the *Essays*, however. He had fought those good fights repeatedly in the press, from his youth onward. His goal now was more ambitious: to offer an analysis of the vitality and future of Western parliamentary institutions. To do this, he needed to examine the conceptual and psychological bases of political authority in the Liberal democracies, and he found that those bases had been badly eroded. Lippmann remained a Liberal: elections and rational procedure were the basis for morally legitimate and empirically effective political authority. He did not subscribe either to the elitist justification of authority implicit in the twentieth-century work of Gaetano Mosca and Robert Michels, or to the rationale for revolutionary authority laid down by Marxism-Leninism. He favored a strong executive, but within the bounds of natural law and constitutionalism, reason and consent.

CHAPTER 6

Conclusion

W ALTER Lippmann's writings do not constitute a comprehensive system of thought, but part of the pleasure of reading any political theorist is gained from accepting the author's tacit invitation to engage in a dialogue. Extending, testing, and amending a theorist's work is a task open to any serious reader. This book has taken one approach to rounding out Lippmann's thought, by understanding him to be a sympathetic revisionist working within the tradition of modern Liberalism. In conclusion, we shall inquire into Lippmann's place in American intellectual history. What influences helped shape his theory? How does he contribute to the discourse on society and politics in the twentieth century?

I

The Liberal tradition is a house of many mansions, and it sometimes seemed Lippmann was bent on dwelling in all of them—as socialist, Progressive, diplomatist, skeptic, moralist, advocate of *Realpolitik,* natural lawyer. Lippmann's ultimate beliefs were partially concealed by this succession of analytic postures. But none of his stances is inconsistent with his commitment to Liberalism as a political method—a system of limited government and individual liberties, of elections and representation, persuasion and compromise.

There are elements in Lippmann's life which go far toward explaining his studied aversion from openly stating his basic beliefs. For one thing, he lacked the support of an academic vocation or membership in an ideological movement. An academic career would have given him insulation from events, focused interests, and a specialized competence. A confessional commitment would have made him spokesman for a movement and provided him with a fixed perspective on issues; but Lippmann was never for long, and never

184

wholly, part of a movement. Though he declared himself a Progressive, that term covered a congeries of groups with convergent claims, and he never identified himself with any single group within the loose alliance. His twin patrons were the anonymous attentive public and the much smaller audience of the policymaking establishment.

While he did display the courage of the lone critic, his reticence concerning his final values went well beyond the requirements of intellectual self-respect. C. Wright Mills, for example, is often mentioned as a social theorist whose isolation was matched by his integrity. Yet Mills did not hesitate to discuss his indebtedness to, and his differences with, such major figures in his field as Max Weber and Karl Marx. Lippmann's special reticence is evident in this matter. He failed to come to terms with the front-rank political theorists of the nineteenth and twentieth centuries. He more characteristically responded to events than to the handful of recent political philosophers who have striven to transcend events.

Over his long career, Lippmann repeatedly displayed a strong attraction to officeholders who wielded power. It is noteworthy that the first leader whom he especially admired was Theodore Roosevelt. It is surely not coincidental that the major themes of Roosevelt's life and leadership found a permanent place in Lippmann's thought. Consider the parallels: Roosevelt was a campaigner who was a recognized scholar, an aristocrat who vigorously attacked the materialism of America's business culture, a war hero who exalted the value of public service, an executive who sought to balance contending groups and classes "in the public interest," a paternalistic figure who saw himself as both the tribune of the people's true interests and their educator as to the nature of their interests.

Lippmann's chosen role as the establishment's theorist confined him to a very short radius of speculation. Limited by his concern for a direct impact upon policymakers, his writing betrayed the narrow range of choice permitted by the American party system to one on the Left. His aloofness served to mask and counterbalance his desire for involvement, his wish to keep his theorizing functional, in the tradition of William James's Pragmatism.

Lippmann's reserve concerning his ultimate values was evidently also connected to his turning away from his Jewish ancestry. He had received religious instruction at his parents' synagogue, had gone through his *bar mitzvah,* and had experienced exclusion from Harvard's eating clubs because he was Jewish. He was deeply concerned with the disorientation of the individual in contemporary society brought on by the dissolution of tradition. Yet in all his writing Lippmann acknowledged his Jewish identity in a significant fashion only once—in a 1922 issue of *The American Hebrew* devoted to a symposium on anti-Semitism.

In that article Lippmann almost offhandedly traced anti-Semitism to the offensive behavior of "the rich and vulgar and pretentious Jews of our big cities," and to poor Jewish immigrants who "when they are at last, after centuries of denial, free to go to the land and cleanse their bodies, now huddle together in a steam-heated slum." Jews are singled out as a group, Lippmann wrote, because of such behavior, linked with the distinctiveness of their surnames and their physical appearance. As a defense against intolerance he counseled uprooting these causes of prejudice, through the practice by Jews of "the classic Greek value of moderation." Lippmann's lack of moderation makes these remarks startling. Whether his essay reveals guilt, self-rejection, or something more complex, it dramatically illuminates his failure to integrate his Hebraic heritage into his personal sense of identity, or to employ it as a resource in his theorizing. On the evidence of this intemperate and simplistic article, which appeared the same year as his sophisticated treatment of stereotypes in *Public Opinion,* it is apparent that the inadmissibility of his ethnic-cultural background was an important source of his reticence concerning his deepest beliefs.[1]

II

In his early prewar writings Lippmann rejected the individualistic Liberalism of laissez-faire. He favored the sort of technocratic collectivism which was widely favored—whether it was called Liberalism or socialism—by moderates on the parliamentary Left in England and the United States. Like other Liberals of the day, he expressed confidence in progress. More specifically, drawing on Pragmatism, he believed in an evolving social construction of reality. Social symbols and institutions, even though not usually consciously designed, are neither unchanging nor sacred. They arise in response to problems, he held, and they can be improved or replaced through the deliberate intervention of human intelligence.

This conception of society put Lippmann in line with the researches of social scientists and the work of social reformers. These inferences also laid the groundwork for the theories developed in *Public Opinion*. His belief in the provisional nature of social arrangements led him to stress the importance of economics in politics, and as an indispensable dimension of justice. Yet this conception of society was a theoretical vehicle without a motor. By acknowledging the functional and changing character of social institutions, Lippmann seemed to imply the presence of forces which impel change and are more fundamental than the social forms themselves. Yet he gave no clear, consistent account of what these forces are, or how they operate. Lippmann gives a pre-Copernican account of society, in which we behold the movement of institutions but lack convincing explanation of the movement.

Lippmann did suggest science would nurture and protect Liberal values in the twentieth century. The old Jeffersonian reliance on the family farm and frontier as guarantees of liberty had ceased to operate in an industrial urban society. Superficially more plausible, but also outmoded in the strategic sectors of the economy, was the business community's cherished ideology of entrepreneurship and competition. Lippmann hoped that science would provide social support for Liberalism in the twentieth century. But the absence of careful institutional analysis vitiates Lippmann's conception of science. It remains as an institutionally disembodied *geist* ("spirit") in his theories. Lippmann had not yet grasped the usefulness of technology for social control, terror, and warfare. His use of social scale as a related explanatory concept was far less helpful than, for example, Max Weber's concept of the rise of bureaucracy. Because Lippmann did not meticulously analyze the new large-scale institutions, and the groups which benefited and suffered from their advent, in terms of status, income, and political affiliation, his remarks on the growth of scale in the Great Society remain vague and unsatisfying. His failure to ask specific questions as to the consequences of large-scale institutions for affected groups renders his apotheosis of the scientist, the professional administrator, and the engineer unconvincing. C. Wright Mills aptly remarked that "The technical knowledge of managers and their relation to production is one thing; their class position, political loyalties, and stake in the current system is quite another. There is no intrinsic connection between the two."[2]

III

Lippmann's adopted role of educator of public opinion was nowhere more evident than in his writing on international politics. He wrote of the "great healing effect of publicity" in foreign affairs and he consistently strove to contribute to that process. His tempered reasoned approach rarely faltered, and his careful treatment of such topics as international organization and balance of power introduced those subjects to large numbers of Americans. He became the best known of the publicists who encouraged the reading public to support a permanent role for the United States in world affairs.

His distinction in this field did not rest upon original theorizing. Instead, it was his judicious application of established concepts to the shifting patterns of events which earned him esteem. More important than Lippmann's impact on the study of international relations is the impact of international politics on the structure of his thought. The new global perspective brought on by the war, Wilson, and the League wrought deep and lasting changes in the formulations of American Liberalism; and Lippmann played a leading part in developing the new views.

The plunge into world affairs had a chilling effect on Liberal militancy for several reasons. In domestic affairs Liberals had operated on the premise of the essential equality of all persons and had striven to create institutional arrangements which would mirror and honor equality. In foreign affairs inequality between states was ineradicable. In fact, one of the arguments used by Liberals to urge American intervention in World War I was that the smaller states which were neighbors of the Central Powers lacked the population and economic base to defend themselves against invasion, resources which the United States possessed in abundance.

In domestic society, a basic aim of Liberals had always been to minimize the use of force and violence; Lippmann suggested that elections were sublimated civil wars. In the external affairs of nation-states, resort to force was a constant possibility. The earliest modern Liberal theorists, Thomas Hobbes and John Locke, had pointed out that lacking any higher common authority, states were in a presocial "state of nature" with regard to one another.

The predominant realities of inequality and the use or threat of force meant that in international politics calculations of power must accompany and overshadow claims of right. This was retrogressive behavior for American Liberals, who had sought a distribution of power within society so equitable that "power" would signify nothing more than the merited weight of numbers in the membership of contending groups. As the war dragged on, Liberals found claims of right increasingly clouded and relative, and calculations of power indispensable to the successful conduct of the war and in setting the terms of peace.

On a global political spectrum, furthermore, American Liberals found themselves outflanked by adversaries on the Left as well as on the Right. The Liberals became self-conscious centrists. They discovered that they had never been as militant as most of them had believed themselves to be. Daniel Boorstin has suggested as a measure of the temperature of American Liberalism that we compare the slogans of the French Revolution ("Liberty, Equality, Fraternity") and the Russian Revolution ("Peace, Bread, and Land") with the slogan of the American Revolution ("No Taxation Without Representation"). To make this comparison is to be reminded of the cautious and constitutional character of American Liberalism, the character which again became evident as American Liberals tried to cope with world war.

The war also dampened dissent and reform by prompting calls for a martial national unity, which would override domestic division and enable the United States to make a maximum war effort. The drive for national unity reinforced the tendency of students of international politics to view each nation as a unified actor with a single stable set of national interests. Lippmann gravitated to a Platonized version of diplomacy as a rational discourse and drama, which in extremity became a contest of arms without altering the objectives of the players. He appeared insensibly to adopt, as did many Liberals, Leopold von Ranke's concept of "the primacy of foreign policy" in national life. This premise of national solidarity helps explain Lippmann's later insistence on the existence of a single objective "public interest."

It should also be noted, however, that his acceptance of the autonomy and decisive importance of international politics and the vital character of nationalism in the twentieth century, left him free to reason during the reactionary waves which swept the country during the Red Scare following World War I and the Cold War following World War II.

A further consequence for Lippmann and other Liberals of American entry into world politics was the acceptance of greatly enlarged executive authority. The development of Lippmann's judgment on this point was gradual. He had always found strong Presidential leadership appealing. His early wartime writings, however, had expressed hope for a greater measure of democratic control of foreign policy, as well as for the advancement of representative democracy by the terms of any peace settlement. By 1922, in *Public Opinion*, his basic reform thrust was more qualified. The "intelligence bureaus" he proposed would enlighten public opinion so that it might more effectively influence the limits of acceptable policy. But by this time Lippmann was too skeptical to rely only upon the direct democratic restraint of public opinion. The bureaus were also to have served as an added check and balance within the institutional framework of government. In his final major work, *Essays in the Public Philosophy*, the public's share in executive power had virtually vanished. The chief executive's responsibility was to the Constitution and to his conscience rather than to a transient majority of a partially informed electorate. Lippmann's final position came close to the view of executive authority laid down by Theodore Roosevelt. "I don't think," Roosevelt had written, "that any harm comes from the concentration of power in one man's hands provided the holder does not keep it for more than a certain, definite time, and then returns to the people from whom he sprang."[3] Roosevelt had been a peacetime President, moreover. The stature of the executive had been further enhanced when the cold calculations necessity made by heads of government in international relations were matched against the irrational mass psychology of nationalism in time of war. In no other sphere of politics did the executive exhibit so much rationality or the people so little.

The development of Lippmann's thought toward a "realist" position is to be found also in his use of the concept of balance of power. One political scientist has remarked that "The realistic tradition in political thought is generated and maintained by preoccupation with conflict, tension, opposition, contradiction, paradox—the antinomies of human experience."[4] After Lippmann had developed the concept of balance of power in his thinking on international politics, he employed it in his theory of moral psychology. There is a permanent tension between the "two natures" of persons in society, he argued, between existence and spirit, between the appetitive self and the social self. The individual "is drawn between the two disparate realms of being, and the tension within [*sic*] them is the inexhaustible theme of human discourse."[5] Lippmann shared the realist position with other social theorists, most notably his contemporary Reinhold Niebuhr. Both men were concerned to demonstrate what Lippmann called "the finite and obscure quality of truth and justice." Both of them were convinced of the truth value of paradoxes in politics. Both were sure that the inner life of the moral man must be characterized by tension. Both believed that concentrations of power in social life can never be abolished, and therefore must be balanced. These concerns and beliefs have become so widely shared that they may be said to have become part of a twentieth-century neo-Liberal synthesis in American thought.

Lippmann was also an important figure in the recovery of an understanding of America's relatedness to the rich heritage and the contemporary ferment of European culture. American social thinkers had long concentrated on the distinctiveness of their own society. Their pride and their misgivings alike were tinged with chauvinism. Theorists like Jefferson, Madison, and Calhoun seemed most effective when analyzing American conditions in perfect isolation. Lippmann's writing on the eve of World War I marked a turning point. He drew freely on British and European thinkers such as Shaw and Wallas, Marx, Sorel, Durkheim, and Freud. Henceforth, Lippmann and other American theorists dealt with European thinkers with increasing ease and studied America in relation to European culture. This cosmopolitan perspective gradually supplanted the older premise of "exceptionalism," which held that the United States was so specially and favorably situated, geographically and historically, that European experience was no burden and no help here. It may well have been that the reappropriation of European theory, to which Lippmann contributed, helped persuade him that ". . . the central and critical condition of the Western society" is that "the democracies are ceasing to receive the traditions of civility. . . ."[6]

IV

Theoretical originality of the order Lippmann displayed in *Public Opinion* eludes full explanation: the theorist transcends the circumstances which occasioned his work. Nonetheless it is possible to identify some of the conditions which contributed to Lippmann's accomplishment.

First, there was the rapid collapse of Liberal hopes in 1919–1920. The vengeful terms of the Versailles peace, the defeat of the League in the United States Senate, the disappearance of Wilson from the American scene, the Republican victory in the national elections of 1920—all these developments combined to make it evident that American Liberalism had run aground. Liberal counsels had gone unheeded. Further programmatic thinking was hardly in order, with Progressives fighting a defensive battle to hold some positions in Congress and state governments. As he was to do again in another period of Republican "normalcy" three decades later, Lippmann withdrew from close analysis of events in order to do more basic theorizing. He took a leave of absence from his editorial responsibilities on the *New Republic* in order to work on *Public Opinion*.

Second, the war had had a moral "leveling effect" on Europe's governments in Lippmann's eyes. In their conduct of the war, the parliamentary governments had placed themselves on a plane with the Central Powers. Defense against aggression, the rights of neutral countries, restoration of a balance of power—these professed goals, to which Lippmann had subscribed, had come to appear nothing more than makeshift propaganda for the exertion of Allied military power. The war raised the fundamental question of the importance and direction of public opinion in time of war, a novel issue for American analysts. Was public opinion in fact, as Lippmann had earlier argued, one of the true springs of policy in the Liberal democracies? Did public opinion operate, as Liberals generally had supposed, in favor of peace, and as a restraining influence in time of war? Or was it impelled by aggressive nationalism, stimulated by media and leaders for narrow national advantage? The conduct of the war and of the peace conference had badly twisted the design of Liberal hopes. Lippmann would try to identify what had gone wrong and to discover some line of advance for the Liberals into the future.

Third, Lippmann had observed, as a minor official perched high in the Wilson Administration, the importance of propaganda in the United States at war. The report of the Creel Commission, for which Lippmann had worked, was disingenuous in a way Lippmann could not have failed to notice. It offered lengthy documentation of the propaganda campaign at home, which it labeled "patriotic," "informational," and "educational." Little detail was provided for the programs conducted overseas, but the Creel Report made the dramatic claim of having reversed sentiment overseas, from initial resentment and resistance, to support and favor for the United States. The report contended that this reversal would produce significant economic and political advantages for the United States in the postwar world.[7] If public opinion in foreign nations had indeed been turned about by the efforts of our government, what was the significance of the domestic propaganda barrage? The Report did not speculate on this question; Lippmann would do so.

Fourth, Lippmann had an early and continuing interest in the relationship between psychology and politics. Graham Wallas had been correct, Lippmann believed, in seeing the centrality of the study of human nature to the study of politics. But Wallas had not himself developed an adequate psychology of politics. The work of Freud and James seemed to bear most promise, and the theories of both these men would be subversive of the received Liberal conception of human nature. Freud saw the ego as the often insecure social agent and *persona* for a human self in conflict, caught between stringent social claims and instinctual needs which operated largely outside the individual's awareness. James saw both the self or subject and world or object as constructs out of that vortex or "pure experience" which we conventionally call the human person. If Freud and James were right, the philosophical psychology on which Anglo-American Liberalism had relied, the empiricist and utilitarian psychology of Locke and Smith and Mill, had assumed a rationality and simplicity and uniformity in mental life which falsified the human condition. The inner economy of the libido, in Freud's terminology, would have to be understood and related to the outer economy with which Liberalism had heretofore been concerned. The behavior of individuals and groups in the war provided much grim but impressive evidence for the theories of Freud and James.

Fifth, the waging of the war and the battles of propaganda had coincided with radical advances in gathering and disseminating news. Telegraphy, radio, high-speed printing, even motor transport contributed to a bewildering compression of geography and history. Never had the demands of knowledge rested more heavily on the common citizen. Never had the flow of knowledge appeared so vulnerable. Never had the artificiality and mutability of the social world been so apparent to the reflective person. For these reasons Lippmann concluded that the twentieth-century crisis in representative democracy was a crisis in journalism.

In retrospect it is easy to see the course of Lippmann's life converging with larger political events to produce *Public Opinion*. It was natural that he should discern a crisis in Liberalism and interpret it as one within the purview of his vocation as well as within his Liberal world view. He could not know in 1922 how deep and extensive the crisis would come to be in the decades that followed. The crisis he perceived and his vocation were to remain enmeshed in one another for the rest of his life, each helping to define the other for him. Understanding the moral possibilities of human life, as they were conditioned by social psychology and the dangerous new technological environment of the twentieth century, remained the underlying concern which informed the rest of his writing. Freud remarked that Western man had not fallen so far as he supposed in World War I, because he had never risen as far as he imagined. Lippmann developed a similar judgment, while like Freud (though they used the terms in different senses) he remained convinced that the chances for a humane and just society depended upon forging a successful bond between rationality and morality. This idea was central to Enlightenment Liberalism, but its lineage could be traced back to Socrates.

In *Public Opinion* Lippmann set his face decisively against economic interpretations of the crisis in Liberal institutions. He had never been a convincing materialist. His element was the life of the mind, and meanings which he could discover and interpret must lie there. It is a minor irony that *Public Opinion* should have attracted acclaim as a pioneer essay in social science, for it is with this work that Lippmann turns conclusively aside from the concerns of empirical social scientists and takes up those of a moral philosopher.

V

Lippmann's treatment of epistemological and moral issues established him as a serious social theorist, at the same time that it contributed to the deepening of political discourse in twentieth-century America. *A Preface to Morals* continued the consideration of these matters which Lippmann had opened in *Public Opinion*. Both books treated the manner in which knowledge is grounded in personal needs and experience and conditioned by society. Both works argued for the importance of subjectivity in the working of social institutions.

When *Public Opinion* and *A Preface to Morals* are read together, they develop a single critique of Enlightenment Liberalism parallel to the celebrated argument advanced by Carl Becker in 1932 in *The Heavenly City of the Eighteenth Century Philosophers*. The argument is that the Enlightenment Liberals were themselves a credulous company, bound together by a faith fully as strong as the religious faith they strenuously repudiated. The Enlightenment was dedicated to the end of man's self-imposed tutelage. Humanity had come of age and was seizing control of its destiny. Self-rule was the new maxim—for the individual, the group, and the nation. No longer would men submit to the fables of priests or the commands of princes unlegitimized by consent. No longer would men scan history for signs of divine purposes at work. Men would apply their own purposes to their affairs. The old Christian teleology was overthrown, in natural science and history alike.

As Lippmann framed his critique there were two basic errors in the thinking of Enlightenment Liberals. One was that the Liberals had themselves unwittingly adopted a premise of faith, a teleology or automatism. Their "reserve power of guidance" was popular sovereignty, and Lippmann discussed it in *Public Opinion*. The other error was the Liberals' supposition, buttressed by their own faith in the people, that enlightened society required no faith or final morality. *A Preface to Morals* disputed this assumption.

In the *Preface* of 1929 and in the *Essays* of 1955, Lippmann linked these defects in Liberal theory to other Liberal precepts. The benevolent secularism of Liberals cast doubt upon any beliefs concerning first and last things and devalued them as a subject of political theory. When this attitude was tied to a belief in the privacy of conscience, it led to the dangerous conclusion that faith and morals are matters of personal taste with no public consequence. In what began as an earnest effort to avoid coercion and indoctrination, Liberals ended by banishing from civic discussion the most fundamental questions of social order. As a result, what thinking had been done on these subjects had been by an unexamined hand-me-down moral psychology which blended rationalism, associationism, and the pleasure-pain calculus. Ironically, in trying to safeguard freedom and diversity, Liberals had raised barriers to an understanding of the rich emotional variety beneath socially patterned behavior and of the constant exchanges between mental life and political conduct.

Lippmann wanted to cut beneath these Liberal assumptions, to appeal directly to experience. Carl Becker stated the situation neatly: "The fact is that we have no first premise. Since Whirl is king, we must start with the whirl, the mess of things as presented in experience."[8] When Lippmann did confront experience directly, what he found was anxiety, alienation, disorientation. Amidst unprecedented freedom and abundance, secular man was not at ease with himself or his world. In a society in which there was no god in the process, no supporting automatism, no new orthodoxy to resist and adapt, freedom became threatening to many. The previously unthinkable possibility that many in a Liberal society might choose to regress to an authoritarian political system had to be acknowledged.

Lippmann struggled to find a hopeful prescription for Liberal society. He took up the old Liberal theme, reworked by Freud, that the development of society is a process analogous to personal growth and that the surmounting of institutional religion creates a situation analogous to the crisis of adolescence. Lippmann echoed Freud's hope that a new mature human type would emerge after the trauma of unresisted disbelief had passed. Lippmann parted from Freud and earlier Liberals in asserting that the "highest" traits of the old religious personality would be preserved in the new humanism. Lippmann believed he had found a series of cultural correlations which would prove decisive—correlations between "high" religion, depth psychology, physical science, philosophy, and statecraft. All of these forms of cultural art rested upon disinterested reason. It could realistically be hoped, Lippmann argued, that the loss of the dependencies, continuities, and simplicity of the former society would induce disinterested reason as a favored trait in the race's mental struggle for survival. In business administration, in public service, and above all in personal life, disinterested reason would demonstrate its superiority in the competitions of modern social life. Individuals and organizations guided by it would succeed more often than their counterparts who lacked it.

Lippmann held out no hope for a final stage of history. There would be no social consummation, no resting place in history. But in a generous spirit, without any bitterness, he held up the hope of the Socratic humanist, the man of reason who could represent a new human type, succumbing neither to the desire of hedonism nor to fear.

VI

Essays in the Public Philosophy was the consummation of Lippmann's career as a political theorist. The most difficult of his books, it is based on the deepest scholarly research. It presents the longest view of history. It pursues to their terminus the major arguments developed in his early works.

The principal thrust of the book is very simple. Lippmann was a rationalist, and in this work he warns that Liberal civic culture is being subverted by a spreading nominalism. Because issues of moral psychology have not been effectively addressed in Liberal society, there is no shared understanding of the structure of human nature, or the pattern of personal development followed by the individual. Since the individual's choices have been protected as his own to make as he sees fit, those choices have led to the absolutizing of personal preferences, the absolutizing of individuality, at the very time when the inner structure and dynamics of individuality are less well understood as an integral part of political theory than ever before. Any and all choices by individuals are valued equally, and there are no canons for examining the basis of knowledge and choice. Under these conditions conservative pharisees are indeed left confronting radical cynics. There are no agreed upon standards for choosing between competing claims or for objectively establishing the meaning of justice or the public interest in a given situation. Instead, "justice" and "the public interest" are taken to be no more than ideological epithets, symbolic weapons for contending parties.

Such civic agnosticism had not disabled Liberal societies earlier only because of their covert faith in gods of the process. In the year-to-year workings of their social system, Liberals had been confident that the process of group competition automatically would eventuate in close approximations of justice. In the longer process of institutional development, Liberals had seen the spread of their form of government as an irreversible tide. Here again Lippmann found irony: with their trust in the automatic operation of history, it was precisely the beauty and terror of human freedom that Liberals had forgotten. Men could prove masters within the indeterminism of history only if they could reopen and sustain reasoned discourse upon the moral choices made available by historical situations.

Lippmann shares, therefore, with other American political theorists of his time—Reinhold Niebuhr, Erich Fromm, and Hannah Arendt, for example—a recognition of the need for norms which transcend the Liberal epoch. Niebuhr turned to Christianity, Fromm to the traditions of psychoanalysis and Marxism, Arendt to the rigor that was Greece. Lippmann was the exponent of the life of reason.

Since he was not a naturalist or a materialist, he was prevented from pursuing the insights of the most universally influential theorists in his century, Marx and Freud. Nor would he surrender his intellectual detachment for impassioned advocacy of equal rights for the poor and racial minorities in American society. His gaze fixed on the long view, he took little notice of the openings to the Left in his theories.

For an appreciation of his achievement, we need only turn the preceding paragraph upside down. Lippmann provided a valuable Idealist component to the mid-century synthesis of Liberal thought in America. A variety of creeds and disciplines is represented in this synthesis, which now appears stable, though necessarily unfinished. A Liberalism which can forego human perfectibility and assured historical triumph, a Liberalism which can remain self-critical while resisting external foes, is the heritage of their efforts. It was not a failure of nerve, but a sustaining of courage, to which he contributed.

Socrates was the hero of civility for Lippmann. Paul Tillich has written that "In Socrates . . . courage . . . was made rational and universal. A democratic idea of courage was created as against the aristocratic idea of it. Soldierly fortitude was transcended by the courage of wisdom."[9] Lippmann wrote that authoritarian thought is more instinctually natural,[10] since it rationalizes the primitive impulses to dominate and submit, to command and to seek protection. Liberal thought, he said, was more precarious, like the clearing for a garden in the jungle, perenially threatened by its environment and in need of constant care: "It is not an easy task nor one which we in our time can hope to complete." But, he believed, "We can see the promise. . . ."

Notes and References

The following abbreviations have been employed for books by Walter Lippmann.

A Preface to Politics (PP)
Drift and Mastery (DM)
The Stakes of Diplomacy (SD)
The Political Scene (PS)
Liberty and the News (LN)
Early Writings (EW)
Public Opinion (PO)
"The Political Equivalent of War" (PEW)
A Preface to Morals (PM)
The Good Society (GS)
U.S. Foreign Policy: Shield of the Republic (SR)
The Cold War (CW)
Essays in the Public Philosophy (EPP)

Chapter One

1. Mabel Dodge Luhan, *Intimate Memories*, Volume 3, *Movers and Shakers* (New York: Harcourt Brace, 1936), p. 118.
2. John Reed, *The Day in Bohemia* (New York: 1929), p. 42.
3. PP, 81.
4. PP, 85.
5. SR, viii.
6. John Mason Brown, *Through These Men* (New York: Harper & Row, 1954), p. 206.
7. PP, 88.
8. PP, 227–28.
9. Brown, p. 206.
10. See Samuel Eliot Morison, *Three Centuries of Harvard* (Cambridge, Mass.: Harvard University Press, 1936), pp. 434–37.
11. Brown, p. 211.
12. PP, 39.

13. PP, 38.
14. DM, 61.
15. DM, 60.
16. PP, 216.
17. Cited in PP, 99.
18. PP, 104.
19. PP, 113.
20. Brown, p. 211.
21. Brown, p. 210.
22. PP, 159.
23. Brown, p. 211.
24. Cited in Brown, p. 212.
25. Wallas opened his 1914 work, *The Great Society*, with a dedicatory letter addressed to Lippmann.
26. Justin Kaplan, *Lincoln Steffens* (New York: Simon and Schuster, 1974), pp. 176–80.
27. PP, 123.
28. PP, 21.
29. Ibid.
30. Kaplan, p. 177.
31. Kaplan, p. 178.
32. PP, 14.
33. DM, 87.
34. PP, 204.
35. PP, 237.
36. PP, 237–38.
37. DM, 88.
38. DM, 111.
39. PP, 22.
40. Ibid.
41. PP, 209.
42. DM, 95.
43. DM, 94.
44. PP, 17.
45. PP, 16–17.
46. PP, 104.
47. PP, 32.
48. PP, 34.
49. PP, 32.
50. PP, 7.
51. DM, 100.
52. George Santayana, *Character and Opinion in the United States* (New York: W. W. Norton, 1967), p. 68.
53. PP, 26–27.
54. DM, 39.

55. DM, 146.
56. PP, 225.
57. DM, 79.
58. DM, 77.
59. PP, 22.
60. DM, 78.
61. DM, 77.
62. DM, 81.
63. DM, 82.
64. DM, 85.
65. DM, 97.
66. DM, 40.
67. DM, 99.
68. DM, 98.
69. DM, 70–71.
70. DM, 74.
71. DM, 71.
72. DM, 49.
73. DM, 45.
74. Ibid.
75. DM, 31.
76. DM, 37.
77. DM, 39–40.
78. DM, 43.
79. DM, 50.
80. DM, 35.
81. DM, 43.
82. DM, 37.
83. DM, 37.
84. DM, 50–51.
85. DM, 169.
86. DM, 168–69.
87. DM, 58.
88. DM, 57.
89. PP, 211.
90. DM, 19.
91. PP, 183–84.
92. Christopher Lasch, *The Agony of the American Left* (New York: Knopf, 1969), p. 35.
93. DM, 167.
94. DM, 167.
95. PP, 12.
96. DM, 170.
97. DM, 172.
98. PP, 201.

 99. DM, 64.
100. DM, 66.
101. DM, 63–64.
102. New York: Scribner, 1932.
103. DM, 61.
104. DM, 62.
105. DM, 61–62.
106. DM, 65.
107. DM, 59.
108. PP, 140.
109. DM, 123.
110. DM, 125.
111. DM, 128.
112. DM, 129.
113. DM, 54.
114. DM, 55.
115. DM, 171, 53, 54, 46.
116. DM, 53.
117. DM, 52.
118. DM, 16–17.
119. PP, 200–201.
120. PP, 214.
121. PP, 226.
122. PP, 196–97.
123. Ibid.
124. PP, 114.
125. DM, 59.
126. PP, 90.
127. Ibid.
128. PP, 91.
129. DM, 50.
130. PP, 1.
131. DM, 103.
132. DM, 51.
133. DM, 104.
134. DM, 103.
135. DM, 102.
136. PP, 230.
137. DM, 146–47.
138. See PP, 243.
139. DM, 176.
140. PP, 223.
141. DM, 116.
142. DM, 148.

143. DM, 151.
144. DM, 137.
145. DM, 137–38.
146. DM, 152.
147. DM, 168.
148. PP, 153; DM, 169, 170.
149. DM, 139.
150. PP, 62.
151. PP, 153.
152. PP, 57.
153. PP, 68.
154. (Vienna, 1913), Vol. 2, no. 4, pp. 452–56.
155. PP, 42–43.
156. PP, 107.
157. PP, 65.
158. PP, 91.
159. DM, 51.
160. PP, 83.
161. PP, 84.
162. Ibid.
163. DM, 15–16.
164. PP, 139–40.
165. PP, 91, 236–37.
166. New York: Macmillan, 1914.
167. PP, 177.
168. Ibid.
169. PP, 177–78.
170. PP, 166–67.
171. Quoted in Ronald Steel, "Walter Lippmann, 1889–1974," *New Republic* 171, no. 26 (December 28, 1974), p. 6.
172. See *Current Biography*, 1962, p. 266.
173. See Walter Lippmann, "Political Analyst, Dead at 85," *New York Times*, December 15, 1974, pp. 1, 66.
174. James Reston, "His Thought and Writings Are Very Much Alive Today," *New York Times*, December 15, 1974, p. 66.
175. "Lippmann: Philosopher-Journalist," *Time*, December 23, 1974, pp. 56–57.
176. "Walter Lippmann, 1889–1974," *Newsweek*, December 23, 1974, p. 45.

Chapter Two

1. DM, 167.
2. SR, viii–ix.
3. SR, ix.

4. SR, ix–x.
5. SR, ix.
6. See Charles Forcey, *The Crossroads of Liberalism: Croly, Weyl, Lippmann, and the Progressive Era 1900–1925* (New York: Oxford University Press, 1961); Lasch; Benjamin F. Wright, *Five Public Philosophies of Walter Lippmann* (Austin: University of Texas Press, 1973).
7. PS, 65.
8. EW, 277; PS, 75.
9. SD, 214.
10. EW, 274.
11. EW, 289.
12. SD, 229.
13. SR, 174.
14. See Forcey, pp. 163–77.
15. SD, 10.
16. Cited in Forcey, p. 228.
17. EW, 24.
18. Forcey, pp. 242, 260.
19. Ibid., p. 232.
20. Ibid., p. 231.
21. Ibid., pp. 275–76.
22. Ibid., pp. 256–57.
23. Ibid., p. 257.
24. Ibid., p. 258.
25. Ibid., p. 284.
26. Edward L. Schapsmeier and Frederick H. Schapsmeier, *Walter Lippmann: Philosopher-Journalist* (Washington, D.C.: Public Affairs Press, 1969), pp. 33–34.
27. See Cary, pp. 39–61.
28. "Notes for a Biography," p. 252; Lovett, *All Our Years*, p. 172.
29. Weingast, pp. 15–18.
30. Cary, p. 62.
31. SD, 25.
32. SD, 8.
33. SD, 36.
34. SD, 29–30.
35. SD, 36.
36. SD, 50.
37. SD, 20.
38. EW, 271.
39. SD, 41–42.
40. SD, 171.
41. SD, 7.
42. SD, 189–90.

43. SD, 163.
44. SD, 60.
45. SD, 89–90.
46. SD, 50.
47. EW, 47.
48. SD, 56.
49. SD, 199.
50. Ibid.
51. Ibid.
52. SD, 195.
53. SD, 35, 54, 56.
54. SD, 51.
55. SD, 179.
56. SD, 180.
57. SD, 165.
58. EW, 28.
59. SD, 94, 166–68.
60. SD, 190.
61. SD, 119.
62. SD, 159.
63. SD, 105.
64. SD, 106.
65. SD, 72–74, 104–106, 151–54.
66. SD, 193.
67. SD, 113.
68. SD, xi, 170.
69. SD, 115.
70. SD, 115–16.
71. SD, 191–92, 93.
72. SD, 169.
73. See SD, 90, 164.
74. SD, 135, 190.
75. SD, 4; SR, viii–ix.
76. EW, 57.
77. EW, 48.
78. EW, 54–56.
79. SD, 205.
80. EW, 18.
81. EW, 56.
82. EW, 5.
83. SD, 217.
84. SD, 228.
85. SD, 221.
86. SD, 216–18.

87. EW, 47.
88. EW, 48.
89. SD, 210.
90. PEW, 181.
91. PEW, 182–83.
92. PEW, 183.
93. PEW, 182.
94. PEW, 187.
95. EW, 66; see PS, 41.
96. SD, 221–22.
97. EW, 42–43.
98. SD, xvi, xix.
99. SD, xiv.
100. SD, xiii.
101. SD, xiv.
102. SD, xiv–xviii; EW, 74.
103. PS, 9–10; see EW, 66–67.
104. EW, 72.
105. Ibid.
106. See Cary, chap. 4.
107. SR, vii–viii.
108. SR, 58–59, 7.
109. SR, 49.
110. SR, 9.
111. SR, 8.
112. SR, 12.
113. SR, 17–19.
114. SR, 21.
115. SR, 28–29.
116. SR, 37–39.
117. SR, 52–53.
118. Cited in SR, 61.
119. SR, 63, 162.
120. SR, 86.
121. SR, 109.
122. SR, 199.
123. SR, 138.
124. See SR, 120–21.
125. SR, 105, 93.
126. SR, 81–82, 101, 85.
127. SR, 102.
128. PS, 40–45.
129. "Britain and America: The Prospect of Political Cooperation in the

Light of Their Paramount Interests," *Foreign Affairs* 13 (April, 1935), 363–72.

130. SR, 74.
131. SR, 144–45.
132. SR, 129.
133. SR, 72–73.
134. SR, 146.
135. Ibid.
136. SR, 147.
137. PS, 70–71.
138. SR, 148–52.
139. See Cary, p. 167.
140. SR, 168; see SR, 164–74.
141. Cited in CW, 11.
142. Letter to Schapsmeier.
143. CW, 45.
144. CW, 15.
145. CW, 21–22.
146. CW, 23.
147. "The World We're In: An Interview with Ronald Steel, *New Republic* 165, no. 20 (November 13, 1971), p. 19.
148. CW, 60–61.
149. CW, 59.
150. CW, 38–39, 50–51.
151. CW, 41–42, 56; see Schapsmeier, p. 114.
152. CW, 52–54.
153. CW, 44.
154. "Today and Tomorrow," *New York Herald Tribune*, September 27, 1949.
155. "Walter Lippmann: An Interview With Ronald Steel," *New Republic* 168, no. 15 (April 14, 1973), pp. 16–20.
156. See Schapsmeier, p. 116.
157. Interview with Steel, 1973, p. 17.
158. "Breakup of the Two-Power World," *Atlantic Monthly*, April 1950; "Let's Face It—And Get On," *Ladies' Home Journal*, November, 1950.
159. Cited in Schapsmeier, p. 117.
160. See Schapsmeier, pp. 124–25.
161. "Today and Tomorrow," *New York Herald Tribune*, June 18, 1951.
162. "Today and Tomorrow," *New York Herald Tribune*, September 4, 1958, September 23, 1958.
163. "Lessons for Survival," *Atlantic Monthly*, February, 1951, p. 28.
164. "Today and Tomorrow," *New York Herald Tribune*, May 25, 1954.
165. See "Today and Tomorrow," *New York Herald Tribune*, September

10, 1959, and December 29, 1960. See also Hari Dam, *The Intellectual Odyssey of Walter Lippmann*, pp. 149–52.

166. S, 147.
167. S, 150.
168. Ibid.
169. S, 153.
170. Ibid.
171. S, 157, 159.
172. Interview with Steel, 1971, pp. 22, 23.
173. SD, 178.
174. EW, 3.
175. SD, x.
176. See SR, 156–57, 167, 175; and Cary, p. 96.
177. PS, 6.
178. PS, 4.
179. PS, 8.
180. SD, 226–27.
181. PEW, 187.
182. SD, 158–59.
183. SD, 155.
184. See PS, 18; PEW, 186.
185. EW, 84.
186. EW, 78–79.
187. EW, 82.
188. EW, 82–83.
189. PS, xiii.
190. PS, ix.
191. EW, 89.
192. PS, 33.
193. PS, 32, 35, 36.
194. PS, 73.
195. PS, 60–65.
196. PEW, 183–84.
197. SD, xxii.
198. Cary, p. 72.
199. Cited in Cary, p. 83.
200. Cary, p. 98–112.
201. SR, 174.
202. SD, 141.
203. SD, 136–37.
204. SD, 142.
205. SD, 133–35.
206. SD, 130–49.
207. SD, 156–57, 183.

208. SD, 183–88, 143.
209. SD, 135.

Chapter Three

1. See Henry Adams, *The Education of Henry Adams* (New York: Houghton Mifflin, 1918).
2. William H. McNeill, *The Shape of European History* (New York: Oxford, 1974), pp. 3–4.
3. Sigmund Freud, "Thoughts for the Times on War and Death," *The Complete Psychological Works, Standard Edition* (London: Hogarth, 1963), vol. 14, pp. xiv, 277.
4. Freud, "Thoughts for the Times," p. 280.
5. Cited in EPP, 17.
6. *New York Times*, December 15, 1974, p. 66.
7. GS, 3–4, 15–18.
8. PO, 15, 205, 7.
9. PO, 15.
10. PO, 29.
11. PS, 16.
12. PS, 80.
13. PO, 80–81.
14. PO, 58–63.
15. PO, 65–69.
16. PO, 69.
17. PO, 71.
18. PO, 42–43.
19. PO, 40–41; see 36–39.
20. PO, 44.
21. PO, 46–47.
22. PO, 43.
23. PO, 93.
24. PO, 81.
25. PO, 119.
26. PO, 171.
27. PO, 49–50.
28. PO, 51.
29. PO, 50.
30. PO, 51–57.
31. PO, 120.
32. PO, 122.
33. PO, 123.
34. PO, 125.
35. PO, 122–23.
36. PO, 126.

37. PO, 109.
38. PO, 110.
39. See PO, 114.
40. Cited in PO, 23.
41. PO, 112.
42. PO, 27.
43. PO, 96.
44. PO, 222.
45. PO, 222–23.
46. PO, 96.
47. PO, 98.
48. PO, 99.
49. PO, 74.
50. PO, 124.
51. PO, 154.
52. PO, 161.
53. PO, 163.
54. PO, 168.
55. PO, 162.
56. PO, 164.
57. PO, 177.
58. PO, 178.
59. PO, 179–80.
60. PO, 171.
61. PO, 171–72.
62. PO, 172.
63. PO, 174.
64. PO, 174–75.
65. PO, 175.
66. PO, 28.
67. PO, 173.
68. PO, 180.
69. PO, 204.
70. PO, 188.
71. Ibid.
72. PO, 205–206.
73. PO, 193.
74. PO, 223.
75. PO, 224.
76. PO, 228, 234.
77. PO, 229–30.
78. PO, 239.
79. PO, 236, 238.
80. PO, 247.

81. PO, 248.
82. PO, 256.
83. Ibid.
84. PO, 257.
85. PO, 256.
86. PO, 257.
87. PO, 256, 257.
88. Cited in PO, 258–59.
89. PO, 148, 260.
90. PO, 261.
91. PO, 253, 254, 320.
92. PO, 254.
93. PO, 274, 275, 311.
94. PO, 319.
95. PO, 321.
96. PO, 322.
97. PO, 326.
98. PO, 322–23.
99. PO, 333.
100. PO, 321.
101. PO, 335–37.
102. PO, 358.
103. PO, 360.
104. PO, 361.
105. PO, 363.
106. PO, 365.
107. PO, 410.
108. PO, 369.
109. PO, 370.
110. Ibid.
111. PO, 381.
112. PO, 384–85.
113. PO, 374.
114. PO, 375.
115. PO, 371, 387.
116. PO, 394–95.
117. PO, 397.
118. PO, 406.
119. PO, 390.
120. PO, 407.
121. PO, 408, 416, 414.
122. PO, 409.
123. PO, 407.
124. PO, 409–10.

125. PO, 410.
126. PO, 407.
127. PO, 410.
128. PO, 411–12.
129. PO, 417.
130. PO, 418.
131. LN, 5.
132. LN, 8–9.
133. LN, 62–63.
134. LN, 103.
135. LN, 101.
136. PP, 151.
137. PP, 150.
138. PP, 155–56.
139. PP, 173.
140. PP, 114.
141. PP, 128.
142. PP, 138.
143. PP, 144.
144. C. Wright Mills, Introduction to Thorstein Veblen, *The Theory of the Leisure Class* (New York: Mentor, 1953), p. xvii.
145. Max Lerner, "Editor's Introduction," *The Portable Veblen* (New York: The Viking Press, 1961), p. 48.
146. In Irving Louis Horowitz, ed., *Power, Politics, and People: The Collected Essays of C. Wright Mills* (New York: Oxford University Press, 1963), esp. pp. 257–58.
147. *Between Capitalism and Socialism* (New York: Random House, 1970), pp. 30–31.
148. *The New Industrial State* (Boston: Houghton Mifflin, 1971), pp. 70–71, 298–308.
149. See Don K. Price, *The Scientific Estate* (Cambridge, Mass.: Harvard University Press, 1967); Peter F. Drucker, *Technology, Management, and Society* (New York: Harper and Row, 1970); Daniel Bell, *The Coming of Post-Industrial Society* (New York: Basic Books, 1973).
150. *The Pentagon Papers* (New York: Quadrangle Books, 1971), pp. xiv, xv.
151. *The Pentagon Papers*, p. 244.
152. *Papers on the War* (New York: Simon and Schuster, 1972), p. 18.
153. *Congressional Quarterly Weekly Report* 32, no. 47 (November 23, 1974), p. 3151.
154. John Kenneth Galbraith, *The New Industrial State* (Boston: Houghton Mifflin, 1967), chap. 2; cited in Michael Lipsky and others, *American Government Today* (Del Mar, California: CRM Books, 1974), p. 323.

155. Henry A. Kissinger, "The Policymaker and the Intellectual," *Reporter* 20, no. 5 (March 5, 1959), pp. 30–35.

156. See Richard Neustadt, *Presidential Power* (New York: Wiley, 1960); and Theodore Sorensen, *Decision-Making in the White House* (New York: Columbia University Press, 1963).

157. Hannah Arendt, *Crises of the Republic* (New York: Harcourt Brace, 1972), p. 7.

Chapter Four

1. PM, 321.
2. SR, 512.
3. SR, 412.
4. PM, 3–4.
5. PM, 5, 6.
6. DM, 17.
7. PM, 9.
8. PM, 7.
9. PM, 10.
10. PM, 8.
11. PM, 9.
12. PM, 8.
13. PM, 10.
14. PM, 233.
15. PM, 164.
16. PM, 19.
17. PM, 15.
18. PM, 233.
19. PM, 20.
20. PM, 228–29.
21. PM, 23.
22. PM, 24.
23. PM, 32.
24. PM, 195.
25. PM, 201.
26. PM, 216.
27. PM, 200.
28. PM, 195.
29. PM, 45.
30. PM, 145.
31. Ibid.
32. PM, 164–65.
33. PM, 196.
34. PM, 192.
35. PM, 42–43.

36. PM, 160.
37. PM, 43.
38. PM, 182.
39. PM, 193.
40. PM, 197.
41. PM, 55.
42. Ibid.
43. Ibid.
44. PM.
45. PM, 73.
46. Ibid.
47. PM, 74–75.
48. PM, 70.
49. PM, 78.
50. PM, 82, 111.
51. PM, 76, 61–63.
52. PM, 59–60.
53. PM, 243.
54. PM, 268–71.
55. PM, 273.
56. PM, 275.
57. PM, 277.
58. PM, 278.
59. PM, 278–79.
60. PM, 275.
61. PM, 282.
62. PM, 283.
63. Ibid.
64. PM, 125.
65. PM, 132–33.
66. PM, 122–23.
67. PM, 117, 27, 132.
68. PM, 127.
69. PM, 238.
79. PM, 239.
71. Ibid.
72. PM, 240.
73. PM, 246.
74. PM, 247.
75. PM, 245.
76. PM, 249, 250, 254.
77. PM, 257.
78. PM, 258.
79. PM, 314.

80. PM, 209.
81. PM, 208.
82. PM, 316–18.
83. PM, 77.
84. PM, 319.
85. PM, 306.
86. PM, 305.
87. PM, 302.
88. PM, 113.
89. PM, 114.
90. PM, 4.
91. PM, 137.
92. PM, 208–209.
93. PM, 313.
94. PM, 219–20.
95. PM, 220–21.
96. PM, 209, 224.
97. PM, 225.
98. PM, 319.
99. PM, 168.
100. PM, 320.
101. PM, 175–83.
102. PM, 328.
103. PM, 219.
104. PM, 204.
105. PM, 197.
106, H. L. Nieburg, *In the Name of Science* (Chicago: Quadrangle Books), p. 122.

Chapter Five

1. See Wright, chap. 5. See also on this question, David Elliott Weingast, *Walter Lippmann: A Study in Personal Journalism* (New Brunswick, N.J.: Rutgers University Press, 1949), chaps. 3–5.
2. GS, ix-xi, 342–43, 345, 346, 258.
3. GS, ix, 164.
4. GS, xiii.
5. GS, xix–xxi, 181–85.
6. GS, xi, xiii, xiv–xv, 52–53.
7. GS, xxiii, xxiv, 287–89.
8. GS, 124–25, 115, 117.
9. GS, 118.
10. GS, 51–53.
11. EPP, 11.
12. EPP, 12, 13.

13. EPP, 19–20.
14. See Schapsmeier, pp. 131–37.
15. EPP, 79.
16. EPP, 18.
17. EPP, 12.
18. EPP, 18.
19. EPP, 80.
20. EPP, 102.
21. EPP, 16.
22. Ibid.
23. EPP, 17.
24. EPP, 82.
25. EPP, 83–84.
26. EPP, 82–83.
27. EPP, 79–84.
28. EPP, 12.
29. EPP, 15–16.
30. EPP, 15.
31. EPP, 29, 30–32.
32. EPP, 45.
33. EPP, 48.
34. EPP, 47.
35. EPP, 31.
36. Ibid.
37. EPP, 19.
38. EPP, 72–73.
39. EPP, 73–74.
40. EPP, 120.
41. EPP, 131–34.
42. Cited in EPP, 111.
43. EPP, 128–35.
44. EPP, 90.
45. EPP, 93.
46. EPP, 94.
47. EPP, 97.
48. "Today and Tomorrow," May 28, 1967; cited in Schapsmeier, p. 160. See discussion, pp. 156–60.
49. EPP, 97–98.
50. EPP, 98.
51. EPP, 99.
52. Ibid.
53. EPP, 98.
54. EPP, 22.
55. EPP, 24–25.

56. EW, 82.
57. EPP, 25.
58. EPP, 18.
59. EPP, 24.
60. EPP, 18.
61. EPP, 64, 32, 42.
62. EPP, 26.
63. EPP, 54–61.
64. EPP, 24.
65. EPP, 27.
66. EPP, 24.
67. EPP, 24–27.
68. EPP, 23.
69. EPP, 18.
70. EPP, 19.
71. EPP, 35.
72. Ibid.
73. EPP, 19.
74. EPP, 39.
75. EPP, 28.
76. Ibid.
77. EPP, 37.
78. EPP, 27.
79. See EPP, 13, 22, 98–99.
80. EPP, 18.
81. EPP, 29.
82. EPP, 44.
83. EPP, 48.
84. EPP, 73.
85. EPP, 73–74.
86. EPP, 117.
87. EPP, 107.
88. Ibid.
89. EPP, 134.
90. Ibid.
91. EPP, 133.
92. EPP, 40.
93. EPP, 78.
94. EPP, 81–87.
95. White, pp. 274–75.
96. Ibid., p. 275.
97. Ibid., pp. 276–77.
98. Ibid., p. 278.
99. Ibid., pp. 264, 272.

100. (Austin: University of Texas Press, 1973).
101. Wright, p. 153.
102. Ibid., pp. 132, 154.
103. Ibid., p. 130.
104. Ibid., pp. 127–28.
105. Ibid., p. 142.
106. Ibid., p. 153.
107. David Spitz, *Patterns of Anti-Democratic Thought* (New York: Macmillan, 1949), pp. 95–110; Heinz Eulau, "From Public Opinion to Public Philosophy," *American Journal of Economics and Sociology* 15 (July, 1956), 439–51; "Wilsonian Idealist: Walter Lippmann Goes to War," *Antioch Review* 14 (Spring, 1954), pp. 87–108; "Mover and Shaker: Walter Lippmann as a Young Man," *Antioch Review* 11 (Fall, 1951), pp. 291–312; "Man Against Himself: Walter Lippmann's Years of Doubt." *America Quarterly* 24 (Winter, 1952), pp. 291–304.
108. Wright, p. 152n.
109. EPP, 38.
110. EPP, 55.
111. EPP, 81.
112. EPP, 104.
113. EPP, 105.
114. EPP, 15.
115. EPP, 30–31, 44, 46, 48.
116. EPP, 15–18.
117. EPP, 49, 50.
118. EPP, 88.
119. EPP, 115.
120. EPP, 124.
121. EPP, 107–108.
122. EPP, 88.
123. EPP, 64.
124. EPP, 128.
125. EPP, 85.
126. EPP, 76, 78–80, 82, 84, 85.
127. Herbert Marcuse, *Five Lectures* (Boston: Beacon Press, 1970).
128. EPP, 102; emphasis supplied.
129. EPP, 112.
130. See EPP, 110–13.
131. See, for example, *Man and the State* (Chicago: University of Chicago Press, 1951), pp. 84–97.
132. Paul Ramsey, *Nine Modern Moralists* (New York: Prentice Hall, 1962), p. 212; see pp. 212–23, *passim*.
133. Edmond Cahn, *The Sense of Injustice* (New York: New York University Press, 1949).

134. Edmond Cahn, *The Moral Decision: Right and Wrong in the Light of American Law* (Bloomington: Indiana University Press, 1955).
135. Pp. 212–13; see pp. 223–28, *passim.*
136. EPP, 119.
137. EPP, 133.
138. (New York: Wiley, 1960).

Chapter Six

1. See Walter Lippmann, "Public Opinion and the American Jew," *The American Hebrew,* April 14, 1922, p. 575; Eulau, pp. 439–451; *passim;* and John Murray Cuddihy, *The Ordeal of Civility: Freud, Marx, Levi-Strauss, and the Jewish Struggle with Modernity* (New York: Basic Books, 1974).
2. C. Wright Mills, "A Marx for the Managers," in *Power, Politics, and People,* p. 61.
3. Quoted in *The Writings of Theodore Roosevelt,* edited by William H. Harbaugh (New York: Bobbs-Merrill, 1967), pp. xxxii–xxxiii.
4. Avery Leiserson, "Realism and Commitment in Political Theory," in *The Post-Behavioral Era: Perspectives on Political Science,* edited by George J. Graham, Jr. and George W. Carey (New York: David McKay, 1972), p. 144.
5. EPP, 117; see 117–22.
6. EPP, 75.
7. *Complete Report of the Chairman of the Committee on Public Information* (Washington, D.C., 1920), p. 7.
8. *The Heavenly City of the Eighteenth-Century Philosophers* (New Haven: Yale University Press), p. 16.
9. *The Courage To Be* (New Haven: Yale University Press, 1952), p. 11.
10. GS, 343–44.

Selected Bibliography

PRIMARY SOURCES

Lippmann's unpublished papers are held in a collection at Yale University Library. His principal journalistic writings are to be found in *New Republic*, from 1914 to 1920, *The New York World* editorials, from 1924 to 1931, and the "Today and Tomorrow" column in *The New York Herald Tribune* from 1931, with few interruptions, through 1959.

The Cold War, A Study in U.S. Foreign Policy. New York: Harper, 1947.

The Coming Tests with Russia. Boston: Little, Brown, 1961.

The Communist World and Ours. Boston: Little, Brown, 1959.

Drift and Mastery. New York: M. Kennerley, 1914.

Early Writings. Ed. Arthur M. Schlesinger, Jr. New York: Liveright, 1970.

Essays in the Public Philosophy. Boston: Little, Brown, 1955.

The Essential Lippmann. Ed. James Lare and Clinton Rossiter. New York: Random House, 1963.

The Good Society. Boston: Little, Brown, 1937.

Liberty and the News. New York: Harcourt, Brace, 1920.

Men of Destiny. New York: Macmillan, 1927.

The Method of Freedom. New York: Macmillan, 1934.

The Phantom Public. New York: Harcourt, Brace, 1925.

The Political Scene. New York: H. Holt, 1919.

A Preface to Morals. New York: Macmillan, 1929.

A Preface to Politics. New York: M. Kennerley, 1913.

Public Opinion. New York: Harcourt, Brace, 1922.

The Stakes of Diplomacy. New York: H. Holt, 1917.

United States Foreign Policy: Shield of the Republic. Boston: Little, Brown, 1943.

United States War Aims. Boston: Little, Brown, 1944.

SECONDARY SOURCES

ARENDT, HANNA. *Crises of the Republic*. New York: Harcourt Brace, 1972.

BECKER, CARL. *The Heavenly City of the Eighteenth-Century Philosophers*. New Haven: Yale University Press, 1932.

221

BELL, DANIEL. *The Coming of Post-Industrial Society.* New York: Basic Books, 1973.

BERNSTEIN, RICHARD J. *John Dewey.* New York: Washington Square Press, 1967.

BROWN, JOHN MASON. *Through These Men.* New York: Harper, 1956.

CAHN, EDMOND. *The Moral Decision: Right and Wrong in the Light of American Law.* Bloomington: Indiana University Press, 1955.

――――. *The Sense of Injustice.* New York: New York University Press, 1949.

CARY, FRANCINE CURRO. *The Influence of War on Walter Lippmann, 1914-1944.* Madison: State Historical Society of Wisconsin, 1967.

CHILDS, MARQUIS, and RESTON, JAMES, eds. *Walter Lippmann and His Times.* New York: Harcourt Brace, 1959.

Complete Report of the Chairman of the Committee on Public Information. Washington, D.C.: Government Printing Office, 1920.

"Congress Gets Ford Requests, Overrides Vetoes," *Congressional Quarterly Weekly Report* 32, no. 47 (Nov. 23, 1974), 3151.

CRICK, BERNARD. *The American Science of Politics.* Berkeley: University of California Press, 1959.

CUDDIHY, JOHN MURRAY. *The Ordeal of Civility: Freud, Marx, Levi-Strauss, and the Jewish Struggle With Modernity.* New York: Basic Books, 1974.

DAM, HARI. *The Intellectual Odyssey of Walter Lippmann.* New York: Gordon Press, 1973.

DRUCKER, PETER F. *Technology, Management, and Society.* New York: Harper & Row, 1970.

ELLSBERG, DANIEL. *Papers on the War.* New York: Simon and Schuster, 1972.

EULAU, HEINZ. "From Public Opinion to Public Philosophy." *American Journal of Economics and Sociology* 15 (July, 1956), 439-51.

――――. "Man Against Himself: Walter Lippmann's Years of Doubt." *American Quarterly* 24 (Winter, 1972), 291-304.

――――. "Mover and Shaker: Walter Lippmann as a Young Man." *Antioch Review* 11 (Fall, 1951), 291-312.

――――. "Wilsonian Idealist: Walter Lippmann Goes to War." *Antioch Review* 14 (Spring, 1954), 87-108.

FORCEY, CHARLES. *The Crossroads of Liberalism: Croly, Weyl, Lippmann and the Progressive Era, 1900-1925.* London: Oxford, 1961.

FREUD, SIGMUND. "Thoughts for the Times on War and Death." In *Standard Edition of the Complete Psychological Works of Sigmund Freud,* translated and edited by James Strachey, vol. 14, pp. 275-88. London: Hogarth, 1915.

GALBRAITH, JOHN KENNETH. *The New Industrial State.* 2nd ed. Boston: Houghton Mifflin, 1971.

HEILBRONER, ROBERT. *Between Capitalism and Socialism.* New York: Random House, 1970.

JONES, ERNEST. "Review of Walter Lippmann's *A Preface to Politics.*" *Imago* 2, no. 4 (Vienna, 1913), 452–56.

KISSINGER, HENRY. "The Policy-Maker and the Intellectual." *Reporter* 20, no. 5 (March 5, 1959), 30–35.

LASCH, CHRISTOPHER. *The Agony of the American Left.* New York: Knopf, 1969.

_____. *The New Radicalism in America, 1889–1963: The Intellectual as a Social Type.* New York: Random House, 1965.

LEISERSON, AVERT. "Realism and Commitment in Political Theory." In *The Post-Behavioral Era: Perspectives on Political Science,* edited by George J. Graham, Jr. and George W. Carey. New York: David McKay, 1972.

LERNER, MAX. "Editor's Introduction." In *The Portable Veblen.* New York: Viking, 1961.

LIPSKY, MICHAEL et al. *American Government Today.* California: CRM Books, Dec., March, 1974.

LOVETT, ROBERT MORSS. *All Our Years.* New York: Viking, 1948.

LUHAN, MABEL DODGE. *Intimate Memories.* Volume 3, *Movers and Shakers.* New York: Harcourt Brace, 1936.

MCNEILL, WILLIAM H. *The Shape of European History.* New York: Oxford, 1974.

MARCUSE, HERBERT. *Five Lectures.* Boston. Beacon Press, 1970.

MARITAIN, JACQUES. *Man and the State.* Chicago: University of Chicago Press, 1951.

MILLS, C. WRIGHT. "Introduction." In *The Theory of the Leisure Class* by Thorstein Veblen. New York: Mentor, 1953.

_____. *Power, Politics, and People: The Collected Essays.* Edited by Louis Irving Horowitz. New York: Oxford, 1963.

MOORE, EDWARD CARTER. *William James.* New York: Washington Square Press, 1965.

MORISON, SAMUEL ELIOT. *Three Centuries of Harvard.* Cambridge: Harvard University Press, 1936.

NEUSTADT, RICHARD. *Presidential Power.* New York: John Wiley, 1960.

NIEBURG, H. L. *In the Name of Science.* Chicago: Quadrangle, 1966.

PRICE, DON K. *The Scientific Estate.* Cambridge, Mass.: Harvard University Press, 1967.

RAMSEY, PAUL. *Nine Modern Moralists.* New York: Prentice-Hall, 1962.

ROOSEVELT, THEODORE. *Writings.* Edited by William H. Harbaugh. New York: Bobbs-Merrill, 1967.

RUBINSTEIN, ANNETTE. "Disinterestedness as Ideal and as Technique." *Journal of Philosophy* 28 (August 13, 1931), 461–66.

SANTAYANA, GEORGE. *Realms of Being.* 2 vols. New York: Cooper Square, 1972.

————. *Winds of Doctrine and Platonism and the Spiritual Life.* Glouces- ter: Peter Smith, 1971.

SCHAPSMEIER, EDWARD, and SCHAPSMEIER, FREDERICK. *Walter Lippmann: Philosopher-Journalist.* Washington, D.C.: Public Affairs Press, 1969.

SHEEHAN, NEIL et al. *The Pentagon Papers: The Secret History of the Vietnam War: The Complete and Unabridged Series as Published By The New York Times.* New York: Bantam, 1971.

SORENSEN, THEODORE. *Decision-Making in the White House.* New York: Columbia University Press, 1963.

SPITZ, DAVID. *Patterns of Anti-Democratic Thought.* New York: Macmil- lan, 1949.

TILLICH, PAUL. *The Courage to Be.* New Haven: Yale University Press, 1952.

WEINGAST, DAVID ELLIOTT. *Walter Lippmann: A Study in Personal Jour- nalism.* New Brunswick: Rutgers University Press, 1949.

WELLBORN, CHARLES. *Twentieth Century Pilgrimage: Walter Lippmann and the Public Philosophy.* Baton Rouge: Louisiana State University Press, 1969.

WHITE, MORTON. *Social Thought in America: The Revolt Against For- malism.* 2nd ed. Boston: Beacon Press, 1957.

WRIGHT, BENJAMIN F. *Five Public Philosophies of Walter Lippmann.* Au- stin: University of Texas Press, 1973.

Index